Cross-Cultural Analysis of Values and Political Economy Issues

Cross-Cultural Analysis of Values and Political Economy Issues

Edited by
Dan Voich, Jr.
and Lee P. Stepina

Foreword by George Macesich

Westport, Connecticut
London

Library of Congress Cataloging-in-Publication Data

Cross-Cultural analysis of values and political economy issues /
  edited by Dan Voich, Jr. and Lee P. Stepina ; foreword by George
  Macesich.
      p.   cm.
  Includes bibliographical references and index.
  ISBN 0-275-94638-X (alk. paper)
    1. Comparative management. 2. Management—Cross-cultural studies.
  3. Corporate culture—Cross-cultural studies. 4. Social values—
  Cross-cultural studies. I. Voich, Dan. II. Stepina, Lee P.
  HD30.55.C76 1994
  658—dc20   93-5442

British Library Cataloguing in Publication Data is available.

Library of Congress Catalog Card Number: 93-5442
ISBN: 0-275-94638-X

First published in 1994

Praeger Publishers, 88 Post Road West, Westport, CT 06881
An imprint of Greenwood Publishing Group, Inc.

Printed in the United States of America

The paper used in this book complies with the
Permanent Paper Standard issued by the National
Information Standards Organization (Z39.48-1984).

10 9 8 7 6 5 4 3 2 1

Contents

Figures and Tables

Foreword

This book fills an important gap in the search for insights into the operation of different social, political, economic, and, particularly, managerial systems. The essays are the fruits of extensive research by a group of scholars coming from different cultures and disciplines who are interested in the development of "values, attitudes, and behaviors" within a political economy context. The scholars are all members of the International Consortium for Management Studies.

In this book, the authors address urgent issues for all societies and economies. They analyze and explore various experiences of different countries with different socioeconomic and political conditions as these nations become more fully involved in a global economy.

As befits a book in comparative systems, the authors analyze different systems from various viewpoints. The chapters describe historical and current developments from the perspective of both the individual and society. They provide important insights about the emergence and evolution of social standards, economic initiatives, political priorities, and family- and work-related values.

The authors' examination of current developments comes at a time when the major theme of world affairs is rapid change. We can see major changes occurring throughout the world relating to people's values, organizational and institutional configurations, and national and international initiatives. These types of changes reflect deep-seated emotions and initiatives, and they provide a major forum for research.

In this book, the authors have supplied a comprehensive breadth of view combined with an examination of the common threads of value, issues, policies, and initiatives of the countries studied, resulting in an analysis that is far more than a catalogue of cases. This effort will provide a sound foundation for the analysis of the empirical data compiled by the authors on values and political economy issues, which is forthcoming in a companion volume to this book.

Tallahassee, Florida   George Macesich
November 18, 1993

Preface

The International Consortium for Management Studies has been involved in a major research project dealing with a cross-cultural comparison of people's family, workplace, and cultural values and with how these values relate to people's perceptions of various social, economic, and political issues at the organizational, national, and international levels. The consortium includes multidisciplinary faculty in universities throughout the world who are interested in the development of "values-attitudes-behaviors" of people of different cultures who live in countries with varied socioeconomic and political attributes. Faculty from eight countries initially formed the consortium (Chile, Federal Republic of Germany, Japan, Peoples Republic of China, Russia, United States, Venezuela, and Yugoslavia). During the past year, faculty from France and Mexico also participated in the consortium, which provides a dynamic forum for research and the exchange of ideas for the countries of the world, which are experiencing rapid change as they become more fully integrated within a global economy.

Members of the consortium have been collaborating on two major research projects. One of these is the development of this book, which contains historical and analytical surveys of the relevant literature and ideas about values and issues in each participating country. The chapters contain a mix of some of the applicable theories, concepts, and emerging trends concerning values and issues in each country. The topics were presented and discussed at the annual meeting of the International Consortium for Management Studies in November 1991.

This book contains four major groups of chapters. The first group discusses the general nature and selected classifications of values. The authors then analyze values within an organizational and societal framework. Finally, global values in transition are reviewed. This introduction to the nature and importance of values is followed by a survey of selected "values, beliefs, and attitudes" and their historical development in research (Chapter 1). The first group of chapters concludes with a general overview of Western culture, business, and management, including the historical evolution of Western culture and its current goals, values, and issues (Chapter 2).

The second group of chapters deals with values and issues in Western Europe. The values and perceptions of political economy issues in Germany are discussed, including a synopsis of current research and major trends (Chapter 3). Next, a review of changes in values and requirements of German managers, including the organizational culture of German firms, is presented. This review is followed by a discussion of the consequences of unification and a single European market (Chapter 4). The final essay in this group offers perspectives from a number of noted writers about French managerial values and issues within the context of social, cultural, political, industrial, and technological issues and topics (Chapter 5).

The third group of chapters focuses on the Socialist/Communist values and issues in the transition to a postCommunist era. The political challenges involved (Chapter 6) and the role and transformation of mass media (Chapter 8) in this transition away from Communism are discussed, with Yugoslavia as a focal point. The main trends in the system of personal and social values in the former Soviet Union are discussed within a historical context, culminating with a review of the changes occurring during the socioeconomic and political transition away from Communism and toward the formation of the Commonwealth of Independent States (Chapter 7). A review of historical empirical studies of values (Chapter 9) and a survey of recent value priorities (Chapter 10) pertaining to Yugoslavia are discussed which provide important insights about the ethnic and social-economic-political divisions that exist. Finally, constitutional-legal reforms are discussed (Chapter 11) as they relate to the transition of a society from Communism to decentralization.

The fourth group of essays involves two cultures in Central and South America. An analysis of changing values in Venezuela within its historical context is presented, including a review of current values and issues in that society (Chapter 12). Then, the evolution of the value profile of the typical Mexican is presented, including the current search for a Mexican identity within the context of this country with its very young population (Chapter 13).

The book concludes with a summary of future research directions (Chapter 14) of the International Consortium for Management Studies. This research involves a large-scale empirical survey which has just been completed. The analysis of these empirical data will be completed next year, and the results will be the subject of a second book on comparative family and workplace values and political economy issues. One major theme of this research is the measurement and comparison of people's individualistic versus socialistic values in different societies and of how these values influence perceptions of political economy issues at the organizational, national, and international levels.

In summary, this book represents the first important multi-country/ multi-cultural comparative analysis of values and issues and will provide a general foundation for analyzing the empirical data that have been compiled relating to values and issues. We are pleased to acknowledge and thank all members of the International Consortium for Management Studies who participated at our annual conferences in discussing the initial ideas and the materials included in this volume, and especially the contributors of the specific chapters in this book. A special thanks to Deshia Eady and Kelly Shrode for their outstanding professional assistance in helping the consortium in preparing this manuscript for publication.

Dan Voich, Jr. and Lee P. Stepina
For the International Consortium for Management Studies

Professor Nina V. Andreenkova
Institute for Social and
    Political Research
Moscow, Russia

Dr. Ljiljana Bačević
Institute of Social Sciences
Belgrade, Yugoslavia

Assistant Professor Peter Balogh
Florida State University
Tallahassee, Florida, U.S.A.

Frederic Brunnel
Ecole Superieure de Sciences
    Comerciale (ESSCA)
Angers, France

Professor Mijat Damjanović
University of Belgrade
Belgrade, Yugoslavia

Professor Aleksandar Fira
University of Belgrade
Belgrade, Yugoslavia

Dr. Vladimir Goati
Institute of Social Sciences
Belgrade, Yugoslavia

Professor Rosalind Greaves
  de Pulido
Universidad Metropolitana
Caracas, Venezuela

Dr. Andres Minaro Llagostera
Universidad Catolica Andres
  Bello
Caracas, Venezuela

Professor Hans Günther Meissner
Universitat Dortmund
Dortmund, Germany

Assistant Professor Joel
  Nicholson
Illinois State University
Normal, Illinois, U.S.A.

Professor Dragomir Pantić
Institute of Social Sciences
Belgrade, Yugoslavia

Professor Yolette Ramirez
Universidad Catolica Andres
Caracas, Venezuela

Professor Leonardo Rodriguez
Florida International
University
Miami, Florida, U.S.A.

Professor Alfonso Rodriguez-Coss
ITESM Campus Queretaro
Queretaro, Qro., Mexico

Assistant Professor Heike Simmet
Universitat Dortmund
Dortmund, Germany

Professor E. Ray Solomon
Florida State University
Tallahassee, Florida, U.S.A.

Associate Professor Lee P.
  Stepina
Florida State University
Tallahassee, Florida, U.S.A.

Dr. Mirjana Vasović
Institute of Social Sciences
Belgrade, Yugoslavia

Professor Dan Voich, Jr.
Florida State University
Tallahassee, Florida, U.S.A.

Professor Luis Werner Wildner
University of Santiago
Santiago, Chile

Professor Fengzeng Yan
Changchun University of Earth
  Sciences
People's Republic of China

Cross-Cultural Analysis
of Values and Political
Economy Issues

Introduction

Dan Voich, Jr., Lee P. Stepina,
Mijat Damjanović, and Peter J. Balogh

As national boundaries have changed and new economic collaborations have emerged, the world is going through an increasingly turbulent era. In the face of the virtual death of communism and the end of the Cold War, relationships between groups of like-minded individuals have become the basic impetus of world affairs. These individuals act in concert because they share a very basic thing: a culture. The understanding of culture and its role in shaping both political and economic events is the focus of this book.

Defining culture has proven to be a difficult exercise. Volumes have been produced by anthropologists attempting to pin down the concept. One area of general agreement is that individuals in the same culture share common values. Values are deeply held assumptions about how things should be and about how these ends should be achieved. Values, in turn, lead to a set of specific ideas, persons, or objects in the form of attitudes. Finally, attitudes are the precursors to behavior.

While there is general theoretical agreement concerning the relationship between the variables described above, there has been little empirical research on how values, beliefs, and attitudes vary cross culturally. Beyond G. Hofstede's groundbreaking research on values and numerous polls on attitudes, few researchers have gone beyond simple two-country comparisons. Further, there has been no research on how specific values and beliefs lead to important variations on attitudes toward national and international issues.

This chapter provides an introduction to the nature and importance of values, a review of selected classifications of values, and a look at values within organizational and societal frameworks. Within this framework, values also are discussed in the context of cross-cultural similarities and differences.

GENERAL NATURE AND IMPORTANCE OF VALUES

A simple but useful way in which to view the nature and importance of values is as follows: values shape attitudes which, in turn, influence behavior. In these basic relationships, values reflect the fundamental beliefs and need criteria of people acting individually and within group, organizational, and societal settings. In this way, values reflect a general purpose or philosophy of life, and the absence of values usually results in nondirectional behavior. Thus, values provide a unifying force, mission, or objective function, which shapes attitudes and influences behavior.

Attitudes can be viewed as perceptions about conditions that exist within the environment. These conditions often relate to organizational, national, international, and socio-political-cultural issues, and they are often assessed in terms of how they may affect people's needs as dictated by their values. In other words, the environmental conditions are perceived based on the value-driven attitudes of people. Thus, the analysis of values provides a basis for understanding people's attitudes in terms of how they perceive opportunities and threats in their environment.

The ultimate result of this "values-attitudes-behavior" process is reflected in the behavior of people in terms of their actions to resolve problems or conflicts or to take advantage of opportunities and make needed changes. This behavior in response to environmental conditions or stimuli is shaped by the value-driven attitudes that people form over time. As such, people's behavior reflects a value-based purpose or objective.

Let us look at a few examples of how this process of "values-attitudes-behavior" works. A work-oriented value will influence a person's attitude toward incentives offered by an organization. An incentive based on individual productivity is perceived to be more desirable, thereby leading to behavior or work actions that result in higher productivity. In the case of influencing the behavior of consumers, the marketing mix must attempt to shape the attitudes and perceptions of potential customers by appealing to their values and beliefs as they relate to their product needs. If a customer is an environmentalist, these appeals will represent an attempt to influence the attitudes and perceptions of the customer by emphasizing how the product contributes to a clean environment. From a political perspective, if a voter believes in private property and individualism, a political platform should be developed so that the voter perceives that less governmental bureaucracy will occur, thereby influencing the action of the voter on Election Day.

The values-attitudes-behavior cycle reflects a process of motivation, as shown in Figure I.1. Even though we usually view the motivation process as it relates to the individual's behavior, the relationships shown in Figure I.1 apply in a general way to groups, organizations, and larger societal units. The motivation process includes three major levels of relationships: individual, organizational, and societal. For example, an individual's values are directly shaped by current and historical situations, each of which is influenced by socioeconomic and political organizations and societal relations. These values, in turn, shape the individual's attitudes and how he or she perceives various work, family, and societal issues. Subsequently, the combination of values and attitudes combine to produce behavior resulting in specific efforts and actions, hopefully producing desirable results.

After this cycle of values-attitudes-behavior has been completed, the individual will experience an emotional response or feeling about what has transpired. This response or feeling is shaped by several factors, including the economic and work-related compensation received and the attitudes of others in the organization or community regarding the results achieved. Especially critical to this emotional response is the amount of mental congruency that has been achieved between values and the results. In other words, the values-attitudes-behavior cycle embodied in the process of motivation is highly subjective and emotional, even though the efforts and actions involved may include highly measurable work activities.

As we know, emotions are often the primary considerations for sustaining high levels of morale and productivity. We also know that the values that drive the attitudes and behavior that create emotional responses are shaped by many things. These include individual personality and the norms and expectations of groups, organizations, and socioeconomic and political issues at the local, national, and international levels. Throughout these relationships, family, ethnic, and cultural values are often very critical.

**Figure I.1
Values-Attitudes-Behavior**

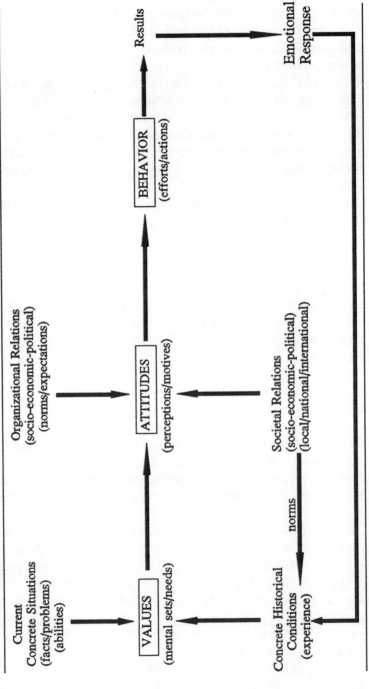

SELECTED VALUE CLASSIFICATIONS

There are a wide range of value classifications which have been developed over time in psychology and sociology reflecting individual group, organizational, and societal values. This section discusses a selected group of value classifications that reflect a mix of individual, work, societal, and cultural value classifications, as shown in Table I.1.

Perhaps one of the most widely recognized values classifications is A. H. Maslow's needs hierarchy. This hierarchy of basic needs reflects value criteria that influence workers' attitudes toward incentives designed to influence work behavior. These needs range from lower-level physiological and safety needs to higher-level needs of esteem and self-actualization. The underlying notion embodied in Maslow's needs hierarchy is to develop work conditions and incentives that motivate people according to the needs that have not been satisfied.

Somewhat related to Maslow's need hierarchy is the classification of work belief values of R. A. Buchholz. This values classification includes two extreme sets of work values relating to a work ethic versus a leisure ethic. The other values inherent in Buchholz's classifications include several socially oriented belief systems: the organizational, humanist, and Marxist. Again, the underlying notions are to better understand workers' work value criteria and to design better motivational systems to influence behavior.

Table I.1
Selected Value Classifications

Maslow	Buchholz
Self-Actualization	Work Ethic
Esteem	Organizational Beliefs
Love	Humanistic Beliefs
Safety	Marxist Beliefs
Physiological	Leisure Ethic
Allport	Hofstede
Aesthetic	Individualism vs. Collectivism
Theoretical	Masculinity vs. Femininity
Religious	Power Distance
Political	Uncertainty Avoidance
Social	Paternalism
Economic	Timeliness

A third value classification is provided by G. Allport and relates to general societal needs or value criteria. To be viable, each society as a whole must satisfy a number of basic economic, social, political, religious, theoretical, and aesthetic needs of humanity. The combination of these needs as a set of societal values reflects the general culture of society. In a healthy and viable society, some minimum mix of each of these needs usually is found.

The cultural value dimensions advanced by Hofstede comprise a fourth value classification that is useful for analyzing culture and society. These value dimensions focus on a society's emphasis on individualism versus collectivism, masculinity versus femininity, power distance, and uncertainty avoidance, which exist in individuals within cultural and societal groups. The initial four-part classification has been expanded to include two other value dimensions, a society's emphasis on paternalism and timeliness. Using Hofstede's values classification helps provide an understanding of the stronger inherent values in a culture or society. This understanding provides useful input not only to develop socioeconomic and political initiatives, but also to gain acceptance for the need for changes.

In a very general way, the above four value classifications reflect several major themes. First, there appears to be a continuum of values that cluster around an individualistic ethic, on one end, and a social ethic, on the other. The values inherent in the individualistic ethic are those associated with a work ethic, economic productivity, individualism, power distance, masculinity, and self-actualization. These values reflect the Protestant, market, and liberty ethics derived from the cultural rebirth and they provided the foundation for the industrial revolution. The work-related values inherent in the social ethic are those associated with organizational, humanist, and Marxist belief systems. The cultural values inherent in the social ethic include collectivism, femininity, and uncertainty avoidance, while societal values include social, political, religious, theoretical, and aesthetic value dimensions within the social ethic.

While the above values, which are inherent in the individualistic-social ethic continuum, are not mutually exclusive, this classification provides a useful way for analyzing major cultural and societal trends. On one hand, the essence of humanity is viewed by the individualistic ethic as inherent in the individual, and not in social relations, while the social ethic views the essence of humanity as inherent in social relations, and not in the individual. In other words, a basic tenet of the individualistic ethic is that improving individual productivity for individual gain will result in the greatest benefits and satisfaction for the individual, organization, and society. The opposite view of the social ethic is that the satisfaction of the group will optimize individual and organizational productivity and, therefore, provide the greatest overall benefits for society.

The central issue relating to values seems to be the priority placed on individual freedoms, private property rights, local and state rights, and the opportunities provided to take individual risks and develop initiatives. The individualistic-social ethic continuum of values that are selected directly involves how individuals will be treated in organizational work situations and how they will be affected by socioeconomic and political initiatives at the local, national, and international levels. The next section presents and discusses how values, attitudes, and behavior interact within an organizational and societal framework.

ORGANIZATIONAL AND SOCIETAL FRAMEWORK

In assessing the values-attitudes-behavior relationship, a fundamental premise, if not an axiom, is that this assessment must include the interaction that takes place between individuals within groups, organizations, and larger societal relationships. The analysis of a single person's values does not provide a full understanding unless it is viewed in relation to the values of others. If a person does not come in to contact with other individuals, his or her values are probably of no importance. This section uses this premise to present a framework to discuss the values-attitudes-behavior (VAB) relationship. The focus of this discussion is that people are both influencers and evaluators of organizational actions.

Perhaps one of the most general models of any organization is the input-output system developed in systems theory. Figure I.2 provides one example of this model, which reflects two major cycles. One cycle relates to the flow of resources, including technology and knowledge, into a series of transformation or production processes within an organizational setting. These processes consume resources obtained from other organizational transformation processes in order to create value in terms of products and services. The pattern of this flow of resources, in terms of quality, volume, timeliness, technology, and cost, into and through organizational value-creating transformation processes is directly

Figure I.2
Input-Output System

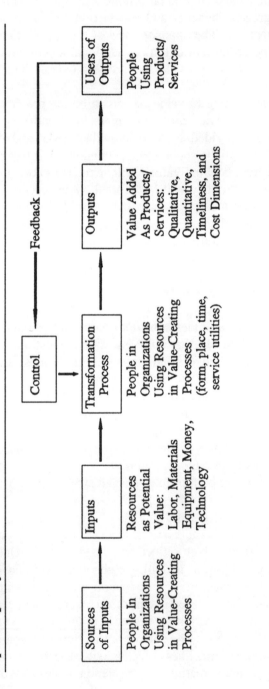

shaped by the values and attitudes of potential users, suppliers, workers, managers, and environmental interest groups (social and political).

The decisions relating to qualitative, quantitative, timeliness, and cost of this organizationally added value reflect the assessment of the values (and needs), attitudes (and perceptions), and likely behavior (and actions) of potential users (or customers). This assessment before-the-fact, plus feedback relating to these decisions comprises the second major cycle of this input-output model. In other words, the effectiveness of the organization depends on (1) an assessment of potential users' values-attitudes relationships, and (2) feedback from users as to the level of satisfaction they receive from the products and services.

The organization must also obtain and assess feedback about major current and emerging socio-economic-political values, attitudes and behavior. The social system directly influences the political processes and economic system within a society. The goals and values of the social system influences the decisions made by economic organizations directly, through users of products and services, and indirectly, through political initiatives, laws, and regulations. This socio-economic-political interaction of goals and values may be further influenced by other goals and values that emerge from or influence the social system. These include some of Allport's religious, theoretical and aesthetic societal values or needs, as well as environmental, international, and cultural/ethnic considerations.

The modern communications media play a major role in assessing, conveying, and modifying values-attitudes-behavior in work organizations and other societal groups. To be most effective, multimedia systems must exist so that greater diversity in communications occurs and, hopefully, media objectivity will increase. The internal communications and information systems of organizations generally focus on customer and public opinion issues that might affect economic growth and productivity. Sociopolitical communications focus on more macro issues, which usually involve socio-economic-political trade-offs or issues at the local, national, and international levels. These communications attempt to objectively interpret developments for the public, but in reality, they try to influence public opinion.

As societies mature, values, attitudes, and behavior evolve, often driven by major economic and social events, international conflicts, technology developments, or cultural issues. In a general way, we can identify differences in values-attitudes-behavior between nonindustrialized and industrialized societies. R. Inglehart's (1977) model of materialist-postmaterialistic value preferences provides a useful framework with which to assess societal values-attitudes-behavior changes in response to economic productivity and growth. This model relates generally to Maslow's needs hierarchy as it pertains to an individual's economic status.

However, in the case of all models, which are only general representations of reality, we can see that factors other than the solely economic can and do drive societal values-attributes-behavior changes. One such major factor is the need for safety or security in terms of protection from other societal, cultural, or ethnic groups.

GLOBAL VALUES IN TRANSITION

In recent years we have seen major changes in various parts of the world concerning individualism versus socialism. Today there are a number of major value-oriented trends which seem to be moving in different directions. For example, the significant changes in values, beliefs, and attitudes of German people that have emerged are influenced by the dynamic process of the unification between East and West Germany, and in particular, in connection with the critical economic situation in East Germany. In addition, the completion of the Single European Market on January 1, 1993, created new environmental factors that support the process of transition. These developments, as well as the opening of the Eastern European countries, have influenced the minds of the German people--consumers as well as entrepreneurs--in a significant way. As a consequence, empirical analyses, such as the annual survey title "Sorrows of the Nation" (see Chapter 3) reflect pronounced shifts in the value system of German people. In this context, it has to be stressed that significant differences between values, beliefs, and attitudes exist in East and West Germany due to the two regions' different political, economic, and cultural historical backgrounds. The prognosis for the creation of a common value system of German people is, therefore, a long-term process. As another example, the movement away from centralized societies and economies in Central and Eastern Europe and in the Commonwealth of Independent States reflects a general shift toward the individualistic ethic. However, within each of these new societies, as well as in the old ones, the patterns of development are different depending on each society's previous position, its ethnic and cultural makeup, and the strength of its economic system.

For example, the relative progress in making effective changes seems to be greater in Hungary than in Poland, and in the Czech Republic compared to Slovakia. The current problems in the Balkans represent the most chaotic transition to new societal, economic, and cultural arrangements. The developments in the former Soviet Union also are not without problems. Many of these are economic, but they also include cultural and ethnic divisions.

Moving to West Europe, however, the European Community developments reflect a more centralized arrangement between different nations seeking common economic and political initiatives and cooperative ventures. This is similar but to a lesser extent, to the recent trading bloc agreements between Mexico, the United States, and Canada, and between China, Korea, Japan, and other Asian countries. Moreover, throughout Latin America we have seen changes from failing import-substitution strategies and the sale of state-owned enterprises to the encouragement of foreign investment in order to improve the economic well-being of a country.

The central theme cutting across all these developments is based on an economic motive or value criterion. While the developments reflect multinational cooperation between somewhat different cultures, the underlying value criterion served is economic protectionism, or at least economic trading preferences using fewer trade barriers. Within the United States there is currently considerable dialogue between the pros and cons of economic protectionism as a national policy initiative. The support of protectionism is driven by the high unemployment levels in the United States, the federal and trade balance deficits, and fears about a further loss of jobs to other countries.

During recent years, the driving force or value criterion has tended to be economic, which is a natural tendency during recessionary periods. It is difficult to change the attitudes of people to accept (and pay for) initiatives and programs that are sociopolitically oriented and are perceived by people to reduce their economic status. The recent Earth Summit Conference held in Brazil in 1992 is a case in point as it relates to the position of the United States. It is clear that the economic value criterion was used by President George Bush as the primary reason for opposing certain provisions advocated in the conference because of the negative economic viability and private property impacts on the United States.

The economic value criterion seems to gain considerable strength as the economic productivity and employment within a country decreases, and has done so especially during recent years when these factors have been low worldwide. Thus, the individualistic ethic seems to be driven in several ways by Allport's economic value criterion. On one hand, you might expect that Buchholz's work ethic, Hofstede's individualism, and Maslow's higher level needs would be reinforced by the greater emphasis on the economic value criteria and the need for increasing economic productivity. However, what appears to be the case is that when unmet economic needs within a society occur in a recessionary period and reach a critical level, there is greater support for values that support economic and social protectionist, and even welfare programs. These values also encourage organizational and humanist values and are often accompanied by more pronounced ethnic divisions.

The above circumstances are central to the major dialogue surrounding the republican and democratic platforms in the United States in the 1992 election year. In other words, the conflict exists between protectionist, social welfare, and health care programs versus reliance on open free-trade mechanisms, enterprise zones, and market-system supplied health care. In the process of changing societal and cultural values, the economic value criterion is the major determinant of change, especially when economic conditions are poor. In periods of prosperity, the society and culture usually can absorb, and even support, hybrid values, which are inherent in both the individualistic and social ethics.

The question that remains is which ethic produces the best economic conditions for society? In other words, do the benefits derived from individual innovation, risk taking, private property and political pluralism outweigh the possible inequality of income to people, thereby increasing the need for social welfare and health care programs? Put another way, do the benefits derived from social and human rights equity, and from more centralized socioeconomic policies and initiatives, outweigh the possible dilution of the work ethic and encouragement for risk taking and innovation? The answer to these questions can only be analyzed in terms of people's basic values relating to work, family, culture and society within the context of international developments.

However, the careful assessment of people's values is difficult because their basic underlying values are not easy to identify or measure in terms of relative strength. Their strength only seems to appear when a crisis occurs, and then they often become very personal, emotional, and, often, selfish. When major changes occur in socioeconomic and political systems, such as those in the former Soviet Union and in Eastern and Central Europe, people tend to cooperate more easily within common social or ethnic groups rather than in more diverse sociopolitical systems. The extent of this cooperation is, in part, related to the seriousness of economic conditions (i.e., the more serious the conditions, the greater the clustering of social and ethnic groups).

While it is difficult to discern people's basic underlying values, it is essential to attempt to do so. This is necessary so that we can develop organizational and societal initiatives that address the needs embodied in these values and result in the implementation of meaningful programs over time.

From the above discussion of selected major changes occurring throughout the world, we can see that the general scarcity of resources and the widespread hostility in our global environment are fundamental forces that influence people's values. These values shape the specific economic, social, and political needs of people, and these needs create various forms of organizations. Thus, people in organizations are used as major mechanisms for producing both economic and noneconomic goods and services to satisfy people's needs. Figure I.3 summarizes these relationships between environment, values, needs, organizations, goods, and services. To analyze how values change, we must look at two major segments in these relationships. These two segments in a general way are differentiated by time as well as by their impact on basic values.

The first segment is the relationship between the environment and basic values. Changes in values that occur because of scarcity and hostility in the environment tend to be less frequent in the short run; however, when changes do occur, they often are of major importance. One important example is the recent shift from a socialist to a market-system economy throughout Central and Eastern Europe (CEE) and in the Commonwealth of Independent States (CIS). Another important example is the dilution of apartheid in South Africa. Moreover, the large shift from conservatism to liberalism in the United States during the most recent presidential election reflects significant changes in people's basic values caused by increasing scarcity and rising hostility in their environments.

Because these changes in basic values are driven by scarcity and hostility issues that have worldwide impacts as well as origins, these changes in basic values tend to spread throughout different regions or nations of the world. Consider as prime examples the large scale formal movement toward economic protectionism which is reflected in the recent formation of the European Community (EC), and the development of the

Figure I.3
Resource Scarcity and Environmental Hostility

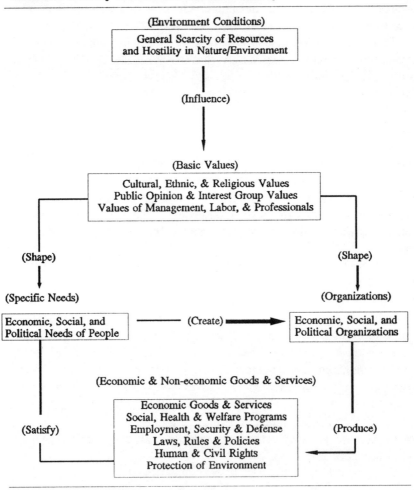

North American Free Trade Agreement (NAFTA) between the United States, Mexico, and Canada. Two sets of basic values are embodied in these developments: free trade between members and preferences to the countries in the EC or the NAFTA relative to non-members. It must be noted that these types of values consensus were influenced by scarcity and hostility conditions perceived in each respective environment, in this instance, world competitive markets.

It is also interesting to note that in each of these two trading blocs there are some signs of internal dissatisfaction among some members concerning the possible loss of income and jobs in certain industries and the potential dilution of national socioeconomic and political independence. Thus, on one hand, the formation of the trading bloc occurs to improve economic conditions and reduce hostility, yet individual countries (especially the more productive ones) lobby for exceptions. When you superimpose the differing nationalistic tendencies on these issues and agreements, the search for consensus becomes more difficult and more emotional.

Building a new consensus of values takes a long time simply because a large number of people are involved. Consensus occurs when a scarcity of resources and the amount of hostility in the environment are perceived to be so severe that people unite to correct these conditions. This is often accompanied by changes in basic values which usually result in new types of socioeconomic and political organizations or initiatives. Subsequently, there also may be different priorities for the economic and noneconomic goods and services produced. It should be noted that in periods when scarcity and hostility in the environment are improving and becoming less severe, it is more difficult to change people's basic values, even though sporadic issues arise.

The second segment is the relationships among needs, organizations, and goods and services. These relationships tend to be more involved in the ongoing production, delivery and consumption of economic and noneconomic goods and services within a society or nation. These socioeconomic and political processes continue to function to satisfy the needs of people as reflected in a general level of values consensus. This does not mean that no changes occur in the short run; however, these changes tend to take the form of selected sociopolitical initiatives that have less centralized impacts on segments of society.

The basic societal and cultural tenets, such as capitalism, socialism, private property rights, pluralism, and so forth, are not overturned by these periodic initiatives. Thus, the fundamental values may be questioned, but a consensus for change usually is not achieved in the short run. Indeed, it is not until new generations of people in society emerge that major changes occur.

As we proceed to the end of this century, there appears to be a great potential for change in the basic values of individual societies throughout the world. A major impetus for change seems to be coming from younger generations, somewhat similar to the antiestablishment movement in the 1960s, but perhaps with a more specific thrust. Certainly, the basic values inherent in Mexico's young population (50 percent is less than 25 years old) will soon provide a major influence on socioeconomic and political initiatives in that country. In the United States, the new generation of political leaders, who are relatively young in terms of the established (and, some feel, outdated) politicians are making major inroads in influencing socioeconomic initiatives. Racial tensions (if not hatred) in the United States are accelerating, especially among young people. In Germany, there is a serious antiforeigner sentiment which also can be observed in many countries throughout the world.

The emerging changes embody hostility, protectionism, and competition for scarce resources and markets and are fueled by racial, ethnic, and national priorities. While these features are not necessarily new, the points of conflict seem more emotional because of the recessionary influences that exist and the greater levels of socioeconomic and political hostility in the environment. A number of the more important areas of disagreement or conflict that are evident and are likely to continue include:

1. The Individualistic ethic and capitalism versus the social ethic and collectivism;
2. Free trade versus economic protectionism;
3. Decentralized versus centralized social welfare and health programs;
4. Materialistic versus postmaterialistic goals;
5. Income and employment versus environmental protection;
6. National versus world governance and multinational priorities;
7. Tax incentives for the rich versus for the poor;
8. Individual human and civil rights versus governmental bureaucracy;
9. Local and states rights versus federal bureaucracy; and
10. Conflicting values according to age, sex, race, religion, ethnicism, economic status, and education.

The above 10 areas of disagreement or conflict will likely continue to be sensitive throughout the remainder of this century. With the advances in communications and the expansion of the media, regional, national, and world events and issues will be debated within the context of each nation or society's environmental conditions and people's basic values. Challenges to existing values, needs, organizations, products, and services will be easier to develop and promote. Perhaps the cycle of change relating to basic values will also be shortened.

1

Survey of Selected Research on Values, Work Beliefs, and Socioeconomic Attitudes

Joel D. Nicholson, Lee P. Stepina, and Dan Voich, Jr.

OVERVIEW OF VALUES, BELIEFS, AND ATTITUDES

A number of researchers from various disciplines have conducted studies on the nature and function of values (Brigham, 1986; Cochrane, Billig, and Hogg, 1979; Yankelovich, 1981). One of the earliest psychological researchers to develop a classification of human values was Allport (Allport, Vernon, and Lindzey, 1931). He categorized values into six different types or groups: theoretical, economic, aesthetic, social, political, and religious. Rokeach (1968, 1973, 1979) added precision to the description of values, defining them as global beliefs that guide actions and judgments across a variety of situations. He saw values as individual attributes that affect attitudes, perceptions, needs, and motivation. They are formed from experience over time in conjunction with parents, friends, school, external referent groups, religious organizations, and the media. Values are the learned mental programming that results from living within and experiencing a cultural setting.

Kluckhohn and Strodtbeck (1961) saw values as central tenets of a society's culture. They defined values as explicit or implicit desires of individuals or groups which influence the selection from available means, ends, and actions. Values are both consciously and unconsciously held. Cultural values can be viewed as relatively general conceptualizations that define what is right or wrong or that specify general preferences. They can be shared by all or most members of social groups, they are something that older members of groups try to pass on to younger members, and, as with morals, laws, and customs, they shape behavior and structure one's perception of the world (Adler, 1986).

One of the earlier reviews of values as they relate to organizational behavior was presented by Locke (1976). Locke's work pertained specifically to the indirect relation of values to job satisfaction. He drew on the work of Rand (1964), who described values as something that people act for in order to acquire or retain. In other words, values once again were considered as reflecting desired end states. Locke saw them as a causal force behind both action choice and affect or emotion.

Perhaps the most significant research to date concerning cross cultural comparisons of values is that of Hofstede (1980), which will be discussed in detail later. The four major value dimensions that emerged from Hofstede's work are power distance, individualism versus collectivism, uncertainty avoidance, and masculinity versus femininity. Dorfman and Howell (1988) have added refinements to Hofstede's scales and added two further dimensions, paternalism and time.

While values are preferred end states or means for achieving them, beliefs are an individual's assumptions about the world, the environment within which he or she exists (Schein, 1985). They provide the individual with an information system, a ground against which to interpret reality. They also provide meaning for the individual, setting the stage for organization and coherency in an otherwise chaotic environment (Schein, 1985).

Buchholz (1976, 1977, 1978) has provided a comprehensive research paradigm for the study of individuals' beliefs about the general nature of work. Buchholz developed and refined five work belief dimensions: the work ethic, the organizational belief system, Marxist-related beliefs, the humanist belief system, and the leisure ethic. Buchholz's research and work-belief dimensions will be discussed at length later.

Allport (Allport et al., 1931), a personality theorist, called social psychology the study of attitudes, which he viewed as an affective disposition to respond to social stimuli in consistent and enduring ways. To the social psychologist, attitudes are like individual behaviors. In fact, researchers can only infer attitudes from behavior. The expression of an attitude on a questionnaire is itself a behavior that is reflective of the attitude in question. Attitudes are thus measured principally by self-reports, since it is the respondent who is providing the information to the researcher. Other measurement techniques are used, such as behavioral observation and physiological measures, but they are inferential as well.

Values are held more deeply than attitudes. They are questioned less and do not have specific objects attached to them. For example, a belief in equality is a value, whereas evaluating a political candidate either positively or negatively is an attitude (Brigham, 1986). In Rokeach's terms, values "serve as standards or criteria to guide not only action but also judgment, choice, attitude, evaluation, argument, exhortation, rationalization, and . . . attributions of causality" (Rokeach, 1979, p. 2). Values are more general and central than are attitudes. In a sense, they precede attitudinal formation. People are capable of holding many more attitudes than values.

There is evidence that organizational behavior is affected by the situation in which the person operates, the individual's own personal attributes, and the interaction of the two (Mitchell and James, 1989). Values comprise one of the significant individual components of these dynamics. They are central concepts to individuals, organizations, and regional and national cultures. Along with situational, interactional, and other personal attributes, values predispose individuals to behavior.

Individuals express culture and its normative qualities through the values they hold. Their values also affect their attitudes, which, in turn, influence behavior. England (1975) has noted that one of the most important behaviors that values affect in the workplace is the formulation of corporate strategy. He also noted that values influence many other kinds of organizational behavior, including reward systems, selection, group behaviors, communication, leadership, and leader-member relations.

Adler (1986) has given several examples of how values that differ across cultures can influence organizational behaviors. In addition, work behaviors, in turn, are valued differentially across cultures. It is important to note differences between values, beliefs, attitudes, and behavior. Values are preferred or desirable end states, and sometimes they are general means for attaining those states. Beliefs are the way in which the individual sees the world. They are what the individual perceives to be happening. Attitudes are affective responses to these perceptions of the individual's environment that lead to specific behaviors : values --> beliefs --> attitudes --> behaviors. Understanding these interrelationships is crucial for conflict resolution and for developing viable initiatives in business and government organizations. There are several kinds of attitudes: for example, information-based attitudes, social adjustment function attitudes, ego defensive attitudes, and value-expressive attitudes, to name a few. Attitudes that are value-expressive are the most resistant to change (Brigham, 1986). Attitudes generally flow from values and have specific objects toward which they are directed. Values and attitudes both combine to predispose individuals to behavior, whether positive or negative, vis-à-vis their perceived environments.

Attitudes have been described as having three basic components (Schermerhorn, Hunt, and Osborn, 1988):
1. *Cognitive Component*: Beliefs and values; antecedents to the attitude.
2. *Affective Component*: The actual attitude; a specific feeling regarding the personal impact of antecedent conditions.
3. *Behavioral Component*: Intention to behave in a certain way in response to the feelings. They are the result of an attitude; a predisposition to act in a specific way. However, one must bear in mind that the link between values, beliefs, attitudes, and behaviors is tentative, an intention may not be carried out due to a variety of situational and interactional reasons.

EARLY PERSPECTIVES ON CULTURAL VALUES

Culture evolves wherever groups exist over time, sharing a history, core values, common beliefs, and basic assumptions about their group and its place in the world. The concept of culture can be engaged at various levels of analysis. Identifiable groups can be said to exist at the ecological/national, regional, and local levels, as well as the international levels, to some extent. Culture also exists within organizations at both the macro (organization-wide) and micro (group and departmental) levels.

Perhaps the most traditional and well-developed cultural research paradigms emanate from sociology and anthropology. One of the earliest, and yet most enduring, sociological definitions of culture came from the Canadian sociologist E. Sapir (1924). Sapir viewed culture as something that embraces the general values, attitudes, beliefs, and views of life. It defines the significance of action and thought of a whole group of people across lifetimes, signifying value for them.

Anthropological literature is equally rich in describing cultural systems. The most comprehensive and accepted anthropological definition of culture is from A. L. Kroeber and C. Kluckhohn (1952):
"Culture consists of patterns, explicit and implicit, of and for behavior acquired and transmitted by symbols, constituting the distinctive achievement of human groups, including their embodi-

ment in artifacts; the essential core of culture consists of traditional (i.e., historically derived and selected) ideas and especially their attached values" (p. 181).

Two of the most important cultural anthropologists, F. Kluckhohn and F. L. Strodtbeck (1961), offered a comprehensive set of assumptions that facilitate the understanding of a society's cultural orientation. One of their central assumptions was that each society has a dominant profile or value orientation, with numerous variations or alternative profiles existing within and across cultures. Another central assumption was that in both the dominant value profile and the alternative variations, there is a rank-ordering of preferences for the various alternatives. Kroeber and Kluckhohn (1952) presented these assumptions as characterizing the norms or stereotypes of a culture. They never succinctly characterize or predict the behavior of all people in a culture but rather describe cultural prototypes.

HOFSTEDE'S CULTURAL VALUES

Perhaps the major contributor to advancing cross-cultural management theory and practice from the ethnocentrist positions of the 1950s and 1960s is Geert Hofstede. The earlier prevailing ethnocentrist paradigm held that the management theory and practice used and accepted in Europe and the United States was universally valid. National culture did not play a role. The convergent hypothesis of that time held that if Second and Third World management systems would come around to the European and American frameworks, they would be successful and all major disparities would disappear (Webber, 1969; Barrett and Bass, 1976). During the 1970s cross-cultural researchers began to eschew the convergence hypothesis and to ardently explore national and regional cultures as variables that affect the management process and related outcome variables (Hofstede and Bond, 1984; Ronen and Shenkar, 1985).

Hofstede was a major figure in empirically researching the importance of national cultures. He chose the national level of analysis because nationality is important to management for a number of political, sociological, and psychological reasons. Nations are political units that develop their peculiar identity based on perceived social symbolic value. These national perceptions are conditioned by psychological factors that emerge in different cultures.

Hofstede defined (national) culture in what can be considered social information-processing terms or, in Hofstede's words, "collective mental programming." Such programming reflects the way in which a national group of people view reality and the group's place in it. It includes such things as language, tradition, espoused values, behavioral norms, and laws. A national culture is very difficult to change. Its artifacts are deeply imbedded in society's institutions and in the minds of its people. Hofstede saw traditions and ways of thinking about the world as being in a mutually reinforcing system with a society's legal, educational, religious, and other institutions. Adherence to the tenets of the culture are rewarded, while deviance is punished.

While Hofstede acknowledged the existence and importance of regional or "sub-cultural" groups within and even across national boundaries, his research dealt with culture at the national level of analysis. This was the proper first step at the time, given the general denial of any cultural influences implied by the ethnocentrist convergence hypothesis. In fact, it was Hofstede's work that was the catalyst for the paradigm shift to cultural awareness in general, as well as the eventual methodological refinements in cross-cultural management research, including greater specificity in the level of analysis. As such, Hofstede's work should be, and is, acknowledged for truly breaking new ground.

Hofstede studied work-related values in a major multinational firm spanning 50 different countries. The four major factors (or cultural value dimensions) that emerged from Hofstede's work are individualism versus collectivism, power distance, uncertainty avoidance, and masculinity versus femininity. With the exception of power distance and individualism versus collectivism, the dimensions are independent of one another. The original factor analysis revealed that 50 % of the variance between countries was explained by three factors: power distance and individualism; uncertainty avoidance; and masculinity. Hofstede treated power distance and individualism separately based on his own theoretical reasoning, which has met with virtually no criticism over the past decade.

Individualism versus Collectivism

Hofstede's first value dimension, individualism, has been the most actively researched in a broad variety of situations. As with the other three dimensions, Hofstede calculated an index value for each country surveyed. This value index score represented each nation's relative position along the continuum of individualism versus collectivism, using the mean scores for all respondents within each country.

The individualist end of the spectrum is anchored by national societies in which ties between individuals are quite loose. In such individualistic societies, members are expected to take care of their own affairs. Collective responsibilities extend only occasionally involving only the immediate family. Such relations are facilitated by greater personal freedoms afforded to members by the cultural norms of these nations.

The collectivist end of the spectrum is anchored by national societies in which there are very strong ties between individuals. Members are born into existing in-groups. Extended families are common and are interlaced with responsibilities characterized by intergroup social exchanges. Members are not only expected to look after each other, they are also expected to hold and adhere to the group's norms and values.

Hofstede defined the two ends of the dimension in terms of social integration. Individualist societies are seen as loosely integrated nations, while collectivist societies are seen as tightly integrated wholes. Each of the 50 countries can be positioned along the continuum in relative fashion by use of the individualism index score.

Interestingly, Hofstede discovered that across all 50 countries surveyed, there was a very strong positive correlation between degree of individualism and country wealth, as expressed by gross national product (GNP). Countries that were very wealthy at the time of the first surveys (1970) were also the most highly individualistic. Such countries were all Occidental (e.g., the United States, Great Britain, and the Netherlands). By contrast, the least wealthy countries were also the most highly collectivist (the Latin and Oriental countries). While it is an interesting proposition, the relationship between the individualist value orientation and country wealth has not been given much further research attention.

Power Distance

The power distance dimension measures the extent to which members of a given society accept as legitimate inequalities in wealth and power. Such inequalities exist to a greater or lesser degree in all societies; it is the acceptance of these disparities that is tapped by the measure. For example, large disparities in wealth are accepted in India (which therefore has a high power distance score). By contrast, any existing disparities in Israel or the Scandinavian countries are downplayed (low power distance).

Hofstede related the power dimension to the centralization dimension in organizations. As such, he conceptualized an autocratic, centralized leadership structure as emanating from the mind-set, or mental programming, of the larger society. This mind-set is reflective of both the leaders and the general populace. The value systems of workers and management in such a case are complementary; a sort of psychological equilibrium tends to occur. The dependency needs of the powerless are satisfied along with the leadership needs of the powerful.

Hofstede reported a global relationship between individualism and power distance for selected countries. Collectivist nations were, without exception, high on power distance scores. The Latin European countries (France, Belgium, Italy, and Spain) were characterized by large power distance scores with high individualism. Without exception, all low-GNP (poor) nations were collectivist in orientation with high power distance scores.

Uncertainty Avoidance

Hofstede's third value dimension incorporates the notion of time, something subsequent researchers have considered as an independent dimension. In Hofstede's reasoning, time and uncertainty avoidance were related because everyone is uncertain about the future. Hofstede did discover, however, that cultures varied in how they reacted to this uncertainty. Some react to an uncertain future with acceptance and even philosophical resignation. Such cultures would have a weak uncertainty avoidance score. High uncertainty avoidance scores would characterize cultures that ardently strive to socialize members into systems that aim to engineer uncertainty out of existence, as much as possible. Greater levels of general anxiety, emotionality, and nervousness can be expected in such cultures. More important, such cultures will have institutions that are designed to reduce uncertainty for members by fostering security and reducing risks.

Hofstede found that Latin countries tend to reflect a large power distance and high uncertainty avoidance, while Asian countries tend to reflect a large power distance and low uncertainty avoidance. Germanic countries tend to reflect a small power distance combined with a higher level of uncertainty avoidance, while Anglo or Occidental countries reflect a small power distance and small uncertainty avoidance.

Masculinity versus Femininity

The masculinity scale measures the division of sex roles in a given culture. Most such sex roles are social and are derived arbitrarily. Hofstede noted that typical tasks for men and women vary considerably across cultures. This dimension taps the degree to which societies either maximize or minimize these social role differences for the sexes.

Hofstede defined masculine societies as those in which masculine sex roles deeply permeate the entire population, affecting the mental programming of both sexes. Hence, common values are achievement, materialism, ostentatious behavior, making money, and so forth. In more feminist societies the reverse is true; values that permeate society are more often those typically associated with women: quality of life relationships over materialism, preservation of the environment, helping behaviors, and so on. Heroes, both literary and real, often embody the values of a given society.

It is interesting to note that Hofstede found that Japan is the most masculine of societies. This makes sense given the definition of sex role differentiation outlined above. The Germanic countries are relatively masculine, as are several Latin countries. On the other hand, the Nordic countries are defined as feminine societies.

Conclusions from Hofstede's Research

Organizations are institutions that serve various functions, including reducing systematic uncertainty for members. Hence, the uncertainty avoidance dimension can be considered in organizational structure concerns. Likewise, since organizations institutionalize power distributions among members, the power distance dimension is also of considerable interest. Hofstede used these two dimensions, to describe four implicit models of organization. One model of an organization is the pyramid, a hierarchical structure held together by the unity of command (large power distance) as well as rules (strong uncertainty avoidance). A second model relies on rules for everything (strong uncertainty avoidance but smaller power distance). The third model is like a village market, with no decisive hierarchy but involving flexible rules and the resolution of problems by negotiating (small power distance and weak uncertainty avoidance). The fourth model of an organization is the family, with undisputed personal authority of the father-leader but few formal rules (large power distance and weak uncertainty avoidance).

Hofstede's work provided strong evidence against the convergence hypothesis: the idea that there were universals for both management theory and practice. The ethnocentrist position that management styles around the globe would eventually converge upon the U.S. models was largely a reflection of the post-World War II economic importance of the United States. Not only were the world's markets wide open for industries in the United States during that period, but the bulk of work on management theory was being done in that country. Hence, the preponderance of management practice and theory put forth in the three decades following World War II were reflective of U.S. cultural values. Thanks to Hofstede's ground-breaking research, we now know that U.S. culture is only one of many worldwide and that there are systematic differences between cultures that are important to both management theory and practice.

Examples of ways in which cultural differences affect management abound. For instance, the individualism and power distance dimensions affect the kinds of leadership that will be effective in a given cultural milieu. The kind of leadership that may work in a highly individualistic society such as in the United States will be relatively less effective in collectivist or group centered societies as are found in Oriental or Latin American societies. The power distance dimension is important to the amount of participatory versus autocratic management that will be accepted and effective in a given society. Lower power distance societies, such as found in the Scandinavian countries, will best utilize worker participation, while high power distance countries, such as France, will more effectively engage autocratic leadership.

The individualism-versus-collectivism dimension is important to motivation theory and practice. Whereas self-respect and individual rewards are important in the United States, public "face" is important to Oriental, Latin, and Middle Eastern cultures. Finally, in countries that are high in uncertainty avoidance, security is a highly motivating factor. In summary, Hofstede provided strong data that management theory and practice are culturally dependent. There is much data to suggest that, in practice, effective multinational companies do adapt their overseas management practices to fit local cultures. Hofstede is given credit for providing the watershed research that signaled a paradigm shift away from the ethnocentrist position of the convergence hypothesis and toward research addressing cultural contingencies as potent variables.

Hofstede is also credited with being among the first to empirically demonstrate the counterintuitive notion that, despite ever-increasing global communications, along with the globalization and increased interdependence of world markets, there continue to be distinctive cultural differences between nations and regions. In fact, several researchers have provided evidence that such cultural differences are increasing rather than decreasing (Ali, 1988; Adler, 1986).

Hofstede demonstrated that differences in national and regional cultures show up in work values. He made a convincing case for the consideration of prevailing social values as quintessential variables in understanding motivation and organizational behavior cross culturally (Ali, 1988). Indeed, Bhagatt and McQuaid (1982) have described Hofstede's research as the most significant cross-cultural study of work-related values.

WORK BELIEFS AT THE ORGANIZATIONAL WORK LEVEL

In addition to values, beliefs are critical components of culture at the organizational level. Barney has described organizational culture as "a complex set of values, beliefs, assumptions, and symbols that define the way in which a firm conducts its business" (Barney, 1986, p. 656). Pettigrew (1979) described culture as an amalgam of beliefs, ideology, language, ritual, and myth. Dennison (1984) stated that it is a set of values, beliefs, and behavior patterns that form the core identity of an organization. Schein (1985) depicted it as a pattern of basic assumptions or beliefs. Culture can also be viewed as a mix of values, beliefs, assumptions, meanings, and expectations that members of an organization or group (or subgroup) hold in common and that they use as behavioral and problem-solving guides. Beliefs are an integral element of culture at the organizational level.

There are two important considerations concerning the relationship between national and organizational level culture. These considerations are the reasons for bringing organizational-level culture into the discussion. First, organizational-level cultures do not arise from a vacuum. On the contrary, organizations draw their members from national populations, and members bring with them the values and beliefs operating within their national culture. When culture is being investigated at the national level, one can expect a reasonable degree of general congruence in the structure of value and belief systems among members. Hence, there is a strong relationship between organizational and national culture when the focus is on values and beliefs and the level of analysis is the societal level. Second, and most important, the attitudes and behaviors that flow from values and beliefs do so within organizational contexts. Hence, in order to properly examine the relationship between national-level values and work beliefs, consideration must be given to the two contextual referents for these beliefs: the society and the workplace.

The study of culture can help us the understand many phenomena of organizational behavior, especially those that are not readily understood or seen as rational (Schein, 1985). Siehl and Martin (1984) stated that the content of culture at the organizational level comprises core values and beliefs which, in turn, define the organization's philosophy and mission. Schein (1985) added that culture is the embodiment of the values and beliefs that are so deeply held over time that they become unconscious assumptions of the group members. In other words, through interactions with the environment on critical issues, the organization tends to repeat those things that work out positively for it. As such, beliefs about the nature of such phenomena are learned by group members to be true and beneficial. With repetition and learning over time, these initially conscious expectations, intuitions, and beliefs gradually become unconscious assumptions. No longer demanding attention, they cluster into core values and beliefs. From these core values and beliefs flow behaviors at all levels of organizations. More important, these organizational values and beliefs are engendered from a starting base of shared national-level cultural values and general beliefs about work.

Schein (1985) has examined the deep psychosocial assumptions that form the belief foundations of an organization's particular culture. Schein's dimensions are: humanity's relationship to nature, the nature of reality and truth, the nature of human nature, the nature of human activity, and the nature of human relationships. These core beliefs critically affect the core strategic decisions that organizations will make, such as with their mission statements. The dominant U.S. business culture paradigm is, in Shein's words:

"oriented toward the mastery of nature, holds an active optimistic view of man as perfectible, views society as built on competitive relationships, and has an optimistic future built on a notion of progress . . . [It involves] a pragmatic view of truth and reality, a monochronic view of time, a view of space and resources as being infinitely available, and a view of authority relationships as 'rational-legal' in the sense that power should go to those who have the expertise and are selected or appointed by a process that rests on the democratic principle of consent of the governed . . . We expect relationships to be emotionally neutral, universalistic, specific, and achievement oriented" (Schein, 1985, p. 110).

There have been no studies to date that systematically investigate the relationship between national-level cultural values and beliefs about work. Major stumbling blocks, such as difficulties in the operationalization of culture and a lack of clear distinctions between values and beliefs have hindered such studies in the past. Researchers have previously focused solely on value dimensions cross culturally. The best research that has been done to date on work beliefs is by Schein (1985). However, his paradigm is a qualitative, within-subject design approach that is firm-specific, and studies that provide for a comparison of work beliefs across organizations and across cultures are called for.

BUCHHOLZ'S DIMENSIONS OF WORK BELIEFS

There do exist dimensions of work beliefs that would facilitate research concerning the relationship between values and beliefs. Buchholz provided significant research concerning beliefs that individuals hold about the nature of work. Her research provides a methodology to facilitate comparison of work beliefs across both organizations and cultures. The dimensions of Buchholz' (1978) work belief scales are discussed in the following paragraphs.

The Work Ethic

The work ethic dimension measures the extent to which individuals believe that work is good in itself and bestows dignity on a person. Thus, everyone should work and those who do not are not useful members of society. By working hard, a person can overcome every obstacle that life presents and can make his or her own way in the world. Success is thus directly linked to one's own efforts, and the material wealth a person accumulates is a measure of how much effort that person has expended. Wealth should be wisely invested to earn still greater returns and not foolishly spent on personal consumption. Thus, thrift and frugality are virtues to be practiced in the use of one's material possessions.

Organizational Belief System

The organizational belief system dimension measures the extent to which individuals believe that work takes on meaning only as it affects the group or the organization for which one works and along with one's status and rise in the organizational hierarchy. Work is not so much an end in itself, but more of a means, valued only for how it serves group interests and contributes to one's success in the organization. However, this success is more dependent on one's ability to conform and adapt to group norms than it is the result of individual effort and accomplishment. In other words, success in the organization is more dependent on the ability to get along and "play the game" than it is on individual productivity.

Marxist-Related Beliefs

The Marxist-related beliefs dimension measures the extent to which individuals believe that productive activity or work is basic to human fulfillment. Without work, a person cannot provide for his or her own physical needs. Through work, we create the world and ourselves and keep in touch with our fellow human beings. As presently organized, however, work in the United States does not allow man to fulfill himself as a creative and social individual. The work of the average person mainly benefits the ownership classes of society rather than the workers themselves. In this way, workers are exploited and alienated from their productivity. They should have more of a say in what goes on in corporations and should exercise more control over the workplace.

Humanistic Belief System

The humanistic belief system measures the extent to which individuals believe that work is to be taken seriously as the way in which we discover and fulfill ourselves as human beings. Thus, individual growth and development on the job is more important than the output of the work process, and what happens in the workplace is more important than productivity. Work must be redesigned to allow a person to become fully human and reach higher stages of development than the fulfillment of material or only the basic needs and wants. Work is an indispensable human activity that cannot be eliminated. Thus, work must be made meaningful and fulfilling for individuals and must allow them to discover their potential as human beings.

Leisure Ethic

The leisure ethic dimension measures the extent to which individuals believe that work has no meaning in itself but rather finds meaning in leisure. Jobs cannot be made meaningful or fulfilling, but work is necessary to produce goods and services and enable one to earn the money to buy them. Human fulfillment is found in leisure activities where one has a choice regarding the use of one's time and can find pleasure in pursuing activities of personal interest. This is where a person can be creative and involved. Thus, the fewer hours one can spend working and the more leisure time available, the better.

Findings from the Buchholz Studies

Consistent with earlier propositions by Sheppard and Herrick (1972), Buchholz (1977) found that workers had a work orientation based on humanistic beliefs rather than on the traditional work ethic (i.e., the Calvinist Protestant work ethic which had been dominant for decades prior to the 1970s).

Other results of Buchholz's (1977) research indicated that management also adhered most strongly to the humanistic belief system, least strongly to the Marxist system, and moderately to the organizational belief system and leisure ethic. Buchholz interpreted this to mean that management generally enjoys its work and looks desparagingly at too much leisure time. She found no differences in beliefs due to type of company, size of firm, religion, or education. Some differences were found between lower and upper levels of management on Marxist beliefs, which Buchholz interpreted to reflect the desire among the lower levels for more decision-making authority. A difference across position (and its correlate, age) was found for organizational belief. Buchholz saw this as indicative of increasing commitment to the corporate viewpoint as one grows older and rises in position within an organization.

Buchholz summarized the implications of her results in the following words: "This is a radical departure from the so-called work ethic tradition that was once believed to have been dominant in our society in the past. While the work ethic may once have described the work experience for managers satisfactorily, it apparently no longer does so and has been replaced by a humanistic view of work" (Buchholz, 1977, p. 585).

SOCIOECONOMIC ATTITUDES AND BUSINESS ISSUES

It has been demonstrated that there is significant agreement in the literature that essential elements of national and organizational culture are shared values and beliefs. To a significant extent, organizational cultures derive basic value and belief structures from national cultures. Furthermore, there is agreement that values and beliefs greatly influence organizational attitudes and behavior. To a significant degree, values, beliefs, and attitudes govern behavior and decisionmaking activity in organizations. It is through shared values and beliefs that organizational culture impacts organizational behavior and, hence, effectiveness. A significant problem yet to be resolved in the literature is the question of whether and how cultural values and work beliefs are related.

Attitudes represent the middle link in the chain of Values and Beliefs ---> Attitudes ---> Behavior. One particularly important concern is the question of how cognitive and affective attitudes toward a few significant national and international issues may affect both governmental and business strategic planning and operations.

Importance of Environmental Issues Assessment

The environment, perhaps more than any other organizational element, affects decision making, structure, and other internal activities of organizations (Daft, Sormunen, and Parks, 1988). It has been demonstrated, both in theory and actual practice, that formalizing environmental analysis activities can be extremely beneficial to an organization (Klein and Linneman, 1984; Newgren, Rasher, and LaRoe, 1984). Many successful organizations employ special units and selected personnel solely for the purpose of acquiring, interpreting, and communicating information on a firm's external environment.

Much attention has been given in the strategic management literature to environmental assessment. Competitive firms narrow their focus to those sections of the macroenvironment relevant to their particular domains, their microenvironments (Kefalas, 1990). Strategic objectives are established for the firm by matching its internal capabilities with the capacities of its external microenvironment. Assessing the relevant external microenvironment is the far more problematic task, especially in a multinational setting (Kefalas, 1990).

Competitive multinational firms integrate environmental scanning as a critical component of their strategic planning systems. They consistently evaluate their environment, looking for emerging trends, organizational changes, and emerging external issues that may impact their corporate decision making (Preble, Rau and Reichel, 1988). The two principal reasons for multinational environmental assessment are to enable the firm to detect and minimize potential political and economic threats and risks and to identify and maximize opportunities for profitable involvement (Kefalas, 1990).

It is accepted practice in multinational management to treat the firm's microenvironment as a set of emerging issues that are critically relevant to corporate survival and profitability (Kefalas, 1990). Whereas environmental scanning denotes merely assessing the environment, the more comprehensive, interactive term "issues management" incorporates proactive management of the environment. Coates (1986) described issues management in the following terms:

"Issues management is the organized activity of identifying emerging trends, concerns, or issues likely to affect an organization in the next few years and developing a wider and more positive range of organizational responses toward that future. Business and industry in adopting issues management, seek to formulative creative alternatives to constraints, regulations, or confrontation. Often in the past, the awareness of a trend, a new development, or the possibility of new constraints came too late to frame anything but a reactive response."

Perceptions of Issues as Attitudes Toward the Environment

Perceptions of such issues involve attitudes toward the environment that directly impact the strategic intentions of decision makers (Daft et al., 1988). The timely accumulation of pertinent environmental information can benefit a firm, not only by indicating what environmental changes are likely to occur, but also by providing the organization with the necessary lead time to adjust its strategic planning and prepare for transitions (Hambrick, et al., 1985). Competitive multinational firms must be aware of the attitudes, beliefs, and issue orientations of key stakeholders in their relevant domains (Fahey and King, 1977).

Organizations that conduct international business activities are faced with the added uncertainty of multiple, interactive global environments (Preble et al., 1988). Multinational executives tend to see economics, competition, and politics as the most critical factors that are readily identifiable in their environments (Keegan, 1974). Domestic managers, on the other hand, identify customers first, followed by economics and competition (Preble et al., 1988; Daft et al., 1988).

McCann (1985) pointed out that organizations can collaborate on scanning activities, not only for the purpose of preserving resources, but also to more successfully identify issues that require the most managerial attention. Interorganizational domains are used as the basis for McCann's collaborative scanning theory. Interorganizational domains are shared social space within an industry that is presently occupied by many related, but independent, firms (McCann, 1985).

McCann and Gomez-Mejia: The INUBPRO Project

Among the most valid and comprehensive empirical research in this area is that of Gomez-Mejia and McCann (1986a), who demonstrated the significance to firms of decision makers' perceptions of sociopolitical and economic issues operating in an environmental domain. Significant studies assessing cross-cultural attitudes toward pertinent environmental issues were conducted. These researchers conducted the bulk of their work through the Interamerican Business Project (INUBPRO). One of the aims of the INUBPRO project was to identify, assess, and track attitudes toward trade- and economic development-related issues that are pertinent to the Caribbean Basin region. One result of their work is a set of scales that can be used to assess the important environmental concerns that constitute an issues climate, not only for the Caribbean, but for other regions as well. Such attitudinal assessments represent important information for decision makers involved with corporate and governmental policy to include in the strategic-planning process. This work provided summary findings for both businesses and governments with active concerns in the Caribbean region.

Specifically, the objectives of the INUBPRO environmental scan were:

1. Identification of a set of core trade and economic development attitudes;
2. Assessments of these attitudes by organizations involved in the region in terms of the perceived stage of issue development and impact; and
3. An analysis of these assessments to determine policy implications for the participating organizations.

Forty issues were compared across 20 Caribbean Basin countries. The following is a sample of the kinds of issues assessed:

- Public sector corruption;
- Political violence and social unrest;
- Crime rate;
- Inflation rate;
- Levels of unemployment;
- Political radicalism of workers and labor unrest;
- Favorable attitude toward private enterprise;
- Multinationals as furthering economic development;
- The role of government in local economies;
- Social and cultural values promoting business;
- Nationalism;
- World governance (i.e., the United Nations); and
- World hunger and poverty.

The survey instrument also assessed respondents' intentions to invest in various parts of the region. The guiding research question was whether and how perceptions of issues would relate to intentions to invest. The most important factors predicting intentions to invest were social and political issues.

Gomez-Mejia and McCann drew several conclusions about attitudinal issue orientations from their studies. First, a general descriptive state of the perceived issues climate can be given as a result of the environmental scan for the Caribbean Basin region. Second, there are important implications for firms that are active in the region. Attitudes were found not to be independent of one another. Instead, they tended to cluster together. Several particular issues loaded on more than one factor. This indicated to the authors that firms link issues in their management of the environment. For example, since the issues were not always independent of one another, actions firms took vis-à-vis one issue could be expected to have effects on related issues as well. Skillful issues management on the part of a firm could result in an enhanced exploitation of environmental opportunities and better minimization of environmental risks that were linked together. By the same token, poor issues management on the part of a firm could result in missed opportunities and a higher exposure to risk.

Finally, and most important for strategic management purposes, the studies reveal that attitudes toward social and political issues are of extreme importance. For any regional policy to be effective, much emphasis must be placed squarely on such attitudes. Since intentions to invest are directly linked to perceptions of pertinent issues, such attitudinal sets are important parts of the relevant domains or environments of policy decision makers.

SUMMARY

This chapter has reviewed some major research on cultural values, work beliefs, and socioeconomic attitudes. After a brief introduction to values, beliefs, and attitudes, the ideas of Hofstede (1980), who developed a widely used set of culture scales, and the work of Dorfman and Howell (1988), who refined and added to Hofstede's scales, were discussed. Next, a review of beliefs operating at the organizational or work level was presented, with special attention given to the work of Buchholz's (1978) work belief scales. Finally, Gomez-Mejia and McCann's (1986a) environmental scanning instrument and research were discussed as they relate to assessing socioeconomic attitudes and ways in which they may influence governmental and business initiatives.

2

Western Culture, Business, and Management
E. Ray Solomon and Dan Voich, Jr.

The culture of society reflects the different ways in which people choose to satisfy their economic needs and wants, consistent with their social values and priorities. Various socioeconomic and political institutions and processes emerge to control and regulate the behaviors of individuals, groups, and organizations. In recent years, we have seen a reassessment of how the business institution provides the economic needs and wants of society, consistent with changing values and priorities of its people. Often, diverse cultural and ethnic interests influence local, national, and international initiatives, as well as the operation of the business enterprise. Similarly, the business enterprise often attempts to shape the society and culture that it serves.

This chapter explores the relationships between culture, business, and management and how the business institution has evolved in response to socio-economic-political changes. It reviews the relationships between Western culture and business practice as they have evolved since the emergence of the Industrial Revolution, and examines how these developments have influenced the management of organizations, with special emphasis on the United States. Changing social values and priorities are discussed in terms of their effect on the goals and values that have influenced the development of the business institution and its management. Culture, business, and management in transition are discussed within the framework of management theory and business practice as they exist today, just prior to the twenty-first century.

ROOTS OF CULTURE, BUSINESS, AND MANAGEMENT

Western culture is founded in the tenets produced by the cultural rebirth, the Industrial Revolution and the spirit of capitalism. These three tenets greatly influenced the goals, policies, and management practices of business firms.

Cultural Rebirth

The cultural rebirth that evolved from 1500 to 1700 produced three major socio-economic-political changes that supported the emergence and development of the Industrial Revolution. First, the Protestant ethic emerged as a social force that emphasized the spirit of self-reliance and provided for the social sanction of work. This marked the beginning of the rise in achievement motivation, the work ethic, and the acceptance of business as an honorable profession. The basic tenet of the Protestant ethic as a work ethic emphasizes that if people are productive in their work, they will be satisfied both economically and socially.

The social sanction of work led to the acceptance of the merchant class and gave more importance to commerce and the need to invest and grow financially. Productive work and the reduction of waste became major priorities for individuals. Eventually, the endorsement of a form of social Darwinism emerged which supported the notion of the survival of the fittest. Thus, entrepreneurship, innovation, and self-reliance became important social, as well as economic, goals of society.

The market ethic is the second major change that was produced by the cultural rebirth. It emphasized that economic freedom would increase individual and enterprise productivity. The spirit of entrepreneurship produced by economic freedom would breed innovation and discovery, which would benefit not only the individual entrepreneurs but society as a whole, since science and reason would be applied effectively to resolve economic problems. The necessary technology and innovation would be developed to permit large accumulations of resources to further expand the capacity to produce more and better goods and services needed by society. As the shift from a state-controlled to a market directed economy occurred, mercantilism evolved into capitalism. Trade expansion through economic competition and innovation led to growth in individual prosperity and the development of a middle class in society.

The liberty ethic, the third major change produced by the cultural rebirth, presumed that productivity would be enhanced through individual and political freedom in support of laissez-faire economic policy. The liberty ethic produced the Age of Enlightenment. Private property rights, contracts, the right to profits, constitutional government, and human rights became important working doctrines for business enterprises and individuals. The reliance on these doctrines would permit individuals and business enterprises to develop to their fullest potential, thereby providing maximum benefits to society. The liberty ethic advocated a political system based on law, equality, and justice, rather than on the dictates of the few, within the framework of political freedom and laissez-faire economic policy. Essentially, the liberty ethic provided social endorsement of the Protestant and market ethics through laws and government intended to enable them to evolve and grow to their fullest potential.

The Industrial Revolution and the Spirit of Capitalism

These three changes produced by the cultural rebirth created the environment that led to the emergence and development of the Industrial Revolution and the spirit of capitalism. As the Industrial Revolution grew and spread, the implications for the development of business and management theory were great. The large accumulation of resources by business firms made them capital-intensive, and new ways were needed to finance large enterprises. Moreover, large capital investments created sunk costs and the need for more effective risk management. New planning and forecasting techniques were needed to span considerably longer periods of time and to take into account the risk and probability of severe losses as well as gains.

Larger organizations, in turn required more employees, which led to greater division and specialization of labor. In addition, more extensive delegation of authority and decentralization of operations followed. These larger organizations created various organizational arrangements and management processes that were very different than those needed for smaller, family controlled enterprises. With the greater number, as well as the greater diversity, of people concentrated in large enterprises, understanding how to influence and motivate people at work gained in importance. The cultural and social fabric of the work environment became viewed as an important variable which influenced efficiency and productivity. Different kinds of incentives for labor had to be developed to ensure a steady supply of qualified employees and managers.

As organizations grew in size, more managers were needed. The larger organizations also required new and more formal systems of accounting and control. These systems had to process and analyze a much greater volume and variety of information in a timely manner to ensure that actual (versus planned) performance was optimized. These new systems, in turn, required employees with different kinds of skills and education.

These kinds of developments during the Industrial Revolution led to the recognition that the job of the manager within large, complex organizations must be defined so that the practice of business and management could be studied and taught. Initially, this study focused on technical and manual work systems at the lower levels of production organizations and intended to improve efficiency in the workplace. For example, the scientific management movement applied industrial engineering concepts to improve worker productivity and ensure quality and cost control. Later, with the emergence of mass production techniques and assembly lines, attention shifted to process management, the automation of work, and the job of middle- and upper-level managers.

The large growth in production systems required new types of distribution channels and, eventually, marketing systems to reach and develop widely dispersed geographic markets. As a result, production scheduling, inventory control, and plant location decisions reflected the need to service national and international markets. With this high degree of geographic dispersion and integration of markets, the development of individual marketing concepts evolved into formal marketing theory.

With these changes in production and marketing, other functional areas of business formally evolved and developed. Accounting, finance, purchasing, inventory control, personnel, risk management, and other specialized areas grew in importance as tools to improve the planning, allocation, and control of major resources in the firm within the context of large-scale production and marketing systems. The large capital requirements that were needed by these systems created a need for new financial concepts. As these concepts evolved, theories of corporation finance, investment, and financial institutions emerged.

The extensive division and specialization of labor within a firm created the need for new kinds of planning and control systems to optimize resource acquisition and allocation in achieving organizational goals. The large growth in the formal structure and size of business organizations also created social and psychological problems in the workplace. Informal organizations, interest groups, and differing personal and social values in the workplace were identified and recognized as being significant variables to consider in designing more formal and authority-based management concepts. Eventually, theories of organization behavior, motivation, and leadership evolved, drawing on concepts from psychology and sociology.

CHANGING SOCIAL VALUES AND PRIORITIES

As a result of the large growth in the institution of business during the late nineteenth and early twentieth century, a large accumulation and exploitation of resources occurred. This led to serious public concerns because frontiers began to disappear, labor became exploited, and vast power became centralized in the few. Public support shifted from the exploitation of resources to resource rationalization, and greater attention was given to the equitable distribution of income of the firm and society's wealth. Moreover, these concerns eventually encompassed the need to conserve resources, limit growth, and provide for the protection of the environment. As a result, a reassessment of the Protestant ethic and the rights of the individual began to occur within the framework of providing equity among workers and various social groups, as well as the social responsibility of business. Eventually, the public endorsed a greater role for government in the regulation of business. Various government-sponsored and -funded programs evolved affecting workers compensation, labor rights, and interstate commerce. The Great Depression in the 1930s led to a substantial dilution of the unqualified support of the Protestant, market, and liberty ethics as necessary conditions for a productive and satisfied society. Social pressure led to governmental and regulatory limits on business firms to ensure that extreme negative economic situations would not recur. Moreover, the growth in the power of organized labor required business firms to adjust their policies and practices relating to how employees were hired, compensated, promoted and dismissed.

The traditional focus on optimizing resource acquisition, utilization, and distribution for profit, changed to include an analysis and study of how this resource flow process is, and should be, affected by changing social values and priorities. Through time, an array of views emerged, ranging from those advocating a continuation of a laissez-faire business environment to others urging more government regulation and even the federal operation of some business enterprises. Proponents on one extreme of the dialogue emphasized that the proper role of business is business, the production of economic goods and services. Proponents on the other extreme advocated that business is a social institution created by society and must produce economic goods and services in a socially responsible manner.

CURRENT GOALS, VALUES, AND ISSUES

A major feature of the culture and society of the United States is its hybrid nature. One can find numerous advocates for virtually every social, economic or political initiative at any given time. In many respects, this hybrid nature reflects the personal and organizational freedoms that have been supported throughout history by and that stem from the tenets embodied in the cultural rebirth. In spite of the hybrid nature of culture and society, there seems to be a general consensus of the more important macro goals and values of people in the United States, as summarized in Figure 2.1. Within each of the three sectors shown, there is general support for the particular goals and values. For example, accessible health, education, and welfare services are fundamental goals or values of the social system, as are safeguarding civil and human rights, reducing conflicts and terrorism, and providing equal opportunity to all segments of society. Protecting the environment and conserving natural resources also are fundamental to the social system.

The social system establishes an economic system and a political one. The economic system is responsible for producing the various economic goods and services that the social system desires and for complying with the various social priorities and initiatives relating to the environment and human interaction within society. When viewed by themselves, the goals and values within the economic systems are fundamental to society, and most of them are generally supported.

The political system facilitates and regulates the operation of the economic system, ensuring that the various social, economic, and human needs of society are satisfied in an orderly, equitable, and timely manner. It is also concerned with establishing national priorities and initiatives, and it regulates how various states interact within a system of federalism. When viewed by themselves, the goals and values within the political systems are also fundamental to society, and most of them are generally

Figure 2.1
Goals and Values

Social Goals and Values

Providing access to education
Improving public health
Reducing hunger, poverty, and homelessness
Providing childcare services
Safeguarding the environment
Conserving natural resources
Safeguarding civil and human rights
Reducing racial conflict
Providing equal opportunities for minorities
Reducing international terrorism

Economic Goals and Values

Enhancing economic growth and development
Increasing income and employment
   opportunities
Developing energy self-sufficiency
Providing affordable housing
Developing natural resources
Providing incentives for investing and saving
Enhancing the free-enterprise system
Reducing excessive governmental regulators
Developing effective growth infrastructure
Controlling inflation

Political Goals and Values

Providing for national defense
Maintaining pluralism and constitutional government
Enhancing the liberty ethic
Enhancing federalism between municipal, state,
   and federal government levels
Enhancing private property and contract rights
Reducing government bureaucracy and waste
Increasing accountability of government
Reducing influence of military/industrial complex
   on economic and social priorities
Maintaining world peace, law, and order

supported.

The system of socio-economic-political goals and values reflects the outputs expected by society. While there is general consensus of what most of these outputs should be, how they are achieved often presents differences of opinions by various social, economic, and political factions. This is especially true when serious imbalances occur between the nature of social priorities and the ways in which the economic and political systems respond to resolve these conflicts. For example, a set of issues deals with how to make the economic system effective in producing goods and services and providing for growth and development within increasing demands for providing social services, protecting the environment, and safeguarding civil and human rights. Major intervening variables include government deficit spending, inflation, consumer debt and savings, national defense, crime and corruption, social conflicts and terrorism, and energy self-sufficiency. Additionally, organizational bureaucracy, the dilution of the work ethic, and federalism are important issues and compound these problems.

From a macro perspective, the major issue is achieving the appropriate balance between capitalism and socialism that is needed to enhance economic growth and social services. In many respects, the effort to resolve the balance between capitalism and socialism drives all other issues within society in that initiatives in the social, economic, and political sectors are based on the relative emphasis given capitalism versus socialism. Essentially, this involves a continuum of choices, ranging from individualism and the historic endorsement of the Protestant, market, and liberty ethics, on one hand, to socialism, which embodies a broader concern for equity in the provisions of health, education, and welfare services of society.

The individualistic ethic, which is a central tenet of capitalism, is a decentralization concept that encourages greater freedom of individual action and choice. If this freedom is provided, greater innovation, motivation, productivity, and risk taking should accrue to the benefit of the individual and the middle class as well as to society as a whole, since the overall productive capacity and performance of society should be optimized. On the negative side, individualism may result in or encourage the exploitation of resources by a few, and the resulting concentration of power may not benefit enough members of society. Thus, higher levels of poverty and unemployment may occur.

The benefits and negative aspects of socialism are assumed to be the opposite. For example, the social ethic emphasizes that more equity should occur in the distribution of the society's resources and wealth, thereby reducing poverty and unemployment. However, this may encourage less individual motivation for innovation and risk taking, and toward work generally. As a result, the total production of society may be less. Obviously, the above set of assumptions for the two ethics is not totally true or false in either case. Certainly both ethics have merits as well as problems.

The basic dilemma is how can society maintain the important benefits of the individualistic ethic and capitalism that productive people need and want, and yet satisfy the broader social values and priorities embodied in the social ethic in order to provide an adequate level of goods and services to the less fortunate and less capable. Proponents of social responsibility of business usually discuss the need for business firms to support social policies, programs, and priorities in order to preclude government intervention. Moreover, as a socially oriented enterprise, the business firm might generate greater public support and demand for its products or services, and in the long run, their economic purpose and objectives could be achieved in this manner. Opponents of the social responsibility of business argue that the role and purpose of the business institution in the United States is to provide economic, and not social, products and services for profit. Moreover, if it is profitable, the business firm is fulfilling its obligation to society. If business social responsibility programs of businesses dilute the firm's profits, the resulting economic failure that may occur could increase unemployment and reduce people's standard of living.

Perhaps one of the greatest impacts of imposing social programs on business is on the small business firms which have limited resources. A small business firm usually incurs higher risks in beginning a new business, gaining a market for its products and services and sustaining growth until revenue and profits become stabilized. A society may be imposing too much social responsibility on small firms, if it establishes excessive regulations that increase the cost of doing business. This may discourage an adequate level of new business ventures and the risk taking needed to maintain and enhance competition.

On the other hand, larger firms may have opportunities to use some of their capital for socially oriented programs, and through innovative marketing programs, they may even increase the demand for their products. However, in some cases, this investment may dilute the level of investment in research and development that is necessary to remain competitive in international, as well as national, markets. The relative emphasis placed on capitalistic versus socialistic tenets also greatly influences the rate of technological change in the infrastructure of business and society.

CULTURE, BUSINESS, AND MANAGEMENT IN TRANSITION

The rapid changes in technology, communications, and transportation have made the world's markets, production centers, and financial institutions highly interdependent. A society cannot remain isolated in its socio-economic-political policies and practices. The business firm especially is affected by other major industrial and financial operations throughout the world, and it draws many of its resources from politically and culturally diverse regions and nations. Rates of exchange, inflation, balance of payments, interest, and similar factors are influenced by regional, national, and international developments and initiatives. Multicultural values and priorities also influence business and management. For example, most business organizations employ a multicultural work force. Communities and regions are comprised of various ethnic groups with different value systems and socio-economic-political backgrounds. Access to potential international markets must be gained, not only by the traditional appeals based on product price, quality, and service, but also through the removal or reduction of ethnic and national protectionist barriers.

Because of the diversity in different people's values and goals, management uses various incentives to motivate and influence behavior of workers. We can see that the economic incentives initiated during the scientific management era are still important motivators. Employees derive their personal satisfaction from being productive, as well as through the goods and services they can obtain from higher wages or salaries. However, some employees are motivated by noneconomic incentives, such as opportunities to participate in the design of work systems, interact in groups, and be involved in decision making. The traditional priorities of organized labor, such as equitable distribution of income, seniority, and job security, must be fused into incentive systems.

Management's Response to Cultural Change

Management must fuse these hybrid values and priorities in trying to develop a cohesive, dedicated work force that is committed to organizational goals. Moreover, management needs to stimulate innovation and creativity yet ensure control and accountability through some reasonable and effective level of bureaucracy of work and management. The challenge to management is to recognize the role and importance of group commitment to organizational goals without diluting personal aspirations, needs, and values.

In the business firm, the dynamic interaction between culture and management must be reasonably controlled. The developments that have occurred in our cultural environment and that have shaped business practice and management are brought into focus in the organizational setting. The organization utilizes goal theory and programming to develop its purpose, objectives, and strategies, which are usually stated in terms of products and services to be provided and subsequently reflected in revenues, costs, and profits. The cultural values and priorities influence this process as well as its outcomes. It cannot be effective unless it is responsive to the particular socio-economic-political priorities and initiatives within the cultural environment.

Concepts and techniques in decision and information theory attempt to apply logic and measurement to optimize resource allocation and the control of risk and thus achieve organizational goals. Goal theory and programming, along with decision and information theory, attempt to provide rationality to the manager's job. Although nonrational variables may be included in the analysis, the primary objective function for most of the models and processes used usually emphasizes the measurement of revenues, costs, and profits.

Organization theory provides the formal structure, policies and procedures within which people work to optimize the acquisition, allocation, and disposition of resources for profit. The organization reflects the use of various systems of authority, delegation, decentralization, job design, communication channels, feedback, and control within which employees perform various kinds of technical, analytical, and managerial work. In this way, the formal organization is used to provide some order and certainty with which to guide behavior of employees.

The theory of organization behavior provides concepts and techniques that can be used to influence, motivate, and coordinate the efforts of people within the organizational setting. These concepts and techniques are designed to induce performance and influence behavior in such a way as to generate a commitment to organizational goals utilizing the formal structure and the decision and information techniques that have been designed. To be effective, this inducement and influence of behavior should satisfy individual and group values and priorities yet support the achievement of organizational goals and enhance the stability of operations.

How to achieve this congruence is one of the most important challenges of management education and practice. It is also one of the most difficult to resolve because of the diverse and changing values and priorities that characterize the culture of most societies. People's family and workplace values may differ because of a variety of socio-economic-political reasons, including the state of economic development, literacy, inflation, population growth, political freedom, civil rights, human rights, and others, that exist in their society. People's values are also influenced by developments in the international environment. The search for markets, competition for resources and technology, the need to build political ties all impact people's values as the business firm attempts to achieve greater production, marketing, and financial economies of scale.

Philosophies of Management

In various cultural settings, a number of philosophies of management have evolved that take into account the inherent diversity of people's values as they come to bear in the workplace where the business organization seeks to fulfill its economic mission. All these philosophies are culturally based. In other words, the distinguishing characteristics of management practice stems from the value systems of society, and in most cases, it depends on the relative importance placed on the individualistic versus the social ethic. Within this basic cultural setting, organizations apply and modify various relevant technical, analytical, and managerial concepts and techniques.

The application and modification of these concepts and techniques takes place in the formal organization. One important management philosophy is based on the bureaucratic model, which relies heavily on the use of formal authority. Bureaucracy's reliance on formal authority structures, policies, and rules is often accompanied by highly centralized planning and control systems. This type of management system tends to provide fewer opportunities or incentives for individual innovation or input from lower organizational levels. Various technical, analytical, and managerial concepts and techniques are usually designed by the top management levels and implemented throughout the organization in their original form. Thus, the production work level becomes removed from the decision making level. In addition, the highly centralized planning and control systems often become cumbersome and ineffective in generating and implementing innovation, thus creating resistance to change.

On the other hand, some reasonable level of management bureaucracy is needed in all business organizations to assign responsibility and delegate authority for the use of resources. This is also necessary to effectively monitor, control, and adjust performance and goals. The other management philosophies described below do not discard bureaucracy in organizations but rather shape it to better take into account other social and behavioral factors.

European Industrial Democracy, or co-determination, is a second general type of management philosophy. It provides for the involvement of workers in various aspects of management in specific legislation, usually through the collective bargaining process. Workers are represented on various management boards and work councils at all levels of the organization, to include the firm's board of directors. European Industrial Democracy provides for a very open type of organization. Workers and managers formally and regularly meet to discuss various aspects of work design and performance, managerial policies and practices, employee concerns, and stockholder priorities. The various boards and councils provide a series of forums whereby social and personal values and priorities become integrated with the economic goals of the firm and the employees.

European Industrial Democracy emerged as a major management philosophy somewhat in response to the aftermath created by World War II. The shared hardships experienced by people in Europe gave more emphasis to the social ethic, which eventually carried forward into the workplace. It also influenced political initiatives and business regulation at the local and national levels. A major impact of European Industrial Democracy is that the employees in the business firm have a considerable voice in the design of work systems and in decisions relating to the distribution of the firm's resources. As a result, a greater percentage of resources is allocated to employee wages and social services, such as health care, education, and leave benefits.

A third management philosophy is Management by Consensus, which was derived from Japan's Ringi system. This approach to management builds on familial relationships applied to the work organization. It is a behavioral orientation that uses concepts such as participative management, quality circles, communication and group dynamics. Similar to European Industrial Democracy, the use of Management by Consensus gained popularity because of its successful use in Japan, or conversely, Japan's success was attributed in part to the use of this management philosophy. In truth, Management by Consensus has been used to some degree in other countries, and especially in the United States. One key factor that made it successful in Japan was the tradition of strong family loyalty in Japanese society, coupled with the severe economic and political aftermath brought about at the end of World War II.

The Management by Consensus approach used in Japan does not usually mean that all decisions are made by formal employee votes. Instead, it provides information to employees and gives them opportunities to endorse or provide input to various decisions, the design of work systems, and other policy initiatives. As new generations of employees are drawn from the educational institutions in Japan, we can see some changes occurring in their attitudes. For example, the younger employees are beginning to question the seniority system which has been used extensively for promotion and compensation. They are also more impatient and vocal in relation to the need for, and pace of, change.

Worker-Management is a fourth management philosophy which provides for highly decentralized management. By law, it provides for the extensive involvement of workers in the firm's management. It greatly extends European Industrial Democracy and Japan's Management by Consensus in that workers are responsible for "doing" as well as directly "managing" the means, conditions, and results of their labor. The Worker-Management system often places a very large burden on employees because of this dual role. This comes about not only because of the time involved, but also because of the special expertise that may be needed by employees when dealing with issues and making decisions outside of their respective discipline. The Worker-Management system tends to emphasize the social ethic, and therefore, the share of the firm's resources allocated to employee social services tends to be large. Consequently, incentives for individual innovation and productivity are usually less than needed, or they may not be given a high priority.

A fifth important system may be termed a hybrid management philosophy. Management systems employed in the United States have typically been hybrid systems, using a combination of organization and behavior concepts at different times. We can see a much greater variation in management styles used between U.S. managers of different firms, and even within the same firm. In addition, there have been considerable instances of experimentation in using different managerial concepts to improve organizational productivity and worker satisfaction. The cultural heritage in the United States has usually supported the individualistic ethic, and organizations have traditionally encouraged experimentation and change.

The hybrid model reflecting the management philosophy used in the United States is not a single model, rather it reflects numerous approaches to management using variations of bureaucracy, European Industrial Democracy, Management by Consensus and even Worker-Management, to some degree. The choice of the approach or combination of approaches used is usually the individual manager's prerogative. However, in some organizations, there may be company-wide policies that may require some common managerial practices regarding the involvement of employees in certain matters.

SUMMARY

The transition of culture and management proceeds as two highly interdependent thrusts through time. The practice of management is the synthesis of many disciplines and the product of cultural forces as it attempts to provide the economic goods and services that society demands. The economic environment provides the framework within which the practice of management must function. While the focus of management is in the economic realm, its actions are affected by social values and priorities. People are the primary means for management to fulfill its economic responsibility. The cultural fabric of society produces the values that people bring into the workplace and that influence political and regulatory systems affecting the economic environment.

In many cases, people's values change because of the failure of business to provide needed economic goods and services. For example, the changes that took place during and after the Great Depression in the 1930s not only changed the balance of power between business, government, and organized labor, they also moved employees away from the individualistic ethic toward the social ethic in the workplace. Security and affiliation needs replaced the need to achieve and self-actualize. Government help became more popular than self-help, and the goals of profits and efficiency diminished somewhat in favor of social programs.

Today we can see distinct patterns of social values as they impact business and management. The work ethic is still a dominant force in the workplace, even though the socialization process is important to many employees. One of the dominant forces that has emerged is the idea of entitlement, which many people bring into the workplace. Under this belief, people simply feel that society owes them a living. In many cases, these people have important skills, education, and training but lack motivation. Such individuals present a major challenge for management. People who are less capable pose a different kind of problem for society and business. Providing greater opportunities for training or education may move some of this group into the productive work force.

The mesh of social values and economic initiatives often is translated into political institutions, initiatives, and government regulations. The political environment continues to be very crucial to business and management. Foreign policy, trade policy, federal budget allocations, product regulations, employment practices, environmental protection, social welfare initiatives, human rights, and affirmative action are only some of the many governmental programs that have been developed by the social sector through the political processes. Some of these programs can be found at the local, state, and national levels, and they often become intertwined. They create major burdens on, and increase the costs of, business and management.

Political initiatives and government regulations will continue to impact business and management, and consequently the business firm and large industries will continue to influence future political initiatives and regulations. A major concern that results from extensive political and governmental control and regulation of business, along with the implementation of costly social and environmental programs, is that once implemented, controls are difficult to remove, even when most people agree that they are no longer needed. A second major concern is that these programs and initiatives may tend to dilute the individualistic ethic, which may, in turn, dilute the long-run ability of business and management to provide the economic goods and services for society in a competitive way.

The socio-economic-political environment develops the cultural fabric within society. This is the milieu in which business and management must function in fulfilling their economic mission for society. In working to perform this mission, we are beyond the point at which the business firm can expect to operate without continuing and increasing oversight and regulation from the social and political sectors. The business institution and the practice of management have developed in significant ways since the cultural rebirth of 1500-1700, and through the Industrial Revolution, spanning several major wars, periods of recession and inflation, and various social reforms. The more recent changes that have occurred in Eastern Europe have had a profound effect not only on the importance of the business institution in society, but also on how it should operate to provide society with the economic goods and services that it needs and wants. One lesson from history must show that from the range of choices available, even though there is a clear need for some level of social and political oversight and regulation, substantial support of the individualistic ethic must continue.

Thinking about how to distribute wealth must not overshadow the need to develop new and better ways to produce it for society. Advertising must not be used as a substitute for research and development if productive vitality and competitiveness are to be sustained. Reliance on national planning systems is not a substitute for competition. Incentives and opportunities must continue to be made available to individuals if new ideas are to emerge to successfully build a healthy economic environment.

3

Changes in Values and Perceptions Relating to the Political Economy of the Federal Republic of Germany

Hans Günther Meissner and Heike Simmet

People's values and perceptions are an intensively discussed scientific topic in Western Europe, and especially in the Federal Republic of Germany (Klages, 1984; Raffeé and Wiedmann 1983, 1985, 1988; Windhorst, 1985; Tietz, 1982). The current discussions are focused on the changes in values and perception of consumers and entrepreneurs during the last decades. In addition to the local and nationally based changes in the Federal Republic of Germany, there are comprehensive international influences because of developments in Europe. The most important of these include:

- Developments in Western Europe leading to the Single European Market 1992;
- Liberalization trends in Eastern Europe; and
- Unification with the German Democratic Republic.

These changes have had a great effect on value systems and perceptions, and are already causing reactions in companies' and consumers' attitudes and behaviors in the Federal Republic of Germany.

Scientific interests are focused on the description, theoretical issues, and empirical analysis of these current phenomena. The following chapter provides a survey of the sources of values and perceptions research. In addition, it demonstrates the current main streams in people's values and perceptions in connection with the political economy of the Federal Republic of Germany, as well as their impacts on the scientific research.

SOURCES OF VALUES AND PERCEPTIONS RESEARCH

Today the analysis of people's values and perceptions is a very current topic of scientific discussion in the Federal Republic of Germany, although the research of people's values and perceptions lacks a long tradition in business administration. The value research was traditionally found in the scientific field of philosophy and theology where its aim was to formulate value ethics and theories (Steege, 1986). The newer social-economic scientific interest in values and perceptions research in the Federal Republic of Germany arises from two different sources (Meissner, 1985).

The first source is the psychological and social psychological approach, originating from Max Weber's *Economy and Society*, with special reference to the role of the Protestant ethic in capitalism (Weber, 1956). The Calvanistic attitude was directed against consuming and conspicious consumers with their affluent values and perceptions. Instead, it favored investments. In this way, Weber articulated a consumer-skeptical atmosphere in the German economic consciousness. Today, sociological theory is still extremely critical of consumption and the activities of entrepreneurs.

The other source of people's values and perceptions research originates in the field of economics. The hypothetical figure of the *homo oeconomicus* governed the model-building process in economics and evolved from a model condition to a normative pattern, especially in the microeconomic theory. This approach was adopted in business administration science and dominated it for decades. Above all, the successful German scientist E. Gutenberg focused on the functional relations of the firm. He regarded entrepreneurs (he called them the "dispositive factor") and consumers as being outside the firm, and therefore external to the pure theory of business administration (Gutenberg 1951).

Today, this paradigm of Gutenberg's business administration theory is regarded as antiquated. The reception of marketing theory in Germany especially was influenced by the work of the American researcher Philip Kotler (Kotler, 1982). It changed the focus of German business administration from internal problems to the market relations of the firm and to its social-cultural, economic, and political environment.

Marketing is interdisciplinary in focus. It describes and analyses people's values and perceptions with a view to understanding the background conditions of the transactions between companies and consumers. Marketing theory focuses on the realization of these transactions with the aid of a specific interaction system. One fundamental issue of this interaction system is the knowledge of consumers and entrepreneurs within the scope of marketing research (Meissner, 1986).

The process of change in value systems of consumers as well as entrepeneurs is leading now to new impulses for research on the patterns of marketing research in the Federal Republic of Germany. One consequence of these new impulses considers the change in research methods. The strong influence of values and perceptions research on marketing issues has intensified the importance of using quality methods in marketing research. Another consequence considers the increasing application of other scientific disciplines, so that the interdisciplinary orientation of marketing and marketing research is becoming increasingly significant.

SYNOPSIS OF CURRENT RESEARCH

The current discussion of the priorities and changes in people's values and perceptions toward the political economy in the Federal Republic of Germany is strongly influenced by the works of R. Inglehart, who advanced the thesis about the "change from the material-istical to a post-materialistical society" (Inglehart, 1979, 1980). This thesis posits a decreasing significance of traditional values in industrialized societies (such as business careers, economic growth, materialistic prosperity, etc.), toward a better quality of life, protection of the natural environment, and health consciousness.

The thesis of the postmaterialistic society tends to be widely discussed in the Federal Republic of Germany. Additionally, there are actually contrary trends to be regarded. Juveniles especially are increasingly polarized between materialistic and postmaterialistic orientations (Raffée and Wiedmann, 1985). Besides their sociocultural, political, and natural influences, the sources of the growing significance of materialistic values arise from the change in economic and political patterns as well.

The changes in values and perceptions may not be regarded solely as a generation phenomenon, as the value orientation is not similar in structure across age groups (Baumann, 1990). For example, research by the Konrad Adenauer Foundation has shown that in Germany, the elderly (over 60) and middle-aged (30-60) tend to value duty and acceptance to a greater extent than the youth (18-29). Only long-term changes are taking shape here, but as more people with later birthdates move into the older age groups, the impact of these changes will increase (Baumann, 1990). This assertion agrees with the results of a study of a group from Nuremberg, *Gesellschaft für Konsumharkt, und Absatzforschung*, (Society for Consumption, Markets, and Market Research), "People and Food 2000," which shows the value changes to be differentiated according to year of birth (see Figure 3.1).

As a result, it should be stated that it is not possible to give a general forecast of value and perception changes. Only the registering and analysis of trends in value and perception priorities of selected socio-cultural or life-style groups can be regarded as practicable (Trommsdorff, 1989).

In addition, the current research is focused on international research activities, and especially on strategic international marketing research (Meissner, 1990b). The peculiarity of international marketing research lies in the fact that aspects of the behavior or attitudes of consumers and entrepreneurs that are self-evident to companies selling on the home market must now be clarified by marketing research. The specific culture in which a person happens to grow up and live is decisive in the formation of attitudes and the shaping of consumer behavior patterns. These anthropological bases of international marketing research relate primarily to social processes and especially to the cultural conditions in the foreign markets (Meissner, 1959).

The importance of international consumer research has not previously been awarded sufficient attention, although there are signs that this situation is now changing (Holzmüller, 1986). Thus, for example, a model has been constructed by life-style research (Banning, 1987), which links the cultural aspects of the behavior of consumers and investors with other important criteria for the explanation and prognosis of this behavior. In particular, it makes them amenable to a measure of quantification that is desirable for various decision processes.

MAJOR TRENDS IN CHANGES IN VALUES AND PERCEPTIONS

Social-Cultural Trends

The main scientific interests regarding the description and analysis of the social-cultural environment focus on commonalities and differences

Figure 3.1
The Value Changes among People

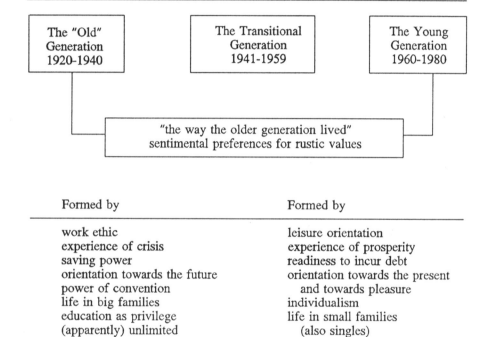

| The "Old" Generation 1920-1940 | The Transitional Generation 1941-1959 | The Young Generation 1960-1980 |

"the way the older generation lived"
sentimental preferences for rustic values

Formed by

Formed by

work ethic
experience of crisis
saving power
orientation towards the future
power of convention
life in big families
education as privilege
(apparently) unlimited
    resources

leisure orientation
experience of prosperity
readiness to incur debt
orientation towards the present
    and towards pleasure
individualism
life in small families
    (also singles)
scarcity of resources

Source: Nestle Group Germany, "Mensch und Ernahrung 2000,"
In-house document, n.d. p. 3 (based on a study by Gesllschaft für
Konsum, Markt, und Absatzforschung.)

in people's values and perceptions between the Federal Republic of Germany and the other European countries. These interests are strongly involved with the consequences of the Single European Market of 1992 (Meissner, 1990a).

Scientific expectations aim towards a consensus of people's values and perceptions in Europe, although important differences on national as well as local levels are to be considered. Assimilations above all are to be expected in selected occupational and social groups, for example, students or bank managers. Nevertheless, a specific connection with national and local particularities is still in existence. These particularities are to be expected, for example, in the different habits of consumption and travel (Meissner, 1990a).

Therefore, an ambiguous situation exists concerning the development of people's values and perceptions in Western Europe. On the one hand, there are assimilation processes to be regarded, which are especially advanced by the internationalisation of new technologies, and particularly the electronic mediums. On the other hand, there is a contrary development according to the simultaneously increasing differences between people's values and perceptions at local and national levels (Meissner, 1990a).

Because of this difficult situation, numerous analyses of European values and perceptions have been developed during recent years. Important analyses were set up by the European market research institutes such as the RISC Institut (Institute for International Research on Social Change, in Nyon/Paris) and the Euro-Panel, an alliance of 15 European market research institutes ("Mafo-Instrumente für das Euromarketing," 1989). Another very practicable typifying analysis was developed by the management consultant Höfner and Associates (Höfner, 1987).

The following statements will give a short survey of Anticipating Change in Europe (ACE), the European value change research system of RISC, which compared the German population with other Europeans (Grimm, 1989). The results of this research are based on about 30,000 representative annual interviews in 12 European countries. The essential part of the study is the observation of 20 European trends.

The German value research points out the following main results:

- German people are currently placing increasingly great value on enjoyment and consumption and are very consumption orientated.
- Many issues are more emotionally regarded than before.

- People's approaches are more relaxed.
- Although environmental protection plays an important part in the political economy, the group of alternatives is declining, except within the age-group of 20-30 years.
- In the age group of under 20 years, materialistic attitudes are again emerging.
- The increasing pleasure in prosperity and consumption, as well as an eventful life, and the new, more positive attitude toward technology and science do not reconcile with an increasing performance orientation.

In research concerning European sociocultural tendencies, Grimm (1989) compared German values and perceptions in comparison with those of other European countries. The research clearly showed that Germans are less progressive than other Europeans, especially the Italian, French, and Spanish. The position of German values and perceptions may be compared rather with those in Great Britain and Sweden; they emphasize traditional values and norms and tendencies toward conformity.

Nowadays, the research activities in the Federal Republic of Germany have broadened the concept of Western European values and perceptions research to integrate the specific sociocultural environment of the former German Democratic Republic in the existing analysis. This is regarded as a new challenge for marketing research as the long separation of the two parts of Germany has shaped two sets of very different sociocultural patterns. The larger German marketing research institutes are very involved in this research.

Economic-Political Trends

The relation of people's values and perceptions toward economic and political issues is strongly influenced by the actual changes in Europe. During recent years, the discussion has concentrated on the economic and political consequences of the Single European Market (1992). On the whole, the European community has developed a new consciousness of its strengths and capacities, which is based on the real processes of growth and change in Europe. In recent years, a whole series of countries of the European community, including the Federal Republic of Germany, have exhibited growth rates of about 4 %, and it is possible that these are due to anticipation of the Common Europe.

The specific strength of the European economy lies in the development of technological systems, intelligent products, and manufacturing. These developments are adjusted to reflect human needs and to minimize environmental pollution caused by industrial production, and they offer appropriate technological solutions. The development of new information and communication technologies has especially influenced the competitive power of European manufacturers as well as retailers (Simmet, 1990). Within the European Community, a new self-awareness has arisen with respect to both creativity and technical efficiency, as well as to the required and necessary economic transformation of the world.

In addition to the infuences of the European Internal Market, the developments in Eastern Europe in connection with the union with the German Democratic Republic are currently at the center of discussions. These developments have displaced the disussion about the Single European Market 1992 to a certain extent, although the importance of the European Internal Market should not to be underestimated.

Sorrows of the Nation

In the Federal Republic of Germany, the *Gesellschaft für Konsum, Markt, und Absatzforschung* (GfK), analyzes the "main sorrows of the nation" annually. The sources of this analysis are the spontaneous answers of German people.

The analysis illustrates that the developments in the former German Democratic Republic and the liberalization trends in the Eastern European countries have exercised a strong influence on people's perceptions who feel that these developments signify that the certainty of peace between the traditional political and economic societies in Western and Eastern Europe has increased.

The union with the former German Democratic Republic especially causes many economic and political discussions in the Federal Republic of Germany, so it is not surprising that the German people are involved in this process. The current discussions are concentrated on the political procedures in realizing the union and on the financial questions concerning investments in the eastern part of Germany.

These events have displaced former priorities such as the burdens of unemployment, which was mitigated by positive economic trends. These trends are partly accounted for by the investments made in response to the creation of the European Common Market in 1992. Nearly every sector, including the manufacturing industry as well as the service sectors, has intensified investments in rationalization in order to strengthen its international and European competitive position. In the European community the real investments increased to 8 % in 1988 and in 1989 to about 6 %. These are values that had not been realized for the previous 20 years (Prognos euroreport, 1990).

The second current concern, protection of the natural environment, also has diminished in comparision to former years. The expectation is that this mitigation is only a temporary phenomenon, therefore, the environmental impact of markets becomes a major political priority as well as a major decision parameter in marketing strategies (Meissner, 1990b). The political lobby for environmental protection has much greater influence than in comparison to former times. In addition, business firms in Germany in the last few years have strongly intensified their activities in producing and developing new products with less environmental pollution (for example, using less harmful propellants and packages that can be recycled).

However, the significance of another problem is growing: the housing shortage is regarded as an important problem in the Federal Republic of Germany. This is caused by increased housing rentals, the fewer number of social welfare houses, and the higher numbers of evacuees, resettlers, and removals of people of the former German Democratic Republic and Eastern Europe.

The other specified themes are also intensively discussed in the German press, but they are not as important in German people's values and perceptions. The burden of social insurance and pensions in the Federal Republic of Germany has diminished during the last years. The foreigner question and asylum problems were also perceived as real, but not major, concerns of people in the Federal Republic of Germany.

CONCLUSIONS

This chapter has illustrated the political economy of the Federal Republic of Germany according to the actual trends of German people's values and perceptions. In addition, it has demonstrated that the patterns in values and perceptions have never before been more stratified.

Research on people's values and perceptions must consider that there are some values and perceptions that conflict with others. For example, on the one hand, the trend of individuality exists, but on the other, there are trends of an increasing social contact. Similarly, the increased hedonism is at variance with an increasing societal orientation. This is a very important phenomenon in the changes in values and perceptions in the Federal Republic of Germany and was effected by the assertion of pluralistic value and perceptions systems over uniform traditional values and perceptions (Raffée and Wiedmann, 1985).

Consequently, consumers and entrepreneurs regard economic, political, and social issues as a unit, which leads to a set of opinions on materialistic and postmaterialistic values and societal as well as individual interests in people's minds. Further research should concentrate on the description and analysis of these changes in the national, as well as the cross-national and cross-cultural, connections.

4

Managing the Future:
Changes in Values and Requirements
of German Managers
Hans Günther Meissner and Heike Simmet

Management and the organization of management are decisively responsible for the development and success of enterprises. A lot of well formulated strategies fail in spite of the consideration of the relevant environmental influences, marketing requirements, technological aspects, and financial supports, because they do not realize the significance of management and the potential of human resources in the company. Management, especially the management of human resources, is not a static, but rather a dynamic, phenomenon. At all times, management must adapt to change in their external and internal environments. This chapter gives an overview of the scientific discussion of management in the Federal Republic of Germany and analyzes the framework conditions of management values and requirements. In addition, it characterizes the actual trends of German managers' values and requirements with special reference to the consequences of the unification with the former German Democratic Republic and the significance for German managers of the Single European Market.

MANAGEMENT SCIENCES IN THE FEDERAL REPUBLIC OF GERMANY

Not long ago, management in the Federal Republic of Germany was regarded as a function of traditional business administration, which concentrated on the rational operations of enterprises, such as leadership, direction, and administration (Gutenberg, 1951). In the following periods, however, parallel to the integration of the Anglo-American management sciences, the behavioral components of management were allocated increasing importance in the Federal Republic of Germany (Hopfenbeck, 1989, p. 409). The former concentration on rational operations has nevertheless led to a strong accentuation of German management science on techniques of management, such as management by objectives, management by exception, management by systems, management by motivation, and so on (Häusler, 1977). These management techniques often represent isolated models of traditional business administration, which suffer from integrated and system-orientated representations. It is significant that there is no equivalent of this strong accentuation of management techniques in the Anglo-American sciences, although comprehensive impulses have nonetheless resulted (Staehle, 1987, p. 49).

Modern management in the Federal Republic of Germany, however, is regarded as a complex system with functional and institutional dimensions, which are combined with the specific behaviors and values of individual managers. Above all, new values and requirements of managers with special regard to the sociological and psychological backgrounds are integrated in the actual analyses of management. Although the integration of sociological and psychological influences nowadays is self-evident in German management sciences, their implementation still has not been completed in a lot of enterprises. Small and medium-sized companies, in particular, suffer from a lack of modern management know-how. These companies are primarily family companies, so that all important decisions (and sometimes the unimportant decisions as well) are made by one person or by a very small circle of persons, and this is linked to an organizational structure which is strictly hierarchical. In such cases, the problems lie both in the form of organization and in the wasted potential of colleagues who are themselves capable of assuming leadership roles. Especially in small and medium-sized companies which are growing and internationally active, this lack of modern management style and organization is still a problem in the Federal Republic of Germany (Meissner, 1990b, p. 58).

FRAMEWORK CONDITIONS OF GERMAN MANAGEMENT

The framework conditions of German management include environmental influences, value changes, and cultures of companies.

Actual Environmental Influences

Environmental factors have comprehensive influences on management, so that they have become a major parameter of the analyses of management values and requirements. These environmental factors, which may be systematized into four types of dimensions:
- Sociocultural,
- Economic-political,
- Technological, and
- International.

They are characterized by intensive change processes. At the same time, management values and requirements are underlying dynamic processes.

One of the main actual environmental factors in German society which is influencing managers' values and requirements relates to the *sociocultural* changes in the Federal Republic of Germany. Changing sociocultural values, for example, the increasing consciousness of consumers concerning the quality of life as well as of products and the growing importance of environmental protection, have implications for the leadership philosophy and organization of German enterprises. Sociocultural changes beyond this are concerned with sociodemographic impulses, especially relating to general generational conflicts and emancipation processes of women managers. One dominant factor of sociocultural changes concerns the new values of the junior staff of management: traditionally, value systems and perceptions of those managers that have influenced the companies for a long time are opposed to the desire for self-expression and independence of the younger generation of management (Hahn, 1988, p. 115). In addition, the new self-consciousness of female managers who are trying to have the same success and career chances in German enterprises as their male colleagues is an example of the influence of sociocultural changes in the German management. Nevertheless, various empirical studies show that only 2 to 4.4 percent of top managers in the Federal Republic of Germany are female (Müller-Böling and Ramme, 1990, p. 39).

Economic-political influences on German management relate mostly to the present business outlook and therefore implicate very dynamic factors that can hardly be prognosed, although the latest election in December 1990 indicated a relatively stable economic-political atmosphere. Economic growth in the Federal Republic of Germany has contributed in a far-reaching manner to the development of a changing value system. The working careers of men and women are increasingly coming to represent only a limited episode in the lives of many people, with the consequence that the era of professional activity is shrinking to a period of transience. The value system of many citizens of the Federal Republic of Germany, as well as citizens of most highly industrialized countries, is undergoing a corresponding change, along with their life-styles and consumer habits. Freedom is being associated with free time, and the quality of life is becoming the ruling paradigm of the "affluent society." Connected with these developments, however, one also finds a critique of culture that advances, in the face of material superfluity, toward inwardness and self-limitation. The economic growth that has been attained and is still continuing in the Federal Republic of Germany, and the quality of life and work that is associated with this growth have therefore led to far-reaching consequences for people's values and perceptions (Meissner, 1990b, p. 31).

Impressive influences on management also are resulting from the development of *technological changes* in nearly every business sector. New information and communication systems in manufacturing, retailing, and administration are increasingly becoming key factors of modern management, so that a lack of participation in these new technological developments may imply special risks or missed chances. As a conse-quence, the whole of management, including the top levels, has to follow a profound learning process with the aim of accepting the use of new information and communication technologies and implementing them in their decision processes (Simmet, 1990, p. 195). Empirical studies illustrate that the acceptance of these new technologies in management is sufficient in the Federal Republic of Germany, compared with its acceptance among average population (Müller-Böling and Ramme, 1990).

Another primary environmental factor that is regarded as a main framework condition for management concerns the *international processes* of German companies and the internationalization of German management. The realization of the Single European Market, the opening of the Eastern European countries, and opportunities in the United States as well as in the Asian markets are leading to an adaptive management organization and a different structure of management styles, as well as changes in management requirements. National management, therefore, is continuing to lose its significance, whereas international management in the markets of the Triad (United States and Canada, Europe, and Japan) is becoming the prerequisite for success for many German enterprises. The awareness of the economic unity of the world is today much more clearly marked than has ever been the case previously in the history of the world economy. A greater awareness of the change that has taken place is to be found among the German companies rather than those of the former colonial powers. As a consequence, the German economy has been more successful in adjusting to this new constellation. These structural changes in management brought about by foreign activities are linked, both for companies and for business management theory, to a paradigm change (Meissner, 1990b, p. 53). Increasing numbers of German companies and their managers are understanding this paradigm change, assimilating it, and employing it strategically.

Changes in Values of German Managers

It is generally accepted that a profound process of value change has taken place in the German society, as it has in other Western industrialized countries. This process of change from the so-called materialistic to postmaterialistic values started at the beginning of the 1960s, and was completed in the 1970s (Rosenstiel, 1989, p. 89). These changing value systems not only affect society, they also influence specific economic sectors. Therefore, managers, and especially management trainees, are also affected by this process. With the beginning of the 1980s a new atmosphere has been established in companies that reflects the consequences of the general value changes. This new atmosphere in companies has created a new vocabulary for the management staff. Instead of discipline, self-control, and sense of duty, which were the main values of the former management and entrepreneur generation, new values such as self-expression, motivation, creativeness, participation, and originality outline the new working atmosphere (Höhler, 1990, p. 188).

The so-called "German working morale," which is often praised abroad, has apparently vanished. Increasing numbers of people in Germany are working in order to live and not living only for work (Rosenstiel, 1987, p. 39). However, enjoyment and work performance do not stand in opposition. On the contrary, these new management values are based on the combination of enjoyment and performance (Höhler, 1990, p. 188). As a consequence, a new fascination with career and performance has thus arisen in the German management. Especially within the younger generation of management, the meaning of work includes these new aspects, which are combined with a distinct will to work and produce.

The positive economic growth of the Federal Republic of Germany has caused another change in German managers' values. Because of the strong competition between the enterprises to hire managers, top managers especially nowadays have far more choice of positions than they did some years ago. Salary is no longer the only decisive parameter, but additional benefits, such as commercial vehicles, insurance, old-age pensions, share in profits, balance of leisure time, and others nowadays play an important role in the selection of a position. In addition, the general atmosphere, and especially the culture of a company, is increasingly regarded as a decisive factor for German managers when they are changing jobs. As a general principle, the diverse values of managers toward work and performance always depend on their respective working and performance conditions and experiences. Therefore, empirical analyses have to consider the subjective values and value systems of managers as well as the actual working circumstances and cultures of companies (Fürstenberg, 1987, p. 17).

Culture of German Companies

In the course of their existence, all companies develop a definite and distinctive culture, which describes the system of values and provides information about the company's modes of behavior. The prevailing system of values of a company determines the courses of action open to it in making specific decisions. Management values multiply the value system of a company, and because of the dynamics of value systems in management, it is evident that the culture of companies has to adopt these new influences.

The traditional company culture of German enterprises largely involved a technical orientation. Technical efficiency and securing the qualitative level of production represented the dominant ideas toward which all other company aims were directed. In addition, the traditional company culture is characterized by organizational and personal ideals. Some companies have developed a pronounced hierarchical culture, whereas others have established a culture marked by centralization around individual leading personalities, which may sometimes resemble a personality cult. In these cases, the leading figure (the firm owner or a member of the board of directors) influences the decision processes of the company to a disproportional extent, which is a hindrance to coping with real-world problems and conditions (Meissner, 1990b, p. 59).

This traditional culture of companies nowadays is overlapping with new cultural values and management orientations. The dynamics of the value systems of entrepreneurs and their staff have formed new identities among German companies. According to these general value changes, so-called "soft factors" (non-economic and quality of life values) are achieving more and more significance in the culture of German companies. The result is a change of management approaches from quantitative to qualitative, and often the use of nonrational values.

The development of new cultures of German companies is actually influenced by the previously mentioned generational problem in management: the generation of people during the economic reconstruction after World War II have retired from their enterprises or will soon. The following generation of entrepreneurs is now questioning the traditional values and, therefore, looking for new contents for the firm's culture. As a consequence, a decreasing significance of the continuation of company traditions is currently recognized. There is a distinct desire to provide security for the family, but no longer an unlimited desire to bequeath the firm (Tietz 1982, p. 95). Consequently, traditional companies are losing, to an ever-greater extent, the connections and the leadership of the former founders and their families.

Beyond this, the traditional culture of German companies is decisively influenced by the actual scientific discussions on the significance of building up a corporate culture of companies, which may be defined as "collective programming of the mind" (Hofstede, 1980, p. 13). The ethical dimensions of corporate culture in particular are obtaining more and more significance in the Federal Republic of Germany (Hoffmann and Rebstock, 1989). Consequently, increasing numbers of German companies are trying to mitigate, or even reverse, their one-sided economic thinking in favor of strategically sensible, ethically oriented economic activity. In particular, the various voluntary measures that German companies are taking for environmental protection illustrate an increasing consciousness of the ethical responsibility of enterprises.

Another indicator of the development of a new culture of German companies is the increasing number of image campaigns, which elucidate the changing corporate orientations. For example the German company Franz Haniel and Cie has started a new image campaign with the slogan, "There's more to life than work." The advertisement illustrates the changing values of the company management and stresses that an increasing number of firms are becoming aware of the fact that nowadays, more important activities than the stabilization of hierarchies and the safeguarding of traditional values should be pursued. Ensuring the adoption of innovations, controlling market inconsistencies, providing for effective control and use of the overload of information, motivating employees to participate in these various processes, and last but not least, creating stimulating visions and opportunities whereby the future of a company is made a reality are the present challenges for those in management.

ACTUAL DEVELOPMENT OF GERMAN MANAGERS' VALUES AND REQUIREMENTS

Consequences Concerning the Unification with the Former German Democratic Republic

The unification of the Federal Republic of Germany with the former German Democratic Republic is regarded as one of the most important challenges for German managers. The actual positive economic development, which is due, not least, to the new market potentials in the former German Democratic Republic, have presented German managers with new opportunities, which include at the same time new risks and new experiences. One of the main interests of German managers concerns the rehabilitation of an adequate economic infrastructure for the new enterprises that are now being established in this area. This process affords increased management activities and, of course, increased financial resources. Many German managers who had problems in achieving an adequate position a few months ago can now avail themselves of new career opportunities in the new federal states. On the other hand, these new opportunities are not attractive for some established managers of the western part of Germany because of the lower level of infrastructure and limited possibilities for leisure time in the new territories of the Federal Republic of Germany. Because of these phenomena, western German managers often have an ambivalent attitude to working and to living in that region.

The unexpectedly fast process of the unification, along with the aggravating consequences for the economy as well as for business administration, have caused German managers to be faced with tasks that are almost or nearly totally new for them. The long separation has produced two countries, with different economic-political, technological, and, especially, sociocultural structures. Even a lot of the vocabulary is different within the old and new members of the Federal Republic of Germany, so that it is sometimes difficult for people to understand each other, despite the existence of a common mother language. In addition, the comprehension of the idea of a free market system and an adequate business administration is still backward in the former German Democratic Republic. This situation necessitates a distinct flexibility for the actions of German managers in the new federal countries. At the same time, a marked pioneer thinking is affordable, because German managers are not able to insist on well-known structures and situations. On the contrary, they have to retrench the traditional doctrines and build up new structures for industry, retailing, and administration.

Another problem concerns the continual management education of the former management staff in the new federal states. New education and the adequate development of human resources still are in the beginning phase. The establishment of new training systems for eastern German managers is expected to require years. Despite the fact that most of the staff of the former state-owned industries are willing to adopt the new economic structures and ideas, some of the former political ideals still exist. In addition, large numbers of well-educated qualified managers of the eastern part of Germany are continuing to leave the former German Democratic Republic to look for better job opportunities in the western part of the Federal Republic. A two-sided and profound learning process, therefore, is necessary for the management to realize a real economic, as well as a complete sociocultural, unification of the German nation.

Significance of the Single European Market

The dynamics of the Single European Market require that German management involve itself to an increasing extent in the various forms of foreign activities in the European market. This orientation toward increasing European activities forces management into both external and internal processes of adjustment. The structures that have been handed down in matters of organization and personnel have to be harmonized with the new dimensions of European activity (Meissner, 1990a, p. 157). In order to cope with the demands of European markets, it is necessary to establish new, suitably adjusted, forms of management organization and a European-oriented personnel policy with special regard to the cross-cultural differences between management styles and attitudes within the Single European Market (Tietz, 1990, p. 381). Management thus undergoes a pronounced structural and functional change as European activities are extended, and a profound change in company culture thereby ensues (Meissner, 1990a, pp. 157).

The scientific discussion concentrates beyond this on the ideal profile of a European manager as well as on the abilities of German managers concerning the challenges of the Single European Market. European business cannot be successfully administered by managers who remain bound exclusively to national norms, rules, and business practices and have been trained solely along these lines. New attributes of European managers are receiving ever-greater significance, and these include not only a higher qualification requirements (for example, additional education in foreign languages and higher skills in communication), but also a higher sociocultural sensibility and strategic competence (Töpfer, 1989).

The staff of German enterprises often suffers from a lack of important attributes of the adjusted European manager, although German enterprises are very involved in international and, especially, European activities. For the realization and long-term expansion of their European options, German companies, therefore, must follow a personnel policy that is conscientious in its planning and specific in its tasks. Personnel recruitment, planning, and training programs of German companies have to adopt the requirements of the unity of the European market in a much stronger way than before, and they must develop strategic concepts to fill up the gap in the following years.

CONCLUSIONS

Values and requirements of German managers are in a situation of upheaval. General changes in values and perceptions in the German society, as well as economic-political, technological, and international processes, have influenced the value systems of German managers very strongly, and have created new requirement profiles for German managers. As a result, a new atmosphere is developing in German companies. This new atmosphere is characterized by more or less strong discrepancies between the companies' values and requirements and the values and abilities of their managers. In the future, it will become evermore significant for German companies to adopt the new impulses originating from their staff. At the same time they have to develop strategies to integrate the different points of view in a new corporate culture.

The unification of Germany, accompanied by very different socioeconomic, political, and cultural values of the former German Democratic Republic, present major challenges for German managers. These challenges will be especially critical as strategies and policies for managing human resources in organizations are designed and implemented, in addition to the challenges related to the movement toward market system business and economics.

5

Contemporary French Managerial Values and Issues: A Review of the Literature
Frederic Brunnel

This chapter summarizes some of the important literature relating to French managerial values and contemporary issues affecting the management of domestic and international French enterprises. The thoughts of several leading French scholars working in the area are presented in capsularized form. The chapter concludes with a summary of some current socioeconomic and political developments which impact business and management in France.

SOCIAL, CULTURAL, AND POLITICAL

Gerand Mermet (1990)

France has experienced a number of changes during the 1980s according to Mermet (1990):
- Improvement of economic activity,
- Creation of new jobs,
- Increases in savings,
- Increases in professional accidents and illnesses,
- Increases in the number of marriages,
- Stabilization of the birthrate, and
- Increases in the spread of income levels.

Additionally, sexual inequalities are becoming greater in France, concurrent with the economic growth of the 1980s, and it seems that there is a lack of regulatory mechanisms that could correct them.

Moreover, the widespread homogamy and endogamy maintain the present social structure.

Social norms seem to becoming stronger overall in France. Media are greatly responsible for this "soft dictatorship." Moreover, the media promote the image of the superman and -woman. However, very few French people correspond to these models. The soft dictatorship of the media pushes the French people to modify their behavior, and to adopt socially correct behavior. The corporate life as well is becoming more codified. Deviant behaviors within the companies tend to be sanctioned. Companies need to be extremely competitive, and they strive for the American style of "management by excellence."

The French people are tending to become more frustrated with their life, especially the ones who do not participate in the economic growth. French people tend to be more stressed and more depressed. This overall frustration has contributed to an ideology crisis and the rise of parties on the far right. Attitudes toward immigrants are becoming increasingly negative. The debate over the immigration issue is not only related to the unemployment problem, but also to the future of France as a society that is becoming more multicultural. Thus, France is going through an identity crisis.

The overall social stratification of the French society is changing. The upper class of the past (medical doctors, professors, lawyers, politicians, etc.) have lost some of their privileges. Management has to become more efficient, for instance, while the middle class is splitting. Single-parent and other nontraditional families are becoming more influential in France. Institutions such as the church, the unions, the political parties, and the state are undergoing a period of change as well. They have to undergo reforms and evaluate the future.

French people see themselves increasingly as in a transition phase, and even in a phase of decline. Environmental problems, acquired immune deficiency syndrome (AIDS), and population growth are often perceived as presenting major threats for the future of the planet, causing some French people to think they are in the last phase of history. The young generation especially is wondering if they are the "last generation."

Because of the crisis there is a growing interest in the notions of solidarity, humanism, and morality. The next century should be spiritual, if not religious. Even though French people go to church less often, their faith appears stable in all the surveys. Sixty percent of the French say they believe in God. They might disagree with many positions of the Catholic Church, but they have a conscience of the necessary relation between private life and morality, between material life and spirituality. The Catholic Church in France has never been very comfortable with the notion of modernism and the republic; however, in these new times of crisis, when fraternity and humanity are needed, the Church might play a greater role and adjust to the society. The new role of the Church can be the one of a counterpower to the political parties, the trade unions, the school, or the media. Today's crisis concerns morals, politics, and cultural and geographical identity: in other words, spirituality. Therefore, it is highly possible that some French people may find a solution to their problems in religion.

New tendencies in French society are emerging. French people are placing an increasing importance in leisure. This may be because of a fear of the future. It also seems that many French people would dream about their own life rather than actually live it, as judged by the fact that they have come to travel more, watch more television, play more games, and even use more illicit drugs.

French people also appear to fear science and its consequences, both ethical and environmental. The 1980s have brought about a major change regarding the attitude toward money. Money is no longer something people are ashamed of, and individual success stories are becoming more important. In order to maintain their standard of living or buy more luxurious goods, the French people have reduced their savings and increased their use of credit. At the same time, they are having more trouble coping with the world around them. The European Community (EC) has not yet been finalized, and at the same time, the United States, Japan, and Scandinavia do not represent models. The French people have trouble finding the geographical area to which they belong: is it the city, region, nation, Europe, or the world? They also show a greater need for culture, in any form, and for a greater mix of audiovisual materials, e.g., television, radio, MINITEL (home information retrieval network).

A major tendency as well is the new horizontal dimension of society. The traditional pyramidal structure is becoming flatter, in the corporations, in the families, and at the state level. The French have a more direct grasp of the institutions around them, and at the same time, it appears that society is leaving out increasing numbers of people (the jobless, homeless, etc.). The French people are also becoming more individualistic. They are beginning to reject the traditional partition of time ("a time to love, a time to work, and a time to rest"). In fact, the

French people do reject the rigid partition of things and the bipolarization of their lives: work/leisure, man/woman, right/left. Instead, they are looking for a new concept of life and society.

Joelle Attinger (1991)

French people pay a lot of attention to tradition and culture. They pursue and live through quality of life, which involves fashion, cuisine, architecture, and the arts. *Savoir vivre* is everywhere in France and is a central component of French culture. Mermet (1990) provided further insights on the French identity, indicating that the French place the highest value on liberty of opinion. Some other values he included in his discussion are democracy, culture, tolerance, language, patriotism, and religion (in this order of importance to the French). Mermet also discussed the importance the French assigned to various words describing a wide range of values. Ranking is different depending on gender. Women prefer so-called "family-oriented" values (ranked from most to least important): love, family, children, friendship, happiness, and home. Men give priority to the professional life and external activities such as work, money, health, leisure, vacations, and peace.

James Walsh (1991)

Walsh (1991) indicated that French people are going through an internal crisis of identity. They feel discontent from both a social and a political perspective. They have lost their faith in the future and wonder about their national identity. Even though France appears to be one, if not the, leader in modern Europe building, French people are feeling lost and disoriented. They do not trust the politicians, and they worry about the competition ahead of them. They especially fear the new German economic power. The Gulf crisis contributed even more to confusion about the French identity. Furthermore, they wonder if they will be able to keep their French spirit in the new Europe. In short, they seem to be losing their bearing, their ideals and dreams.

However, France is still a country with a very good quality of life and standard of living. It also has very competitive technology. One of France's greatest assets is its overall stability as French institutions have shown their ability to provide the country with a stable leadership.

A new challenge for France involves determining how it is going to cope with the new Germany. Germany has been a long-time partner of France, but it seems now that the relationship might be less balanced than it used to be due to the new size of the German economy. How the French will react is still an unanswered question.

From a military perspective, as well, France is wondering where it stands. The Gulf crisis has shown the ambiguity of the French position. Being in and out of the North Atlantic Treaty Organization (NATO) simultaneously is a difficult position to hold. France must rethink its military strategy in the light of Europe, but it must also reconsider its diplomacy, especially vis-à-vis the Arab world. Regarding their relation with that region, French authorities must keep a watch on their internal situation as well. The immigration from North African countries is a real problem in France. The Arab population presents a true challenge regarding its assimilation. One consequence of this is the growing power of the "Front National" of J. M. Le Pen.

The key to answering many of the questions regarding the future of France seems to appear in the role it will be able to play within Europe. Francois Mitterand's policy in the early 1990s, which can be referred to as a new "Gaulism," is still a major factor in the future of France. Under his policy, France should get more involved in the EC through many communi • policies. Even though France has many problems and difficulties, in comparison with other countries, France has a major role to play in achieving European integration since Germany is busy with the aftermath of unification.

Margot Hornblower (1991a, 1991b)

Even though France has a tradition of terre d'asile (land of asylum), the 1980s have raised the question of the amount of immigration that can be assimilated within the French society. The main focus of the immigration issue is on the north and west Africans living in France, about three million of them. Immigration is a key issue in contemporary French politics. It is a key point of the proposition of the far right party of J. L. Le Pen. On the other end, the sons and daughters of immigrants are not at ease. Even though they are citizens, they do not feel French due to rejection they experience from a portion of the population. The overall climate is deteriorating, and incidents of racial violence have increased.

Frederick Painton (1991)

Even though Mitterand is the finest politician of the last decade, because of various socioeconomic problems, an overall feeling of dissatisfaction in the French population emerged in the early 1990s. French people do not feel at ease in their environment. They are not confident in the future and are increasingly intimidated by their overall social and economic situation. The situation is so serious that Mitterand named a new prime minister in 1991. However, the effect he was looking for did not come about, and the situation is not improving. The fears of some analysts that a social explosion like that of 1968 may emerge were realized in the spring 1993 elections. Dissatisfactions ranging from unemployment, distrust of the traditional political parties and politicians, economic protection, and ethic priorities are evident in the social, economic, and political life in France.

INDUSTRY AND TECHNOLOGY

Jean Louis Bassoux and Peter Lawrence (1991)

According to Bassoux and Lawrence (1991), it is important to understand French management practices. Some reasons to pay more attention to France are the following:

- In 1989, France made one-third of all acquisitions in western Europe, adding more in 1990. And in 1991 France has surpassed Japan and the U.K. in acquiring U.S. companies.
- Nuclear power provides just under half of France's power needs, which makes France the largest EC's energy exporter. Electricity is 48 percent cheaper in France than in Britain and 54 percent cheaper than in Germany.

French technology is among the best in some fields; such as Airbus and the high speed train. Many companies are world leaders in their industries; including Michelin, L'Oreal, l'Anliguide, and Alcatel. All these examples call for an understanding of what makes a French manager. Management in France is considered more a "state of mind" than a system of techniques. Management in France is a separate profession, and managers have a different legal status (codes). Management is often seen as being an intellectual activity rather than as action-oriented. An analytical mind, independence, and intellectual rigor are the qualities desired from managers. French managers use, and excel in, quantitative thought. They seem particularly competent when it comes to planning, conceptualizing, research, and system design. However, French managers may be overly logical and lack intuition.

French companies are rather centralized, and the French PDG (president director general) is the equivalent in one person of the CEO and chairman of the board. French managers mainly are graduates from the cities. There are 170 *grandes ecoles* (prestigious university level schools), but only 23,000 graduates a year. Alumni of the *grandes ecoles* have strong networks and act as gatekeepers when it comes to hiring. Lifetime or long-term employment in the same company is a more frequent expectation in France than in the United States.

In conclusion, what Japan achieves through consensus and groupism, France achieves through elite convergence. Even though the French system has some weaknesses, it nevertheless provides managers with a clear logic and rules which provide unambiguous signals that shape managerial action. In addition, it provides French industries with a focus and sense of purpose that the rest of the world should not underestimate as a key to strong economic performance.

William Rademaekers (1991)

France is, without doubt, a leading technological country and can boast some of the finest high-tech achievements of the last decades. Examples include:
- The high-speed train,
- The tunnel under the English Channel,
- Nuclear power plants,
- The Ariane Rocket Program, and
- Products such as fiber optic cables.

These technological achievements, however, may not ensure economic success for France. Nevertheless, they represent only the visible part of an iceberg that may return the fifth largest economic power to its former glory.

Edward Gomez (1991)

France has a long tradition of central planning, observed Edward

Gomez (1991). The key element in French administrative structure has been Paris. Paris and the surrounding area have traditionally enjoyed greater growth and economic power. However, in recent years, the provinces of France have realized that they too can play a key role in the French experience. More power has been given to local authorities, and more initiative is now coming from places other than Paris.

Some example of new important leaders outside Paris are:

- Aliette de Lacombe: jewelry designer in the Basque country;
- Jean Claude Aurousjeau; prefect of the Nord department (representing the national government at the regional level);
- Mark Sandim; commercial director of the party Nautes; and
- Jean Bousquet; entrepreneur and mayor of Nimes.

Claude Pigamiol (1989)

According to Claude Pigamiol (1989), France has a tradition of highly centralized industrial relations. However, because of recent industry restructuring activities, a different approach to work-force consultation has emerged. Many French companies have adopted attitudes that recognize the participation of workers in such consultation. French companies (at least some of them) believe that workers have an important say in the outcome of negotiations. This change of attitude is partly explained by the strategic nature of industry restructuring, as well as by the emergence and recognition of new management theories.

These changes, which have occurred in very specific situations, may in fact, have an impact on the overall industrial relations system of France. The new human dimension is taken into account by managers, both in the decision-making process and during the implementation of decisions.

Jeff Bridgford (1987)

Even though France has had a socialist at the head of the nation, Jeff Bridgford (1987) believed the labor movement to have suffered major losses of its members and experienced a great decline in overall support for labor unions. The decline of the labor unions is particularly at the CGT, the communist union. It seems that the new labor laws are in part responsible for this decline. Unions also have failed to show their strength in the highly unionized industries in that they have not been able to prevent restrictive wages policies. Furthermore, unions have been incapable of attracting workers from the growing tertiary sector, and at the same time have lost members due to the rising unemployment in the industrial sector. Finally, companies have tried to ignore unions by introducing more flexible wage bargaining methods, and by developing participative management.

Frederick Ungeheuer (1991)

Overall, France lacks a strong industrial base. French industries have difficulties in competing internationally and have lost some international markets in the last 20 or 30 years. In 1991, the International Monetary Fund's *World Competitiveness Report*, ranked France at the 15th position (behind most of the European Community members), the worst ranking since 1986. Some of the weak points for France include improving fiscal administration, exercising managerial freedom, achieving export and labor flexibility, and avoiding high corporate and industrial taxes.

The solution that has been advocated by the national government relies on a return to a policy involving state intervention to promote the overall economy and commerce. However, the state may lack the finances to implement such a plan.

SUMMARY

The recent general elections in the spring of 1993 reflect the response to the various social and economic concerns described above that have occurred in the early 1990s in French society. The priorities of the French people include: increasing employment, improving the quality of life, protecting the environment, controlling the influx of immigrants, supporting economic protectionism, and demanding more active state promotion of the economy and commerce. In may respects, these priorities are similar to those which predominated the recent presidential election rhetoric in the United States in 1992.

In the spring of 1993, the French Socialist Party suffered a major defeat in the general election. As the conservative party proceeds to build its coalition and power toward a center-left government, President Mitterrand is likely to stay in office until his term expires in 1995. With unemployment at a record high, the emerging government will need to shape its policies to alleviate this problem, and reflect the priorities which have emerged as summarized above.

6

The Political Challenges
of Post-Communism
Vladimir Goati

The end of 1989 and beginning of 1990 marked a fundamental political turnaround in the East European countries, including Yugoslavia. In the process, the *ancien régime* was swept away with dramatic speed and a system of representative democracy began to be raised from the rubble. The old power structure has been pulled down and a new structure with a new hierarchy of political protagonists is being established. At the same time, new tensions and conflicts are appearing whose regulation will form the core of political life in the future. It will take decades for the political earth to settle after this great quake. Some of the main features of political processes in these countries are examined here.

In the spectacular breakdown of the *ancien régime* the loser in the political contest is easy to pick out: the Communist party, which was the backbone of real socialism's political system. However, it is harder to identify the winning side because it is made up of diffuse parties and movements (the triumphant magma) whose real differentiation only began after they came to power. Most probably, the contouring of the political spectrum in the East European countries will lead to groupings into a number of major parties, which will be reminiscent, with local variations, of the political families of Western Europe. Let us first review the changes on the losing side.

DILUTION OF THE COMMUNIST PARTY

The dramatic upheaval has pushed the Communist party out of the power center and, in places, to its abolition. Within a few months, the Communist parties have thrown off the hard core of their tripartite ideology (the holy trinity): the dictatorship of the proletariat, democratic centralism, and proletarian internationalism. As far as the League of Communists of Yugoslavia is concerned, the third idea was erased from the ideological project back in the 1950s. Parallel with that there was a change in the organizational structure. The principle of organization at the workplace was given up in favor of territorial organization. Additionally, the name of the party was changed. In the feverish search for a new political identity, the Communist parties are adopting goals and values to which they had been hostile until recently: representative democracy, the citizen, the lawful state, the division of power, and human rights. In comparison to this mighty ideological turnabout, the programmatic revisions of the Social Democratic parties of Western Europe in the 1950s was a mere adjustment.

In addition to the changes in ideology, mode of organization, and name, which were swept in by changes from above, there was also a far-reaching change from below. In the course of just a few months, the majority of members left the parties, so that by the beginning of 1990, their membership (in six East European countries: Bulgaria, Czechoslovakia, Hungary, German Democratic Republic, Poland, and Romania) had dropped to about one-fifth of their membership in 1985 (to 2.3 million from 10.5 million).

No recent data is available for the League of Communists of Yugoslavia, but it is clear that there has been a dramatic decline, particularly in Slovenia and Croatia, where the Communists have become the opposition following electoral defeat. The scale of the outflow is indicated by the official estimates of the Slovenian party (SKS-SDP). In June 1990 it had about 20,000 members, or a little under one-sixth of the membership in 1981 (125,206). This process has also begun in the USSR. In 1989, 136,000 members left the party voluntarily, and 82,000 left in the first three months of 1990. Quantitatively, these are small numbers in view of the substantial (19 million) membership of the Communist party, but they are very significant considering that until very recently, there were no voluntary resignations.

Such a process of deserting the sinking ship is no surprise, for it is well known that a high proportion of party members have an exclusively instrumental approach to the party. In the real socialist countries, as well as in the Yugoslav party, membership was a pass, not only to political, but also to professional, promotion, and even people with no interest in politics whatsoever joined the party ranks. This also explains why the majority of members turn their backs on the party when it is relegated to the opposition and can no longer facilitate social promotion. The real question, however, is why the minority (about one-fifth) of Communists still remain faithful to their organization. The answer that they are consistent in their ideological commitments irrespective of the change in political circumstances is not adequate because the Communist parties have abandoned their central ideological ideas.

It is more likely that the reason for remaining is that for these individuals, the party is, above all, a social group in which the individual establishes a network of informal relations that are often stronger than the formal party framework and are independent of changes in the party's ideological program. Consequently, remaining in the party for them is a matter of personal identity, and not primarily an ideological or political act. This is supported by the fact that--at least, judging from initial, still unverified, data--the majority of the remaining members of the Communist parties are of the older generation. In view of this, it may be said that the future of these organizations is not rosy and that the erosion of their influence will continue.

For the East European Communist parties that unwittingly found themselves in a pluralistic setting, the moment of truth came at the first free elections which were held successively in the first half of 1990. These elections actually represented the Communists' trial by fire. Having claimed to express the interests of the whole of society, or at least the majority, and having previously won over 90 percent of the vote at elections they ran, these parties now had to be content with much more modest returns (see Table 6.1).

Elections to the lower house were not free, since 65 percent of the seats were allocated on the basis of prior political agreements. In the elections to the Senate, the Communists only managed to win 1 of 100 seats.

The election returns presented in Table 6.1 show the complete political marginalization of the Communist parties, with the exception of Bulgaria's Socialist party. This is concluded, not just on the basis of the low percentage of votes won, but also from the refusal of other parties to collaborate with the Communists. The disassociation from the Communists in these countries should be seen as a constant in political life and not just a passing feature of the 1990 elections.

Table 6.1
Reform Communist Parties' Shares of the Vote at the 1990 Parliamentary Elections

Party	% Vote
Hungarian Social Party	11
Democratic Socialism Party (GDR)	16
CP Czechoslovakia	14
Socialist Party (Bulgaria)	47
SK Slovenia-SDP (Yugoslavia)	17
SK Croatia-SDP (Yugoslavia)	24

Note: The June 1989 elections in Poland are not included here because they were only partial elections.

Once power was taken from the Communists, Communist party members began to be eliminated from the middle and lower ranks of the political hierarchy and from major social institutions. Although the newly installed government's need to eliminate a cadre sediment that had been built up over decades is understandable, the breadth and the ruthlessness with which this is being done in some countries suggests a rising wave of revanche (primitive anticommunism) which flies in the face of official appeals for political tolerance.

IMPACTS OF CHANGE

The victorious political group (whether party or movement) had shaped its political identity in contrast to those of the ruling Communist party (CP). This was enough to win the elections, but not to run the state. The disappearance of the enemy (personified by the CP) has spurred the growth of internal dissension within the winning groups. Although the new East European governments do not have great freedom of action due to various constraints such as foreign debt payments, rapid restructuring of the economy, marketization, and so forth, they have some options with regard to the participation of particular social groups in paying the price of reform, the pace of change, the scale of privatization, the degree of opening up to foreign capital, and similar efforts. The first cracks are appearing in the process of choosing these options, which indicate the likelihood of changes in the current ruling blocs in the near future. Change of government, although a routine operation in the stable democracies of Western Europe, could produce additional political strains in Eastern Europe and Yugoslavia. Even frequent changes of government in the West (witness France, Italy, and Belgium) did not have lasting adverse effects because stability was ensured by a highly professional bureaucracy (in Weber's sense) which, like an automatic pilot, kept to the course that had been set earlier. There is no such bureaucracy today in Eastern Europe or Yugoslavia, and changes in the ruling bloc could even lead to political crisis.

For these countries at this time, the only way out of a dire economic situation is through a restrictive credit/monetary policy and drastic belt-tightening. This kind of policy is usually carried out by conservative parties in Western Europe. In Eastern Europe and Yugoslavia, the brunt of such policies falls first on those working in unprofitable enterprises and on the overstaffed state administration, pensioners, and first-time job seekers. The two countries farthest along in economic reform, Yugoslavia before the recent political upheaval, and Poland, provide a good illustration of the scale of unemployment.

In Yugoslavia, there were 1.3 million jobless in 1989, with the prospect of this figure rising another half-million in another year. In Poland, 450,000 workers lost their jobs between about 1987, the start of the reform, and June 1990. Since then, the pace of layoffs has been accelerating, and 50,000 people have been losing their jobs every week. Because these are countries with a markedly low personal standard of living and in which the average family does not have any substantial savings, the mass layoffs that are now underway could spark social protests that would be difficult to regulate, given the presently undeveloped democratic institutions. In multiethnic countries like Yugoslavia, national antagonisms are growing. This is largely being brought about by the Communists, who are attempting to lessen their responsibility for the catastrophe and to hold on to power (where they retain it) and shift the blame to other etnic groups in the country.

FUTURE DIRECTIONS AND ISSUES

Given the increasingly dramatic social and political situations, it is most unlikely that democracy will function in the Swedish manner in these countries, as members of the new political elite so naively maintained. As things stand now, political life there is approaching the Latin American, and not the Swedish or any other West European, model. The likelihood of social protests veering off into extrainstitutional waters is increased by the fact that the trade union and political organizations, which are supposed to represent the interests of those threatened most, are weak. Free trade unions are only gradually being established and still lack sufficient negotiating power. Nor are things any better in the political sphere. Discounting the reformed Communists, who have lost all political credibility, the left wing of the political spectrum (judging from the results of the first free elections) is exceptionally weak. Without adequate union and political representation of the threatened interests of those on the lower ranks of the social pyramid of wealth and power, the ranks of the unemployed, which is swelling by the day, could resort to noninstitutional actions that would put the newly established democratic regimes severely to the test. The idealization of the "good old days" when there may have been no freedom but at least enough bread for everyone cannot be excluded either.

We arrive here at a far-reaching contradiction in the East European countries and Yugoslavia between the commitment to representative democracy, on the one hand, and the complete absence of democratic institutions and democratic political culture, on the other. The development of democratic institutions and procedures (the rules of the game) is a long-term process. Of course, the wealth of experience in countries with representative democracy can be drawn upon in this regard. However, the situation with political culture is less promising because the majority of the East European countries cannot boast of any long democratic tradition in the period before World War II. After the Communists came to power, even these weak traces were stamped out, and the political culture was swamped with authoritarian formulae.

In this part of the world, the collapse of the one-party dictatorship has been accompanied by the absolutization of democracy, the belief that it is the absolute cure for all evils. From the psychosocial standpoint, the democratic euphoria is quite understandable because the battle against the *ancien régime* made it necessary to stress the positive aspects of the political alternative which was representative democracy. This explains the exaggerated optimism, not only among the broad public, including the new political establishment, but even in the scientific community. However, these unrealistic aspirations will doubtless lead very rapidly to disappointment. Democracy is no ideal state; it is merely a less bad political order. Even though democracy has demonstrated its relative advantages in prosperous societies, in countries gripped by economic crisis, it has shown its weaknesses and has even failed (witness Italy and Germany before World War II).

A few decades ago, Ignatio Silone said that in the future, the political contest in Italy would be between Communists and ex-Communists, alluding to the fact that an exceptionally high proportion of the members of the Communist party of Italy were leaving the organization and joining other parties. The great writer's prediction has come completely true in Eastern Europe and Yugoslavia today. The majority of key political positions are being taken by former members of the Communist parties, and, moreover, by people from the core structure (*nomenklatura*). Besides them there are the dissidents, who, for the most part, previously belonged to the Communist party!

The reason for this is not some inexplicable weakness of the new system for ex-Communists, nor the Communists' talent to capture important political posts, but rather a sociological imperative. In the middle of the last decade, Communist party membership accounted for an average of about 14 percent of the adult population in the East European countries, and when the ex-Communists (eliminated by purges) are added in, the figure reaches about 20 percent. Members of this group differed from the remainder of the population, not just because, between them, they occupied all the main positions in society, but also because they had a significantly higher level of education and professional qualifications. Clearly, the new regime cannot deprive itself of this manpower resource.

However, the previous involvement of the majority of current political leaders in the Communist party (and often, its inner circle) will certainly have an adverse impact on the political climate generally because these individuals cannot completely shed the codes of political conduct that are inappropriate to democracy. As a result, the political climate in these countries will be tainted by tendencies towards exclusivism, a low level of tolerance, and suspiciousness.

There is another far-reaching effect of the converted structure of the current political leaderships. With the entry into political life of younger generations that have not been socialized in the Communist party, young leaders will begin to rise who, in the race for top positions in the political hierarchy, will be above the reproach of having a Communist past. The contest between the young and authentic (organic) leaders in the new parties can be expected to intensify, and in the coming period, the clash will be an important factor in intraparty dealings, and political dynamics in general, in these countries.

CONCLUDING REMARKS

We have touched on only some of the problems that set the tone of political life in the post-Communist societies of Eastern Europe. Coming to grips with these problems and with the dramatic situation in these countries as a whole, the governments that have emerged from the first free elections have been forced to quickly pass reactionary measures, many of which will crucially worsen the condition of large parts of the population. At the same time, no one can foresee how long the deprivations will last. Hidden behind the unhappy present is a completely uncertain future. Politics, instead of being the traditional "art of the possible," in this part of the world is increasingly becoming the "art of the impossible."

7

Main Trends in the Changes of the System of Values in Soviet Society: A Historical Overview of Research and Current Problems

Nina Andreenkova

In analyzing the broad issue relating to the meaning and purpose of life, the Russian thinkers have traditionally given a significant place to the individual's value oientation. Even though the views on this issue of the most famous writers, F. M. Dostoyevsky, L. N. Tolstoy, and A. P. Chekhov, are well known in Western countries, because of the language barriers, the works of the Russian philosophers and psychologists are practically unknown. For this reason, before beginning an overview of the current empirical value studies in the Soviet social sciences, it is necessary to present a short historical overview of the main ideas that had been were worked out from the beginning of the twentieth century in the Russian philosophical and psychological schools. These ideas, together with the known western conceptions (as reflected in the works of A. N. Maslow, G. Hofstede, and M. Rokeach), provide the theoretical basis for the recent empirical research on this issue.

HISTORY OF STUDIES OF THIS PROBLEM IN THE USSR

The Psychological School

Intensive studies of individual values, and motives of behavior as their moving force, began in Russia in the beginning of the twentieth century. The most fruitful results were produced by psychologists. In the beginning of the twentieth century, L. I. Petrazhitsky (1904) and A. F. Lazursky made the most significant contributions. In the 1920s, in

Russia, a theory of motivation began to develop based on the Marxist approach.

Starting from the 1930s studies appeared that now are considered by psychologists as classic. First and foremost were books by S. L. Rubinstein (1957) and D. N. Uznadze (1961). These works formed the basis of individual schools in the study of the theory of motivation. The Russian psychological school was further developed by A. N. Leontiev (1976). In Leontiev's conception, complex processes of the individual's activity occur as a result of the cultural development of society and the respective development of the individual's consciousness. This brings about a motivational shift which is caused by the changes in the hierarchy of needs, along with the emergence of new needs, making motivation more complex.

The theory of motivation developed by A. N. Leontiev in a number of his studies was most fully expressed in his book, *Activity, Consciousness, Personality* (1976). Leontiev questioned Maslow's scale of motives which classifies them by their closeness to vital (biological) needs. At the bottom of the hierarchy is the need to maintain physiological homeostasis, above that is the motive of survival, further up is the need for confidence and prestige, and finally, at the very top of the hierarchy, are learning and aesthetic motives. In Leontiev's view, the main question is not whether this (or a similar) scale is correct, but whether it is right to establish such a principle of scaling motives. The issue is that neither the degree of consciousness of biological needs nor the motivating power of motives determine's hierarchical relations between them. Such hierarchical relations are determined by the evolving relationships of the individual's activity and by the mediating factors of these relationships, and are, therefore, relative. This also applies to the major relationships between meaning-forming motives and stimuli motives. In the structure of one specific activity, a particular motive can perform a meaning-forming function, while in another activity it adopts a function of additional stimulation.

The same idea is elaborated in P. M. Yakobson's book *Psychological Problems of the Motivation of Human Behavior* (1969). Yakobson noted the importance of establishing the conditions under which these specific characteristics of motivation of certain actions are significant for revealing significant personality traits. Based on empirical data, Yakobson showed that in the case of motivation of creative work, irrespective of the social-economic system, the motives that are related to economic remuneration are not always decisive. Thus, the dominant motives of inventors' creative activities are linked to the wish to promote the economic progress of the country, modernize technology, and to the performance of their plant. Of those polled, 61 percent pointed to the primacy of these motives, while 19 percent referred to the wish to make the work of their colleagues easier and to improve their working conditions as the leading motives. Personal motives related to remuneration, alleviating one's own job tasks, and satisfying one's ambition were dominant among 17 percent of those surveyed.

P. M. Yakobson rightly believes that, besides questionnaires, which permit obtaining statistically significant results, and panel research, which allows observing changes in motives and correlating them with the changes of the factors influencing motivation, one should use a wider range of flexible techniques. These include observation, which elucidates phenomena such as the specific characteristics of the job, the attitude to work, and so forth. Also included are social-psychological experiments which reveal dominant motives determining both the individual's behavior as a whole and the stability of particular motives characterizing the individual's activity in a specific field.

The work of the Georgian school of psychology remains virtually unknown in the West. The founder of the school was D. N. Uznadze (1969), who developed the original theory of the mental set. He proved experimentally that illusions similar to the illusion of weight (where, after objects of unequal weight but equal volume have been compared many times, they become perceived as unequal in volume) occur in all cases where there is a conflict between the individual's immediate mental set and irritants acting on the individual. Uznadze further suggested an experimental method of the so-called fixed mental set, which studies the essence of the mental set by the role it plays in the emergence, development, and fading of illusions. Experimental research identified different kinds of mental set-diffuse, differential, and fixed-and described various properties whose combinations form different types of mental sets.

According to the studies of Georgian psychologists S. N. Chkhartishvili (1958), the mental set is the disposition of the individual. It integrates a person's dynamic relations and mediates the effect of stimulating actions. This is the highest level of organization of "essential human powers." The mental set is the basis for activity by the individual that is aimed at achieving an equilibrium between him or herself and the environment. Being the basis of behavioral cohesion and consistency, the mental set reduces the indeterminacy of any possible form of behavior. In the Georgian school of psychology, the mental set is also taken to mean the psychological content of the interaction between a specific need and its satisfaction, given the constraints within the circumstances relating to the need. This is a prerequisite for the possibility of purposeful and adaptive behavior by an individual. Both of these psychological schools, the Russian and the Georgian, have had a major influence on the study of the problem of the motivation of individual behavior in Soviet society.

The Problem of Values in Soviet Philosophy

A number of Soviet philosophers, such as E. F. Balakina (1965), see the problem of values as a neo-Kantian antithesis to the Marxist understanding of society. Contrary to the neo-Kantian emphasis on universal cultural values, the Marxist philosophy declares that social-class values have priority over universal values. F. Nitzsche, the idol of the twentieth century philosophy, promulgated the notion of "revaluation of all values" on the basis of rejecting the norms of absolute values that exist outside the will of "the superman." This "superman" cannot be content with impersonal and supra-personal values based on intellectual, aesthetic, and moral culture dimensions, but must actively assimilate these values and destroy their autonomy and impersonal character. Marxist philosophy, on the other hand, proceeds from K. Marx's thesis that "the essence of man . . . is not an abstraction inherent to a particular individual, but it is the set of all social relations" (Marks and Engels, 1980, p. 3).

Comprehensive studies have played an important part in our understanding of the individual's outlook, attitudes, and values. While in the nosological field the most prominent relationship is between the object and the subject, in the axiological field, it is the one between the value and the valuer. According to V. Momov (1975), the deontic sphere emphasizes the relationship between the norm (the requirement or obligation) and the executor of the norm. This relationship is manifested in a person's actions. Since a social norm expresses the needs, interests, and will of society (and of a given class in a class society) in the form of synthesized requirements and obligations addressed to the individual, the major question of deontology turns out to involve the relations between the individual and the society. These are obligatory in character, in other words, they require that the individual have a way of life that is in keeping with the needs of the Socialist society. Figure 7.1

Figure 7.1
Relationships of Outlook, Attitudes, and Values

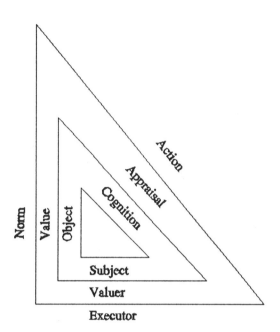

summarizes the relationships between these three views.

Needs, interests, and values are categories of Marxist sociology that denote what a person needs, what the person is interested in and what is dear to the person in life (Zdravomyslov, 1986). In its general philosophical sense, a need is a person's particular want of a certain set of external conditions surrounding his or her existence (a certain demand of external conditions resulting from his or her essential properties and nature). Here, a need is a cause of an activity, but the activity itself also becomes the object of means and brings about the formation of new needs.

In its specific meaning, the notion of *need* includes the daily needs of people, their aspirations and claims that require constant satisfaction. These are material needs such as underlie the Marxist theory. "People, first of all, have to eat, drink, have a dwelling and clothing prior to being able to get involved in politics, science, art and religion, etc. Therefore, the production of immediate material means of life, and thereby every given stage of economic development of a people or an epoch, formed the basis out of which state institutions, legal view, art and even religious ideas of the given people develop, and the basis on which they should therefore be explained, and not the other way round as it was done until now" (Marks and Engels, 1980, p. 27).

In modern society the range of essential needs has significantly expanded. It encompasses needs for movement, communication, education, information, and many commodities. These groups of needs are linked to the development of corresponding systems of production: means of transportation, media, and so forth. One can say that these means are linked to the social functions of people to a larger extent, than to the satisfaction of people's physiological needs. However, they are as necessary for modern humanity as food. The notion of spiritual means includes, first of all, the desire to possess the results of spiritual production: assimilation of scientific knowledge, art and philosophical culture. The ability to extend the range of needs and to generate new needs is an essential aspect of the socialization of people's needs: of the humanization process, which makes them socially significant. Needs are closely linked to interests. An interest is a feature of a social group that essentially affects the social and political behavior of this group, predetermining its most important socially significant actions.

Interests are the bases of the system of values, which we call culture. Culture as a set of values should also be treated as an arena of interaction and a struggle of interests. Every social group is selected in its attitude to the whole complex of spiritual wealth accumulated by humankind. The interests and needs of a given group serve as criteria for selecting its values. The Marxist conception of interests is linked to a concrete analysis of social relations. It proceeds from the primacy of the social system, treating interests as a property, feature, or aspect of the system. Along with the notion of interests, Marxist philosophy uses the concepts of needs, goals, and motives of actions to describe the causes of an event. These categories are closely interlinked: what is a need in one relationship may be a goal in another, and in some cases, the need, the interest, and the goal may totally coincide. It is the interests-their clash and interaction-that determine the cause of the main developments in social life.

Value orientations are seen in Marxist sociology as a system of stable, fixed mental sets of a social subject that are related to the assimilation and creation of specific values. Their character is determined by the type of the social subject (whether an individual, social group, class, or society) and by the content of values. Value orientations are determined by the essential views of the individual and are influenced by the individual's family, by colleagues, and by the society as a whole.

The structure of basic mental sets comprising a value orientation includes three components: cognitive, emotional (evaluating), and behavioral. A social value orientation is formed in the following stages:

1. Becoming aware of one's needs;
2. Comparing one's personal needs with objects and phenomena of the surrounding world and working out one's own position attitude to the world; and
3. Forming a conscious desire for objects, conditions, and forms of satisfying the needs.

The next step involves studying motivation as the moving force of the individual's behavior, his or her disposition and degree of self-awareness, and his or her stability. Figure 7.2 reflects a logical interpretation of the process of motivating . Needs are seen as a source of activity, providing the "ignition" for the whole motivational process. Soviet researchers have paid much attention to the question of the nature of motivation (M. Yaroshevsky, 1966; T. Yaroshevsky, 1973; Diligensky, 1976, 1986).

The motivation of behavior depends on how the individual integrates his or her many components into a coherent appearance. Two approaches toward a definition of motivation can be identified in Soviet literature. In a narrower sense, the motivation of behavior is defined as the motivation of concrete forms of human behavior. In a broader approach (Yakobson, 1969), however, the notion of motivation includes the whole complex of psychological aspects determining the individual's overall behavior with the purpose of studying the motivational sphere of individual and discerning needs and motives of behavior, interests, aspirations, goals, and so forth (Aseyev, 1976). A need is a deep component of the individual. It is object-oriented and dynamic. Among the criteria for classifying needs, Soviet literature uses the correspondence of needs to the basic values elaborated by humankind, the system of socially significant relations, and the meaning of the needs for the individual's particular activity (Leontiev, 1976).

Soviet researchers consider two types of needs: those that are a condition for the development of the individual and those that manifest

Figure 7.2
The Conceptual Model of the Process of Motivation

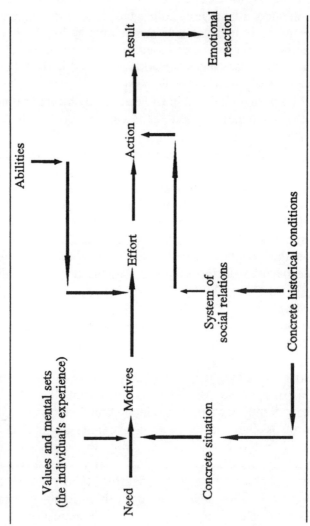

the self (Buyeva, 1968, 1978). The first group includes the needs for physical and psychological comfort, the need for communication, and the need for social bonds, as well as the need for work as a means of getting material remuneration. The second group includes needs related to self-association of the individual, which are manifested through creativity, moral principles, public duty, professional pride, self-respect, and public recognition. N. Z. Chavchavadze (1984) wrote on this complex problem as follows:

> It is said that the individual's activity is motivated by his/her needs, and without having needs the individual would not act. This is probably true. But it is also true that the activity which is totally determined by a need can never be free and cannot create new values of creative activity. As long as the person has a need, the person cannot speak about freedom. The person should, to a certain extent, free himself from this control, and overcome his/her subjugation to the needs and to get above them . . . . Man's freedom always means freeing oneself from the lower values and the struggle for their realization. (p. 29)

Value orientations are essential elements of the inner structure of the individual. They are reinforced by the individual's experience, which, in turn, is shaped by family, people close by, the school, mass media, and other social institutions. One should distinguish between value orientation toward values as specific attitudes of the individual to the norms, customs, and values promoted and reflected by public opinion and value orientation as an inner component of the individual's consciousness and self-awareness.

Such are the main methodological approaches to study values used by Soviet philosophers, sociologists, and psychologists.

OVERVIEW OF CONTEMPORARY SOCIOLOGICAL STUDIES

In the area in question, research was mainly focused on the problems of shaping a harmonious and universally developed personality and on the role of the family, the school, mass media, and other social institutions in the formation of the personality, as well as the role of work and work motivation in the individual's life.

Studies of Personality Formation and Moral Values

This area of research began to be stressed in the USSR starting from the 1960s. It was closely related to the problems of Communist education in attempting to form an all-round personality as a goal of the Communist society. Within the Socialist society, attention was given to both ideological aspects (political views, moral values, etc.) and behavioral aspects (specific life plans of young people and their desire to implement the values declared by the Socialist society). Therefore, among the first sociological studies were those carried out on the initiative of the Young Communist League in 1961 in Moscow, and also in 1963-1966 in a study of Leningrad youth. The methods and techniques used were by no means perfect, and the orientation of these studies was clearly ideological. A special sociological group was set up under the Central Committee of the Komsomol, which carried out fairly regular large-scale surveys of Soviet youth.

In 1961 the Moscow City Komsomol Committee initiated a study of dominant values and life plans of people aged 17 to 28. A total of 1,487 people were polled: industrial workers, engineers, office workers, and college students. The results showed that 60 percent of the respondents who replied to open and differently formulated questions felt that their most significant spiritual value was "clear conscience." The remaining 40 percent chose over 100 other values. These choices were grouped by researchers based on the degree of their closeness to each other. The control study showed that what the young people meant by " clear conscience" was primarily honest work, decency in relations with other people, and abiding by principles of high morality (Sokolov, 1986).

The study of youth carried out by Leningrad sociologists in 1963-1966 yielded a similar ranging of values. Of those who replied, 70 percent responded to the question: "What do you need most of all to be happy?" as follows:

- to have an interesting job I like;
- to be respected by the people around me; and
- to love and be loved.

Only 30 percent of the respondents were oriented toward material values and said that their primary aspiration was to acquire some specific consumer item (Ikonnikova and Lisovsky, 1969).

The research of problems of individual socialization carried out by N. V. Andreenkova (1971) studied the importance of family, school, peers, and mass media in the process of the individual's socialization and the formation of his or her value orientations and mental sets. In 1967, a poll of 805 high-school graduates (16- to 17-yearolds) in Moscow and the Moscow Region, Byelorussia, and Lithuania believed that the main factors in happiness were:

1. Enthusiasm about one's work-74 percent of the respondents;
2. Private life-69 percent (girls rated family life slightly higher than boys at 76 percent and 65 percent, respectively);
3. Respect and love of the people with whom one is in close contact-50 percent;
4. A favorable international situation-31 percent;
5. A favorable situation in the country-25 percent;
6. Material prosperity-17 percent; and
7. The possibility of having fun during leisure time-10 percent.

Undoubtedly, a fairly altruistic attitude toward the financial aspect of life was due to the overall orientation of the Soviet society in the 1960s toward spiritual values and the neglect of material wealth.

A close correlation was revealed between good relations in the family and the attitude of the young people toward others ($r = 0.68$). On the whole, young people in those years were characterized by optimism and great faith in humanity. When asked, "Are you sure that humankind will be able to create a society without wars and injustice, i.e., a happy life for all?" 58 percent answered "Yes," 17 percent expressed doubt, and only 3 percent disagreed. Twenty-two percent had no specific opinion on this subject.

The family and private life were rated second in the hierarchy of values. However, opinions about the age of marriage were fairly heterogeneous in that 52 percent believed that one should get married when sure that one loves the other person, irrespective of other considerations; 31 percent believed that one should only get married when ready to support the family; 27 percent said, when one is mature in terms of age; and 26 percent, when one finishes one's studies (the total is greater than 100 percent because respondents could give two answers). Indicating their attitude toward creating a family, males more often pointed to the necessity to support it materially, while females were more oriented toward love, irrespective of other considerations. At the same time, the overwhelming majority of females were not going to confine themselves to family life, hoping rather to be actively involved in socially useful work. When asked, "What are you going to do after you get married?" 66 percent of females answered that they would try to retain their jobs, 30 percent said that they would quit their job only while taking care of young children, 3 percent thought that they would have to quit their job after the first child was born, and only 1 percent of the female respondents wanted to quit their jobs as soon as they get married.

In 1971-1975, the sociological laboratory of Kharkov University (1977) conducted a study entitled "Communist Ideals and the Formation of a Student's Personality." They polled 6,349 students of Kharkov University and 3,135 students of five colleges in Kharkov. When asked "What do you consider to be the most important thing in your life?" 94 percent of respondents said, "An interesting job one would enjoy"; 64 percent said, "Faith that our society is pursuing the true path"; and 3 percent said, "Achieving individual prosperity."

In 1976-1978, 4,365 industrial workers, engineers, technicians, and students in colleges, specialized secondary schools and vocational schools were polled by Kharkov University (1980). Respondents were selected from Moscow and from Vladimir and the Vladimir Region. With regard to the goal of life, all the groups selected as primary getting an interesting job and having the respect of others. Only the fifth and sixth places were taken by the goals of achieving material prosperity and getting an executive position. Thus, various studies conducted at different times from 1961 to 1982 in different regions and among different social and demographic groups all revealed a common agreement that the most important life values for Soviet people are:

- An interesting job,
- Knowing that what you do is useful to people,
- Public respect, and
- Material prosperity.

Such an orientation evolved as a result of a long period of Socialist construction in the USSR. For the sake of comparison, it will be recalled that the study conducted in 1927 (Gurova, 1977) asked, "What would you do if you could do anything?" Of respondents, 32 percent of the 3,452 said that they would do something for their individual prosperity. In 1967, half as many respondents (16 percent) answered the question in the same way. At the same time, in the 1927 study, 12 percent of respondents chose various kinds of socially useful activity, compared to 52 percent in 1967. In a 1925 study (Smirnov, 1929), over 15 percent of male youths and 21 percent of female youths believed that "the best thing in life" was material prosperity and the possibility of having a calm and care-free life.

There is no doubt that break-down of the whole system of social relations in the country since 1985 is bringing about changes in a system of moral values that had been established over several decades, in the role of the family, in the ways of achieving material prosperity, and in other aspects of social life.

A Study of Work Values and Labor Attitudes

A study of work values and labor attitudes is the most traditional topic in Soviet sociology. From the beginning of Soviet society, all official social institutions supported the absolute unconditional value of work as the basis for existence of the Socialist society and every individual in it. A hierarchic consideration of labor in the process of society's development has become a tradition in the Soviet literature (namely, a necessity). Labor is viewed as a means of satisfying the other human needs: especially the transformation of labor into humanity's vital needs. It was believed that at the initial stages of society's development, labor was, in essence, necessary for satisfying our primary needs for food, clothing, and habitation. In the subsequent stages of development, including Socialist society, labor is, first of all a means of satisfying both material and spiritual needs. During the formation of the Communist society, labor became humanity's first vital necessity, a source of joy, pride, and satisfaction.

Nonetheless, it is becoming evident that at each stage of society's development, labor includes all three main components. In other words, it is always necessary as a source of society's weal, it is a means and a measure for humanity to obtain all the amenities that society has, and, finally, it is a human necessity, depending on labor conditions and content, as well as on our capabilities and proclivity. Society's task consists of enhancing the value of labor for everybody, in both a moral and economic respect (pride for one's good, necessary work, and people's respect) and in a material sense (suitable remuneration for the amount and quality of labor spent).

The violation of the main principle of socialism, "From each according to his capabilities, to each according to his labor," was due to the erroneous interpretation of the principle of equality. Thus, a leveling off of incomes irrespective of labor contribution lowered the value of social consciousness. This did not move Soviet society to social homogeneity, but conversely, it resulted in a negligent fulfillment of people's duties due to their selfish attitude toward labor, and in a lowered efficiency and quality of labor. Ultimately, it resulted in high material and financial differentiation due to the development of the "shadow economy" (a form of black market economy) and the acquisition of unjust incomes by certain strata of the population.

The results found by a panel of sociological researchers who studied labor attitudes showed that in the past two 10-year periods (about 1960-1980), there was a deepening process of the instrumentalization of work. This means that labor became a means to an end rather than a goal in itself. The alienation of work became more intensive first of all among nonqualified workers. This process led to a change in the type of workers: from an orientation toward self realization in the work sphere to indifference for the content of the work and an orientation toward a good wage (Yadov, 1983).

The same tendency was noted in studies about the prestige of different professions in Soviet society (Chernovolenko, Ossovsky, and Paniotto, 1979). Some researchers have stated that the main interests of individuals were oriented toward the production sphere and social-political activity. Now however, they have been displaced into the private sphere (Beliayeva and Kopnin, 1989). According to the 1985 poll conducted by the Institute for Sociological Research in Tambov Region (Andreenkova, 1988), the general estimation of the role of labor in the life of Soviet people was rather high as confirmed by the following answers to the question, "How would you estimate the role of labor in your life?"

Labor is necessary to feed and provide all necessities for my family and myself.	21%
Labor is a means by which I can satisfy my other material and spiritual demands.	19%
Labor is a necessity without which I cannot imagine my life, although, of course, it is also a source of my income and well-being.	60%

The opportunity of seeing the results of one's labor is quite essential for Soviet workers (89.9 percent), as is the need for independence in work and personal responsibility for one's business (87.2 percent), and for respect for one's own and others' occupation (84.7 percent).

On the whole, the degree of satisfaction with one's work was rather high (81.8 percent of the individuals polled reported satisfaction with their work). Seventy-three percent of the respondents prided themselves on their work; 64 percent said that the time sped by; 34 percent said that they worked with enthusiasm, sometimes even on holidays; and 27 percent said that at times, they worked with great enthusiasm. Thirty-one percent of the respondents worked without particular enthusiasm and for only the required span of time. Eighty-seven percent said that they could work better. In their opinion, in order to achieve, the following prerequisites were needed: realization of the necessity to work with complete self-abandonment (69 percent); a change in the general attitude toward labor (68 percent); perfection of labor organization (66 percent); and creation of other conditions (a total of 70 percent of the respondents).

According to the poll, the most significant issues were good relationships in the collective (71 percent) and with the chiefs (62 percent). Overall, the respondents were satisfied with these factors (91.6 and 88.7 percent, respectively). The results obtained reflect, to a great extent, a high level of collectivism in our society, the more so because of the respect on the part of colleagues and chiefs. The respondents were least satisfied with the sports and cultural undertakings at their enterprises (37.5 percent), housing and service (34.5 percent), the level of work organization (32.0 percent), and sanitary and hygienic conditions (29.2 percent), as well as aesthetic labor conditions (27.8 percent), prospects of promotion (27.7 percent), possibilities for technical creativity (25.8 percent), and, in the last place, the level of wages or salaries. The value-related orientation and motivation of labor activity reflect areas or spheres of possible executive and managerial activity that may increase labor productivity and bring about the more rapid development of science and technology.

An analysis of the results obtained leads to the conclusion that the rate of industrial development, given the present stage of the country's advances in the sphere of social and economic achievements, depends on other factors besides the level of educational and occupational competence of the personnel. First and foremost is the desire of people to work, the level of satisfaction with their work as a whole, and separate elements of the production situation. Moreover, the level of understanding of the social significance of production is important, as well as attitudes toward, and commitment to, increasing labor efficiency and the quality of production. Relationships between people in a collective work environment, and their regulation, are acquiring particular importance. Thus, the main thrust of accelerating socioeconomic development is a focus on individuals who work with interest and understanding.

The formation of a conscientious and creative attitude in labor should be based on attention to humanity and the creation of an industrial mechanism that would stimulate people's creative activity and form an environment that conveys an interest in the final results of each person's work. Since the process of *perestroika* taking place in the Soviet Union embraces all the spheres of social life (economic, social, political, and ideological), profound qualitative changes in productive forces and the perfection of production relations are necessary. These need to be complemented with changes in the people's minds and society's superstructure (i.e., the perfection of all social relations, the renovation of forms and methods of work by political institutions, and a deepening of democracy.)

The results of an annual national, industrial, socioeconomic survey that was conducted beginning in 1987 by N. Andreenkova showed that although most enterprises formally adopted new economic conditions on the basis of self-financing and self-compensation, the transition to the present did not have a significant effect on the recent interest of every worker in the affairs of his or her enterprise. These results are shown in Table 7.1.

The workers' level activity, initiative, and interest in enterprise affairs during the last few years did not rise but rather showed a tendency to decrease. Among the factors preventing positive attitudes, lack in labor organization and payment came in the first place. The absence of care for their workplace and of education about the industry from childhood are also of great importance. In the past few years, the workers' interest in performing their work better has decreased. One of the main causes is, first of all, the absence of a direct connection between the quantity and quality of work and its compensation. Most of the respondents said that they could work better with the following conditions: a better labor organization, correlation between payment and real work effort, justice in payment, confidence in the stability of employment, and participation in the consideration of enterprise development. The current unfavorable situation in economics throughout the country influences the affairs of practically every enterprise and the level of job satisfaction, which has had a tendency to decrease. Thus, the work values as part of the common value system are a most clear indicator, not only of the effectiveness of current economic reform, but also of the overall moral health of society.

Table 7.1
Soviet Workers' Responses to Selected Questions from the Annual Industrial Socioeconomic Survey

1. Did you feel an influence from the transition to new economic conditions on your interest in enterprise affairs?

Percent Response

	1988	1989	1990
1. Yes, undoubtedly	13.3	13.3	7.2
2. In a certain degree	24.6	33.3	24.4
3. No, in no way did it influence me	15.5	30.9	39.3
4. My own interest only decreased	2.8	4.0	4.7
5. No, because we didn't pass on new economic conditions	28.1	9.0	11.8
6. Unsure	7.3	9.5	12.6
7. No answer	8.4	-	-

2. Did you note in your collective the rise of activity, initiative, and interest by workers in enterprise affairs (in the present)?

Percent Response

	1987	1988	1989	1990
1. Yes, highly essential	5.5	3.2	4.1	2.5
2. Yes, in a certain degree	53.1	46.2	46.5	33.6
3. No, it practically didn't rise	38.3	41.7	43.2	56.8
4. Unsure	3.1	8.9	6.2	7.1

Table 7.1 (continued)

3. What factors, in your opinion, prevent forming a good relation to work for every worker? (The sum of the answers may be more than 100 percent because respondents could choose more than one response.)

Percent Response

	1987	1988	1989	1990
1. Lack in labor organization	25.2	25.5	24.4	21.8
2. Absence of necessary exactness	10.4	11.0	9.6	9.5
3. Absence of a need in a stable workplace	16.0	17.1	16.3	17.2
4. Imperfection of the payment system	22.9	23.1	27.2	31.1
5. Insufficient number of workers	11.6	9.6	9.2	7.9
6. Absence of industry from childhood, understanding its necessity	13.4	11.7	11.0	10.4
7. Other	0.5	2.0	2.3	2.1

4. Are you now interested in doing your work better than early?

Percent Response

	1987	1988	1989	1990
1. Yes, I am interested	69.2	59.7	55.0	43.8
2. Not very interested	18.5	21.6	30.2	32.2
3. No, I am not interested	9.4	9.5	14.8	24.1
4. No answer	2.9	9.2	-	0.1

Table 7.1 (continued)

5. Do you see close connections between level of payment and the intensiveness and quality of your work?

Percent Response

	1987	1988	1989	1990
1. Yes, my pay directly depends on the intensiveness and quality of my work	37.5	36.0	29.1	31.0
2. This relationship is very relative	38.0	40.8	45.1	42.4
3. No, they do not depend on each other	21.4	21.1	25.8	26.1
4. No answer	3.0	2.0	-	0.5

6. Can you work better than you are now?

Percent Response

	1988	1989	1990
1. Yes, considerably better	32.5	50.0	53.9
2. Yes, I have possibility to work slightly more effectively	25.3	42.2	37.8
3. No, under every conditions	23.8	7.8	8.2
4. Unsure	18.2	-	0.1

7. Are you satisfied with your job?

Percent Response

	1987	1988	1989	1990
1. Yes, I am satisfied	30.5	29.9	27.2	24.4
2. Not quite satisfied	57.2	58.1	60.7	60.0
3. No, I am not satisfied	10.2	9.7	12.0	15.5
4. No answer	2.1	2.3	-	0.1

Note: Totals may not equal 100 percent because of rounding for the above data.

MAIN TRENDS IN CHANGES IN THE SYSTEM OF VALUES DURING THE TRANSITION PERIOD

At the present stage, due to drastic changes in social-economic conditions, the Soviet society is going through a crisis in the system of values. The crisis of values does not mean that values have completely disappeared. What has been destroyed, however, is the system of values that had been promoted by the official propaganda. What we see now is pluralization and a partial dilution of values based on ideology. This is quite a dramatic transition, especially at the level of the individual. For many people whose outlook was shaped on the basis of the system of values of Socialist society (which emphasized the priority of collective interests over personal interests); this means the process of desocialization of the personality. At present, there seems to be two major systems of values.

Collectivist System of Values	Individualistic System of Values
Equality of incomes.	A good income, prosperity.
Priority of ideas, of moral values over material ones.	Comforts, health.
Public recognition.	Self-Expression.
Interesting work, contributing to the good of society.	Success.
Good relationships with one's colleagues.	Power, competition.
Children, caring about future generations.	Living for oneself and not for the future.

At the same time, the current chaotic and uncontrollable transition to a market system (to be more precise, to its first stage, the accumulation of capital) causes an inner protest in many people. This is not because they are, in principle, against the transition to market relations, but first and foremost because of its form, which permits the former party nomenclature and allows undisguised criminal elements to seize a considerable part of what was people's property without changing the system of production. Since the process of transition to a market economy at the present stage brings about reduced production, price increases, and a worsening social, economic, and crime situation, people feel socially unprotected and are losing faith in social justice. The sociological survey conducted in 1967 of those who were born in 1917 (with 650 people polled) showed that the hardest part of their lives had been the years of mass repressions. Many of those polled indicated that the terrible thing that was not only good people were killed, but also the fact that those who remained lost faith in justice. Mutual mistrust became imprinted on the people's souls, and confusion and insecurity invaded people's minds (Vinokurova, 1988).

For many people of older age, the process of tranistion to market relations involves a difficult process of breaking a system of values that has evolved over many years. Concerning the loss of ideals, a significant portion of young people found themselves in a kind of moral vacuum, not believing in anything. Some are seeking a firm ground in religious faith and the church, while a significant portion of people have changed value prioirties in favor of purely pragmatic, utilitarian, and consumption-oriented attitudes. This is frought with the danger of ethical and spiritual transmutation of both individual persons and the society as a whole.

CONCLUSION

The system of values in Soviet society over the past several decades has gone through considerable changes. Several generations of Soviet people have passed from faith in the eternal value of Communist ideals, including their significance and justice, to their complete rejection. At the level of the individual, this has lead to frustration, the loss of stabilisty, and an indiscriminate rejection of anything Soviet. For some peoples constituting the former Soviet Union, this has brought about the rise of ethnic consciousness and nationalist tendencies, often developing into armed conflicts and civil war. Given the general economic crisis, the moral and spiritual vacuum is leading to growing crime, devaluation of the role of work as the basis for prosperity, and other undesirable social consequences. A resurrection of moral and spiritual values is the main way out of the crisis, which should be based on the people's moral health.

8

Transformation of the Mass Media in the Post-Communist Era
Ljiljana J. Bačević

THE TIME OF CRISIS

The late 1980s and early 1990s have been marked by the dramatic, traumatic, and spectacular collapse (and internal breakdown) of the Communist regimes (totalitarian, Real Socialist, and Self-Management) in Eastern, Central, and Southern Europe. Both the theoreticians of these countries and the Western experts (Sovietologists and Kremlinologists) failed to predict this historical change, and they are equally unable to explain it. Scholarly studies have gone no further than providing a description of the phenomenon (some are more accurate than others) and making a post festum analysis of a future that is already a thing of the past. Theoretical generalizations and prognoses are difficult to make because of the wide differences between and within the post-Communist countries in terms of their histories and cultures, as well as their religious, economic, and cultural development and the extent to which the processes of democratization and modernization have progressed. Along with these differences, the post-Communist era is also characterized by sharp political, economic, social, cultural, religious, and other types of conflicts. The principle contrasts are political pluralism versus homogeneity and national intolerance versus tolerance.

The processes of democratization of the media reflect all these conflicts and contrasts. They cannot be surmounted by importing, transferring or adapting Western models of democratization of the media (or, indeed, society). In any case, the dominant paradigms of Western communicology (Lernerian theories of development and the Gerbnerian theory of cultivation) have proven equally unsuccessful in predicting and explaining changes in the mass media in post-Communist countries. The purpose of this chapter is to analyze interdependencies in the situation and the changes in society, in public opinion and behavior, and in the media during the transition from the Communist to the post-Communist period, taking Yugoslavia as a case for analysis.

One of the most striking features of contemporary Yugoslav society is that it has been in a state of profound crisis for a very long time. The symptoms of the crisis (whose roots can be traced to the distant past) became dramatically acute in the early 1980s. A general regressive trend occurred, as reflected in a fall in the growth rate of the gross domestic product (GDP), reduced labor productivity, unemployment, inflation, a mounting foreign debt, and an inefficient utilization of foreign credits. In addition, , poverty and economic and political autarky occurred, as well as a growing friction between national groups and the republic. Morover, the system was unable to resolve the backlog of social problems or to channel social trends.

At the end of the 1980s, in an attempt to remain in power, the ruling (Communits) party literally overnight abandoned its own ideological program of socialist self-management, a consensus economy, and nonalignment, to embrace instead some of the goals and values of civil democracy. Nonetheless, the democratization of society (political pluralism, parliamentary democracy, and a multiparty political system) has proven to be an unstoppable process. It should be noted, however, that in Yugoslavia, as in other post-Communist countries, this process began in highly adverse economic conditions with brewing social unrest. There was a traumatic crisis in ethnic relations in those countries with a multinational composition, leading to the beginnings of ethnic civil wars.

In all these countries, the democratic and pluralistic traditions were stamped out. Now, the majority of the population lacks even an elementary political culture. The removal of the Communists from power unfortunately did not guarantee democracy, although there is no doubt that it indicates democratization. The post-Communist countries face a painful process of building political, legal, and economic instruments and institutions that will guarantee democracy (a multiparty system is only one institution).

The crisis in Yugoslav society has left deep scars on the consciousness of its citizens in the form of an acute value crisis (a moral vacuum, anomy, and conflict of values). These value conflicts are multifaceted (e.g., ideologized communist versus pluralistic, democratic; traditional versus modern; universal versus national values; etc.). The picture is further complicated by cultural and historical differences and different levels of economic and cultural development, roughly corresponding to the different national groups. The general trend of change is nevertheless making itself felt in the form of an accelerated abandonment of the values of the Communist ideological program. For instance, self-management as the pride of the Yugoslav model of socialism has lost more than half its supporters in the last 10 years. The popularity of the policy of nonalignment, which used to have the backing of a fantastic 90 percent of the population, has plummeted, with barely 25 percent of the citizens continuing to give it their endorsement. The preference for social ownership over other types of property relations which was once expressed by two-thirds of respondents in opinion polls, has melted to just over one-tenth, while more than half the citizens surveyed were wholeheartedly in favor of a market economy.

Irreversible changes in the value sphere, however, take a long time, and decades must go by before they become stabilized. Although there are indications of a transformation in the system of values in the direction of modernism and even postmodernism, at the present moment, regressive trends are dominant. These trends are reflected in phenomena such as the retreat into privacy, a return to religion, ethnocentrism, cynicism, and an external locus of control. In the general breakdown of value systems and the resulting confusion, identification with traditional social groups and institutions is a logical reaction. This takes the form of a socalled "return" to national concerns and religion, which are depicted and regarded as a refuge and salvation from the social and individual crisis.

New political parties, including parties that are the successor of the League of Communists, have come to power thanks to national programs in which all interests and conflicts of interest are ideologized as ethnic. If nationalism was once the "last means of the bourgeoisie in their struggle against the working class" (Trotsky), in Yugoslavia, nationalism is the first means to be seized upon by the opposition to remove the Communists during their efforts to remain in power. The identification of all conflicts in society with ethnic conflicts (which, to be sure, buys social peace within the national community) inevitably leads to an escalation of ethnic friction and, most important, blocks all possible solutions for a separate or common life in the territory of Yugoslavia. When interests are ideologized and identified with the nation, a solution to problems is only possible if one of the sides to the dispute will abandon its national interest. Therefore, no solution is possible because it would mean a rejection of national identity (an either-or choice for individual nations). The outcome of such a state of affairs in Yugoslavia is well known: the country is falling apart, and there is civil war with an ethnic and religious basis.

A sense of national homogenization became clear in the mid-1980s as a change in the determinants of the attitudes and value systems of Yugoslav citizens. Up until the end of the 1970s, studies showed that opinions, beliefs, attitudes, and values were primarily determined by social factors (such as profession, income, and status in the distribution of political power). This confirms, in the long run, the thesis that the social structure determines social consciousness. Subsequent studies, however, have revealed that these factors are losing their earlier significance and that national affiliation is becoming the principal differentiating or rallying factor of social consciousness. A consistent homogenization of individual national groups and a resultant differentiation between them are to be seen in literally all the choices stated by the citizens surveyed.

THE MEDIA CRISIS

The Yugoslav media system which was set up at the end of World War II on the Soviet model (involving state-party control, a transmissional and propaganda function, and closeness of alternative ideas and international communication) changed over the course of more than four decades in step with transformations in the political system. The first serious attempt to democratize the media at the end of the 1960s and early 1970s, through decentralization and a controlled introduction of market mechanisms, ended. Moreover, the attempt to democratize Yugoslav society by increasing the number of participants in political power and decision making ended as well. The state-party control of the media was taken over by a larger number of subjects, including political leadership bodies and the leaders of individual republics and provinces and/or local centers of political and economic power.

The introduction of the market into the communications sphere, however, encouraged the appearance of commercial newspapers, which had greater independence from the authorities than the media, which received subsidies. Together with the "recalcitrant" youth, through the form of student and literary publications, they created a parallel system outside the institutionalized system of political communication, which was open to alternative ideas and criticism of the regime. In the mid-1980s, alternative and critical stands and interpretations became normal fare in the so-called central media which included the daily and weekly newspapers with the biggest circulations and government subsidized radio and television-broadcasting organizations.

The litmus test for determining the degree of democratization of media systems has always been reflected in what has been termed *high risk communication*, meaning the communication of political messages. Moreover, it is precisely this category that reveals that the democratization of the media in Yugoslavia is more ostensible than real. In the old, uncomplicated days of the 1950s, the problem of political communication was so simple that it did not even exist: the centralized, monolithic media (in those days, the press and radio) were under state-party control. From their commanding monopolistic position, this centralized media reflected the entire life of society in the service of the interests of the "people," the "avant-garde," the "working class," and so forth, depending on which term was being used to connote submission to the authorities (the Communist party or the League of Communists). Inevitably, as time passed, the image of society as mirrored in the media became farther and farther removed from reality until, in the late 1960s and throughout the 1970s, the media came to let different views and ideas from the cultural sphere, and even from the domains of social policy and the economy, filter through.

History, as well as domestic and foreign policy, however, have continued to remain under strict control. The ostensible pluralization in the treatment of internal affairs in the 1970s and early 1980s was the result of a complete decentralization of the global media system and the creation of republican, provincial, and national subsystems, which were placed in the service of what was purported to be the "national interest." This period was characterized by the outbreak of a "media war." The leadership bodies of the Communist parties skirmished with one another, with daggers drawn on ethic grounds. They disguised the real reason for the conflicts (a struggle for power within Yugoslavia among the ethnocracies) behind polemics in the media over topics having to do with art, culture, education, and history, which ostensibly had nothing to do with politics. By the end of the 1980s, the media war had been carried over into the political and ideological sphere, and the dissolution of the League of Communists removed the last barrier to open clashes between the various ethnocracies.

A peculiarity of the media scene in Yugoslavia is the absence of media with a Yugoslav character (whether in content or coverage). This situation resulted from the polycentric structure of the Yugoslav media system. This system was set up in keeping with the multilingual composition of the population . It was put into practice in an organizational and institutional sense as a collection of autonomous media subsystems of the national groups or the different territorial political units; the republics and provinces. These subsystems had been conceived as organs for the public expression of the various national groups (peoples with different languages, cultures, and traditions), through which the processes of horizontal communication within Yugoslavia as a whole were to take place. In practice, however, the very opposite effect was achieved. Thanks to the numerous mechanisms for wielding control and influence over the media available to the ethnocracies (the right to set editorial policy, financial control, appointment of party members to key editorial posts, etc.), the media came to report the "reality" only as seen through the prism of the national centers of power. Meanwhile, the media accused others of lacking objectivity.

To make matters worse, the circulation of the press between the republics was very limited. For instance, only a little more than one-tenth of the circulation of leading dailies and just under one fifth of the total circulation of all newspapers and magazines were sold across republican borders. Since the beginning of the 1970s, sales of newspapers and magazines, especially daily newspapers in other republics steadily declined. The outcome of this trend, which has become costly, has been a total absence of horizontal communication between different national groups, which is an elementary prerequisite for achieving critical understanding, pursuing a constructive dialogue, and taking creative action on the many problems facing society. At the present, the situation is even more lamentable. The belligerent sides have severed radio and television links, and movement of the press is being prevented. The media of all sides to the conflict are functioning in accordance with a state of war, using all possible techniques to manipulate public opinion and spread misinformation.

A NEW MEDIA MONISM

Just before and after the first multiparty elections in the Yugoslav republics, new processes of media political pluralization were set in motion within the media subsystems. A spate of new publications founded by political parties appeared, independent radio stations were set up, and the national media opened up to a certain extent to the opposition parties (thanks mainly to polarization among the journalists within the media organizations and editorial boards). In contrast to Serbia and Montenegro, where the parties that were the successors of the corresponding republican League of Communists won at the elections, new opposition parties or coalitions of opposition parties came to power in the other republics. The common denominator of all the victorious parties was their national program. In all the newly elected republican assemblies, however, the new opposition became marginalized, regardless of whether this opposition was comprised of the once ruling League of Communists or new political parties.

In some parliaments, such as in Serbia and Croatia, an electoral system based on the majority principle has caused the number of opposition parties to be much smaller than the support shown at the elections. Consequently, the ruling parties with parliamentary majorities enjoy complete control over the parliament and have been able to form one-party governments. The basic problem naturally does not lie in the composition of the assemblies. It is quite legitimate to come to power in a majority electoral system, however, it is not right for the ruling parties to use their majority position to push through or prevent changes that affect the whole of society. In my opinion, such behavior on the part of the ruling parties, especially at a time when decisions that determine the fate of the entire nation are at stake, reflects the weakness rather than the strength of these parties. In the long term, this behavior will lead to political instability. In the short run, however, it would be too much to expect all the citizens to accept as legitimate the realization of the interests of a single political party (which is the net effect of the application of the principle of the majority vote in parliament).

The new political monism has given rise to a new media monism, which I feel is a step backwards, not just in relation to the processes of pluralization of the media that were seen just before and after the elections, but also in relation to the situation that prevailed in the mid-1980s. In comparison with other countries of Eastern, Central, and Southern Europe, the Yugoslav media at that time held a more independent position vis-à-vis the authorities. They were much more open to international communication with Europe and the world, and foreign programs from the West (especially entertainment and educational programs) were much more accessible to the public. Prior to the legalization of the multiparty system, the media were allowed a certain degree of political pluralism, and they were instrumental in shaping a body of democratic public opinion.

After the elections, the trend toward democratization of the media was halted by political decisions of the parties that had come to power (those with a majority of seats in parliament). The results were identical regardless of whether the incumbents were the successors of the League of Communists, which sought to maintain monopoly control over the national media system, or new political parties, which sought to establish monopoly control. The means used to maintain or establish a monopoly have also been identical. Key editorial posts were filled by members of the party, the marginalization of intractable journalists occurred, and so-called "new" press and radio and television broadcasting legislation was pushed through parliament. One-party state control over the media, in combination with the nationalistic programs of the parties in power, intensified the processes of national homogenization and the absolutization of the national interest. Naturally, the present armed conflicts in Yugoslavia are not the result of regressive trends within the media, but there is no doubt that the mass media today are part of the war propaganda machine.

THE CULTURAL ROLE OF THE MEDIA IN A MULTINATIONAL SOCIETY

One of the primary tasks of the Yugoslav media in the domain of culture (in addition to their educational function and their duty to spread genuine cultural values) has been to maintain cultural contacts between members of different national cultures. The media of the different national groups, especially radio and television, had the duty of presenting to their audiences (consisting of one or several ethnic groups) programs of all the national groups in Yugoslavia (and, of course, also from abroad). In practice, this policy was implemented by broadcasting programs produced nationally and from other counties, programs produced nationally and by another national group from Yugoslavia, and programs produced entirely nationally. The dominance of typical products of mass culture in radio and television broadcasting, for the most part, came from imports. By the mid-1970s, programs from West European countries and the United States accounted for between 20 percent and 30 percent of television broadcasting time. This gave rise to sharp polemics between the advocates of cultural universalization and those who wished to preserve the national cultural identity.

In the broad cultural context, there are two conceptually opposed, but empirically visible, trends in the modern world: the trend toward universalization (the creation of a global superculture based on science, technology, and the mass media) and the trend toward reviving and promoting ethnic identity, both of which are present in Yugoslavia. Until 10 or so years ago, there were fears, among both the public and, even, cultural theoreticians and researchers that the trend of globalization would have negative consequences, especially in conjunction with the satellite diffusion of foreign television programs. This fear was not without a theoretical basis in the cultural-imperialistic paradigm (which was inappropriate for Yugoslav society, in my opinion), and not without empirical support (in my opinion, overhasty) in the interpretation of the quantitative data on the proportion of foreign television programs in overall programming and their popularity among all sections of the television audience. Ideological and bureaucratic administrative attempts to stem the flood of universalization are today a thing of the past, for the country is now preoccupied with the tragic implications and effects of the growing emphasis on ethnicity.

In my opinion, neither of these two trends can a priori be described as positive or negative. Both contain internal contradictions that make them ambiguous. For instance, modern, postindustrial, nonmilitant nationalism, which insists on cultural peculiarities and corresponding autonomy as a political solution, is the absolute opposite of aggressive nationalism. The latter insists on cultural isolation, artificial revival of the past, glorification of the national culture, threats from the cultures of other nations, and so forth. Universalization, however, might pose a threat to the survival and development of a national culture, and, in the last analysis, to the preservation and promotion of national identity. However, the absence (or prevention) of international cultural contacts (including exchanges carried out through the mass media) would be fatal for the development of every national culture. The modern world is increasingly interdependent economically and politically, and consequently, there will be growing interdependence among cultures, communications, and the media.

Within the context of the general trends of universalization and the strengthening of ethnicity, Yugoslavia (and indeed, other multinational, post-Communist countries) is a special case. Globalization takes the form of an ever greater opening to Europe and the world, but there has been no parallel strengthening of ties between the national groups living in the country. The expansion of ethnicity completely neutralizes any integrational trends at the level of the country as a whole. Although in Yugoslavia, the general population used to be more or less well disposed to the idea of multicultural contacts. In practice, there were national monocultural trends, and in some parts of the country with a multinational population, these were bicultural trends.

The level of education played the role of an intervening variable in national cultural contacts (i.e., it was not a direct or independent factor). Specifically, a higher level of education had its corollary in a higher cultural level and in stabilization of advanced cultural needs. Advanced cultural needs increased the probability of multicultural contacts, but, in turn, this depended on objective circumstances and conditions. These circumstances or situational factors are not determined simply by unsuitable offerings of the media and other cultural institutions, nor is educational and cultural development a sufficient guarantee of national multicultural contacts.

The culturally most developed and least underdeveloped regions of Yugoslavia, Slovenia and Kosovo, respectively, are precisely those regions where the population demonstrates the least willingness to engage in multicultural contacts and where there is the highest degree of national cultural isolation. These days, the trend towards the production of "ethnically clean" programs, the glorification of the national culture, and the satanization of the cultures of other nations living in Yugoslavia are leading to cultural isolation and the shutting off of what used to be a more or less open cultural area.

The cultural mission of the mass media has been equated in Yugoslavia with the dissemination of works of high cultural standards. However, high standards of culture and the media have for many years been at loggerheads, and in the period of the fast expansion of television, this clash grew into a full-fledged war. Critics have pointed out that the mass media, especially television, spell death to genuine cultural values. Moreover, they are believed to encourage aggressive behavior (particularly of children and young people). Television is blamed for the dehumanization of society. It "anesthetizes" the public and stands in the way of progressive social changes, and it gives an inaccurate picture of the world, society, and social relations. The flaw in these arguments is that their proponents did not deem it necessary to base their conclusions about television on empirical facts, and some of them have never even bothered to watch and analyze television programs.

On the other hand, well-intentioned analysts who regard the mass media as a means of popularizing and democratizing culture (an unquestionably noble objective) have come up against the implacable arithmetics of media opinion surveys. These surveys reveal that radio and, especially, television audiences are primarily interested in these media as sources of entertainment and relaxation, with information in second place and culture and education lagging far behind. (In the culturally advanced parts of the country and among members of those sections of the population with higher levels of education, there is a slightly larger percentage of those who use the media to satisfy their cultural needs.) The differences in respect to the dominant functions of radio and television (entertainment, relaxation, and information) are not very significant, and in regard to television viewers, the differences between the most highly educated and those with the least education were more declarative than real. These conclusions, of course, do not mean that within Yugoslav society there are no differences in cultural behavior and cultural practices (in fact, the differences are often quite significant).

However, I would like to point out that these differences are manifested in other aspects of cultural consumption (books read and attendance at cultural events), while the media sphere, as compensation for the inadequate functioning of other cultural institutions, is an area of cultural equality. However, it still cannot be viewed apart from overall cultural behavior, and media cultural equality does not imply the effective homogeneity of Yugoslav citizens in this sphere. Furthermore, the homogenizing effects of the media in the sphere of culture will most probably be reduced with the appearance of new media (videocassette, cable, and satellite television), thanks to a more varied program and greater control over the media for users (in comparison with traditional media).

INFORMATION AND DECISION MAKING IN WORK ORGANIZATIONS

One of the cornerstones of self-management, which has been highly touted as a superior form of political democracy, is the assumption that everyone is qualified to make important managerial decisions. The implementation of this idea came into conflict, particularly in the practice of work organizations, with the lack of education, professional skills, and incompetence of the majority of self-managers. As a result, major decisions were made within an elite circle of executives, albeit formally and within the competence of the entire work force. In response to efforts to put this ideological tenet into effect, the information systems in work organizations were designed to equip "self-managers" to have a voice in making decisions rather than to foster a feeling of loyalty to the firm, encourage workers to work harder, raise work morale, facilitate communication within the firm, strengthen group cohesion, or other factors.

An influential group of Yugoslav communication experts of the time advanced the hypothesis that information is used as compensation for the inferior status of individuals and groups in the decision-making process. Inferior status includes factors such as lower level of education, lower position in the hierarchy of the work organization, and nonparticipation in political life. After a series of changes in the information systems of work organizations based on this compensation hypothesis, it became evident (and not for the first time) that access to information, instead of being the key to power and influence, was their result. The improved distribution of information did not perceptibly increase decision making since the decisions that they were called upon to make most often concerned problems caused by the malfunctioning and crises in the economic and political systems.

Nonetheless, throughout the 1970s and in the first half of the 1980s, self-management was widely accepted as a social and personal goal and value. That this acceptance was only skin deep can be seen today from the fact that the earlier endorsement of self-management by two-thirds of Yugoslav citizens has dwindled to a minority. With the tacit and, later, statutory abandonment of self-management in work organizations at the beginning of the 1990s, employees were stripped of their rights to take part in decision making.

There is now a very strong likelihood of social unrest because of the effects of the economic crisis in the form of layoffs, unemployment, poverty, and drastic declines in the standard of living. Even though the motivation of workers to take part in self-management decision making has never been particularly great (except when their personal interests were directly at stake), denial of this right at a time when many people will be finding their very subsistence threatened could further complicate an already difficult situation. Notwithstanding all the shortcomings in the distribution of information within work organizations, self-management nevertheless provided the necessary minimum of opportunities for employees to express and articulate their interests and to initiate processes of decision making in connection with these interests. The present blockage of flows of information in work organizations must clearly be compensated for. Independent trade unions, as the natural champions of the interests of the work force, combined with the presence of strong opposition parties, represent the optimal way of preventing a revolt on the part of the poorest strata of the population.

A TIME OF UNCERTAINTY

In historical terms, the crisis of Yugoslavia is part of a general crisis affecting the countries of Eastern, Central, and Southern Europe. Even though the crisis has not affected all these countries with equal severity, and even though the speed with which changes are occurring and the prospects for their success differ, the process of change in their socioeconomic systems (production, property ownership, and political systems) is irreversible in them all. Solutions are being sought in a reorientation to a market economy, reprivatization, decentralization, political democratization (legitimation of the pluralism of political interests), and a moral renewal. In all these countries it is the process of political democratization that has made the most headway (with parliamentary democracy and the multiparty political system). It has left its mark on the consciousness of citizens, as seen in their abandonment of the goals, norms, and values of Communist ideology, and in their political behavior as seen in the results of multiparty elections. The cumulative effects of the crisis have brought home to the citizens of the Communist countries the fact that neither the present nor the future is in their hands or in any good hands. The fall of communism and the transition to the post-Communist period were inevitable

Political pluralism has taken a very distorted form in Yugoslavia. The highly complicated configuration of interests in society has been reduced to simplistic national and religious terms. Traditional (elitist) and populist nationalism have made a triumphant entrance on the political scene. Civil war on national and religious grounds has eclipsed (and, for the moment, pushed into the background) potential conflicts in society arising from the introduction of a capitalist economy. It is only a matter of time before the member of the poorest strata of the population rebel against the growing income gaps and the realization that they will be the ones to pay the price of the economic reforms.

What, then, is the future of democratization in the post-Communist countries, if all it can bring the majority of their citizens, both now and in the foreseeable future, is civil war, poverty, and despair? At worst (in a variant that has already been experienced but not eliminated), there would be a military coup d'état or the coming to power by nonviolent means of authoritarian, repressive, nationalistic regimes. It would be illusory to think that such a possibility would be welcomed only by the military complex and members of the Communist hierarchy who are faced with the prospect of losing their power and privileges. If forced to choose between democracy, hunger, lawlessness, and war, on the one hand, and political disenfranchisement, a minimum standard of living, law, order, and peace, on the other, large sections of the public would opt for the latter set of choices.

At best, we can hope to see stabilization and a continuation of the initial processes of political pluralization. As things now stand, the worst scenario is by far the most likely one. The demise of communism did not automatically result in either a functioning economy or a tolerant democracy. As citizens become increasingly doubtful of the ability of democratically elected authorities to bring about order from the political and economic chaos, it is necessary to make an entire series of historical moves in order to give democracy a chance in the post-Communist countries.

. From the international standpoint, it is clear that economic aid from the most developed countries is a crying need, and as such, it is all the more incomprehensible why it has not been forthcoming and why strings are being attached linking it to the completion of the process of democratization in the post-Communist countries. It should be clear to everyone that there can be no democratization without economic aid and that the advanced countries will pay the price if this process is impeded (through the effects of refugees, a new Cold War, etc.).

From the standpoint of domestic affairs, the problem is much more complex. The anticommunism of the new political forces (parties, movements, and organizations) has not been accompanied by well elaborated programs for the reform of society. In the resulting moral vacuum, it is very difficult to achieve a functional consensus on the list of priorities in social objectives or the instruments for achieving them.

Another evil genie of democratization in post-Communist countries is the absence of common goals and values of the nations living in their territories. The future of democratization in these countries depends on the ability and will of democratic political forces to put forward programs for the transition from postcommunism to democracy which would enjoy elementary support from all, or at least the majority of the citizens. It goes without saying that it also depends on the will of the citizens to accept the democratic alternative being offered.

The democratization of the media, as part of the overall democratization of society, requires as a first step: a new social role and new regulation of the media system. The national mass media of a one-party state should be reorganized according to the model of a public service. In view of the dangers with which a new political and media monism is fraught, legislation should be passed to ensure a voice for political pluralism in practice. In the Yugoslav context, this would mean giving the opposition parties equal access to the media and providing equal time for the expression of their ideas. As governments are formed by a single party, control over the media should be in the hands of a multiparty parliament, and optimally, under a body set up on the parity, and not the proportional, principle. Editorial policy should be left to the editorial boards, which should be made up of highly professional staff who are free from political control. Party political ideas should be presented in the party media.

The freedom of the media from the authorities opens the way to the transformation of the media from champions of the national interest to champions of the public interest. Democracy, as is generally acknowledged, implies the creation of institutions and procedures that guarantee the realization of public and private interests, which can in no way be reduced to national interests. In the post-Communist countries, democracy is regarded, not as a means of realizing public interests, but rather as a means of achieving special-most often national-interests. The functioning media assists in the transition of one-party national governments, and portrays itself as the sole spokesman of the public interest. This reduces the entire interest configuration of society to a uniform national interest, and all conflicts become interpreted in terms of relations between national groups. This has a disastrous effect, not just at the political level, but also in economic and cultural life. This is why an independent position of the media in the territory of Yugoslavia is one of the prerequisites for reaching a consensus on either a life in common under a universal socioeconomic and political structure, or separate existence in this area.

The privatization of the media and the introduction of the market in this sphere will not, in the foreseeable future, seriously threaten the present one-party monopoly over the mass media. Although money has always been readily convertible into political power (and vice versa, for that matter), and although the profit motive as the sole interest of private entrepreneurs calls for as wide a market as possible and supports political forces with a supranational orientation, today there are no private entrepreneurs with large amounts of capital at their disposal in Yugoslavia. Instead, the nationalistic centers of political power are in control of the economy.

The interest of foreign capital in the national media (and, indeed, in other opportunities for investment in Yugoslavia) is virtually nil. The consequences of privatization would be more unfavorable than favorable. If we cast even a fleeting glance on the other side of the fence (whether frontier or ocean), we see that privatization means the sacrificing of the public interest to the interests of proprietors. This will lead to the erosion of the public sphere, greater commercialization, and threats to high-quality cultural productions. Political discussions and cultural programs do not earn profits. Moreover, a polarization of the press into quality prestige newspapers with small circulations versus tabloids with large circulations will occur.

All the post-Communist countries face a highly uncertain future. Possible solutions range from extremely undemocratic to partially democratic systems. Whatever the case, life in these countries in the future will be unpleasant, brutish, and, at worst, short for many. Undemocratic solutions, however, will only postpone the implacable historical processes. The democratization of the media goes in step with the overall democratization of the post-Communist societies. However, the media, as an autonomous element of the social system, can wield an active influence on the processes of democratization and constructive social changes. They certainly do not comprise the main factor shaping the collective consciousness on the state and relations in society, but there is no denying that their influence on the minds and behavior of the citizens in periods of political and economic crisis and turmoil is very great.

The media, then, will also have their part to play in determining whether the post-Communist countries will take the road of genuine political pluralization, whether the citizens will agree to make the sacrifices required for a transition to a market economy, whether modern values will take dominance over traditional and conservative values, and whether the spirit of tolerance will overcome forces of national, religious, cultural, and social intolerance and irrational hate. In other words, the media will influence whether the post-Communist countries will traverse the road that will take them from geographical to civilized

Europe or whether they will be forced to repeat history because they have failed to learn their lessons.

9

A Review of Empirical Studies of Values in Yugoslavia

Dragomir J. Pantić

SIGNIFICANCE OF VALUE RESEARCH AS PERCEIVED IN YUGOSLAV STUDIES

The second half of the twentieth century has seen a noticeable trend in the growth of the number of empirical value studies in all the social sciences. Computer searches have revealed an increase in these studies compared to studies of similar phenomena such as attitudes, beliefs, intentions, and interests. This is noteworthy since up to a couple of decades ago, axiologists claimed that values fall in the atheoretical category and cannot be the subject of inductive, empirical study because of their partiality, which implies arbitrariness and even unethical attempts at their critical assessment. At the turn of the century, under the influences of positivism in sociology (A. Comte) and psychology (J. Watson), the prevailing opinion stated that it was necessary to make a sharp distinction between values and facts. Consequently, values were classified as indeterminable phenomena. Because of their alleged discordance with the empirical approach of positivist sciences, the concept was literally banished from research.

Today, most authors accept the view that no science is entirely void of values and, hence, that it is often impossible to make a distinction between values and facts in the social sciences. Consequently, values can themselves be partly examined as facts. The credit for the success of this approach (i.e., the bridging of the gap between the positivist and normative theories), goes to, among many others, E. Durkheim, K. Marx, M. Weber, A. Maslow, and G. Allport.

As in other countries, and particularly the United States, value research conducted by Yugoslav authors underscores the importance of this concept. Yugoslav authors generally follow the arguments on the signficance of value research put forth by M. Rokeach (1973), A. H. Maslow (1962, 1964), G. Allport (1962), M. B. Smith (1969), E. Fromm (1941, 1947, 1955, 1959), C. Kluckhohn (1952), F. Kluckhohn (1953), F. Kluckhohn and Strodtbeck (1961), C. W. Morris (1956), R. M. Williams, Jr. (1968, 1969, 1979), and R. Inglehart (1977). Yugoslav researchers have accepted the conclusion that values, unlike most other concepts in the social sciences, encourage interdisciplinary and multi-disciplinary research (Rokeach, 1973, 1979). Moreover, they agree that understanding values provide a more holistic summary of complex social and psychological phenomena, including the most general ones such as culture, society, and personality (Alisjahbana, 1966).

In my value research, I have frequently placed emphasis on the warning given by A. Maslow, who was concerned by the anomy that he witnessed among American youth (1962, 1964). He considered that one of the main dangers, especially for the young, is a state of valuelessness. This absences of values is the greatest illness of our time and is more dangerous than ever before. Maslow believed that it is imperative that human beings have a need for a philosophy of life, religion or some system of values. Maslow's views proved to be of special significance in diagnosing the values of Yugoslav youth toward the end of the 1980s, above all with regard to the malignant consequences of mass anomy among young people.

Yugoslav authors perceived early on that empirical value research made it possible, not only to identify existing values, but also to discover new values, which came to the fore particularly in studies of moral values (Popović, 1973; Popović and Miočinović, 1977; Popović, Miočinović and Ristić, 1981, 1984; Miočinović, 1988). They accepted the view that the "planning of values" (Skinner's term) is possible with the help of research, and that the social sciences in general can contribute to the choice of social goals and the establishment of the essence of values that most correspond to the human as a moral being (e.g., Dukes, 1955; Baier and Rescher, 1969; Skinner, 1971; Rokeach, 1973, 1979).

Yugoslav philosophers have attached the most importance to values in their studies of human nature. This is the case regardless of whether they advocate the idea of a universal human nature. All other general, value-imbued concepts used by authors in their research are deducted from the perception of human nature, even when this is only implicit.

In their studies, Yugoslav psychologists adopted Rokeach's viewpoint that the value concept is more central in the sense of greater generality and significance for empirical research, compared to related concepts such as attitudes, which are more unstable and, therefore, less economical for research.

Values are embodied in all normative concepts; for example, economic progress, the development of society, personality growth, and the like are strongly influenced by values. The empirical studies titled, "Maturity of an Individual" (Hrnjica, 1982) and "The Democratic Personality" (Bojanović, 1979) indicated a pronounced value orientation related to these terms and proved that certain values are structurally part of these phenomena. Research into the quality of life and life-styles (Pešić, 1977; Fulgosi and Radin, 1982; Joksimović et al., 1988, Popadić, 1990) has also shown that values are incorporated in the very definition of these important concepts. Thus, Yugoslav authors are in line with those who argue that quality of life cannot be a new and specific concept without encompassing values (e.g., Gross and Springer, 1970, Szalai and Andrews, 1980).

The ideal of many researchers, including those in Yugoslavia, is to discover the conditions that contribute to the better forecasting of behavior. Operationally speaking, the search is for independent variables (antecedent conditions) that enable precise predictions of behavior as dependent variables (consequent conditions). It turned out that, because they are the more general category, values provide better forecasts of behavior than is the case when the independent variables are some other personal characteristics of the individual. This means that we will be more successful in predicting the behavior of individuals if we know their values, especially those that they have firmly espoused, than, for example, if we are familiar only with their attitudes or abilities. Research has even shown that certain values, especially in a combination, are better predictors of success at the university level than ability and achievement motivation put together. Closely related to this is the comparative stability of values in the postadolescent period of the individual's life. Investigations of values frequently reveal the enduring tendencies in a certain social group that enable the discovery of an individual's stable dispositions. Values are most probably successful predictors of behavior because they represent lasting individual characteristics. However, it would be wrong to consider values as absolutely durable and unchangeable once they have been formed (Rokeach, 1973). On the contrary, recent value research in Yugoslavia shows the dependence of values on changes in the social situation, especially prolonged and deep social crises (Radin, et al, 1988; Kuzmanović, 1990; Pantić, 1990a; Bačević, et al., 1991; Vasović, 1991).

A very important, though sometimes overlooked, point is that the use of the value concept enables a person to consider him- or herself as an active individual who strives toward certain goals and ideals. Extreme axiological views reflect that the individual is not an active creator or even exponent of values and that individuals only find, recognize, and discover them as objective realities, have been recently disproved. (These views were held by M. Scheller, N. Harmann, Windelband and others.) Yugoslav theorists and value researchers, on the whole, accept the view of the relational nature of values (i.e., that they are simultaneously subjective and objective). There are, of course, a few authors who define values mainly as subjective phenomena (in terms of disposition, appreciation experience, and direct value experience) and some who prefer objectivistic views (describing values as qualities outside the individual, objectivized goals, norms, or standards). However, apart from theologists, there are no extreme objectivists who would consider values as completely independent entities.

Nowadays there are views that an individual, to a certain extent, creates his or her own values. As such, values represent the person's own reshaped inner potentials which become internalized but also altered, and then externalized, projected, and brought out into the open (Popović, 1973). The process of value creation is, therefore, bidirectional, and it is carried out with the subject's active participation. Of course, exogenous (social and situational) and endogenous factors are inevitable in the formation of values (Pugh, 1978). Nonetheless, it should be noted that the valuative being, as Goethe said, is one of the fundamental human determinants: it represents humanity's specificity. Depending on their theoretical orientation and discipline, scientists are arguing the relative contributions of three kinds of factors in the creation of values: exogenous, endogenous, and autocreational. Yugoslav researchers are inclined to attach the greatest importance to the exogenous factors.

The practical significance of values is also manifold. Investigations conducted in the last three decades in all the social sciences have yielded a wide range of direct specific benefits which are being successfully applied in politics, education, public health care, industry, culture, sports, armed forces, social security, the prevention of crime, and other areas. The countries in which such research is being carried out have a special interest in determining the values of the young generation. For instance, clients in the world of politics, education and mass media are very interested in determining the state of consciousness of today's youth. This is because they wish to gauge the effects of the institutionalized education and civic training through which, among other things, they aim to secure the indoctrination that is more or less specific for their particular system.

The results of value research can be widely applied in the health service fields of prevention, diagnostics, and therapy. In industry, the results are being used especially in the formation of work groups, leadership training, solving organizational problems, measuring the work ethic, testing the quality of interpersonal relationships, examining democracy at work, and the like. In the arts, the greatest accent is placed on studying the nature of aesthetic values, artistic preferences and the tastes of the public, and on defining cultural politics according to the chosen values. In sports, the values of top athletes are considered as indicators of fitness and motivation for success. Values of recreationists, sports fans, and similar groups are also the subject of research. The results of research may also be widely applied in the armed forces in tasks from assessing the capabilities of recruits (in the process of selection) to predicting the accident proneness of top professionals such as pilots. In social protection, criminology, and penology, results of research also have a valuable application, starting from the prevention of juvenile delinquency and extending to the observation of the effects of resocialization. The application of these results is probably the widest in the mass media and, therefore, it is almost impossible to single them out. All the above-mentioned applications of research results have also been used in Yugoslavia, testifiying that the practical significance of the values concept has been realized.

In the past few decades, interest has been mounting among scientists in researching the values of the young generation, mainly because of the realization that such research enables them to gather information about the development of the personality in general. The formation of personality dispositions is of vital theoretical importance in psychology and pedagogy, though it also has significance in other fields: sociology and political science, for instance. The formation of basic cultural values is never a one-way process, and it cannot be reduced to a mere mechanical copying or transfer of values from one generation or one social class to another. Research, including studies conducted in Yugoslavia, has shown that the etiology of values is very complex and that many exogenous determinants are involved in the modeling of every value: historical, cultural, situational, economic, place of work, family, interpersonal, and so on.

TWO PERIODS IN VALUE RESEARCH IN YUGOSLAVIA

Early Research

The first postwar research into values (though these were described as interests at the time) was carried out at voluntary youth work drives between 1947 and 1950 (Smolić-Krković, 1970). The researchers found out that the predominant interests of rural youth lay in politics and economy. The secondary school pupils were also interested in these subjects as well as in engineering. The students manifested chiefly aesthetic and entertainment interests, and the young workers were interested in engineering, sports, and adventure. In a series of studies of similar samples during the 1950s, Supek (1963) discovered, among other things, a strong internationalist orientation among young people.

A study of student samples from all Yugoslav university centers carried out in 1960 (Janićijević et al., 1966) showed a widespread orientation toward material goods and atheism. Towards the end of the 1960s, Dilić (1971) discovered among rural youth in Croatia rather widely distributed traditional values, but also clear signs of a process of erosion of patriarchal authority. A decade later (Dilić, 1977), it was found that the traditional values had considerably weakened and that the gap between the value profiles of rural and urban youth had narrowed. In a comparative study of young delinquents and nondelinquents, Petrović (1973) reached the conclusion that the former group exhibited a more pronounced hedonist orientation. They were more inclined toward anomy and less attracted by distant objectives (terminal values). Moreover, they had a system of values that was less integrated in general and that lagged behind that of their counterparts with regard to value orientations pertaining to work, activism, and learning.

Rot and Havelka (1973) found in a sample of young people in Serbia a marked authoritarianism orientation. They attributed the respondents' considerable authoritarianism to traditional patriarchy which indicates that authoritarianism is, for the most part, determined by cultural rather than psychodynamic influences (for a discussion of this dilemma, the reader is referred to Sanford, 1973). Perhaps this attribution was made because they found that the youths also placed an emphasis on democratic values. The authors also discovered work, cognitive, and altruistic orientations. It was noted that by that time, the differences in values resulting from the social background and status of respondents had become considerable. Respondents from workers' families were found to be rather conservative, hedonistic, and utilitarian, and to strive for power.

Having summed up the findings of several research studies conducted during the 1960s, Tomanović (1971) concluded that the young people of the period had strong egalitarian leanings (preferring the concept of *uravnilovka* or "levelling" over individualism), a deduction for which he found confirmation in later work (1977). This deduction is based on data showing that egalitarian values were found to be rated more highly than those pertaining to self-management, which has long been a leading ideological value. By employing complex indexes, the author decided that the self-management orientation dominated the dogmatic and liberal ones, but also that transitory and mixed values figured highly in the young people's minds. Tomanović found that the respondents had in common a positive attitude toward material goods, but also that this materialist orientation was made up of several strata. It included, for example, material necessity, an inclination to private possession, a consumer mentality, and other factors.

An international comparative study of students from eleven countries in 1969-1970 (Klineberg, et al., 1979) showed that students in Ljubljana were more inclined toward social protectionism (sharing this trait with their peers in France, Italy, the United States, and Australia) than toward internationalism and nationalism. In addition, they were lacking in radicalism with regard to the political role of the university in society and in their protest demands. They had a preference for the correction and improved implementation of models rather than for changing the political system as a whole.

The first youth study covering Yugoslavia as a whole (Pantić, 1974) brought to light significant national, regional, and educational differences in youth egalitarianism. This study showed an egalitarian region (south and east) and a nonegalitarian one (north and west), though at that time, the young people were still rather homogeneous in their self-management orientation and their non-religiousness.

By the early 1970s, a number of studies of youth value orientations had been reviewed in greater detail by Havelka (1975) and Džuverović (1975). In addition, early research of value orientations in Yugoslavia was not restricted only to members of the young generations. There were also several major comparative studies during the 1960s conducted with the participation of the Institute of Social Sciences of Belgrade.

In 1967, Zaninovich (1970, 1971, 1973; Barč, 1970) used a quota and not fully representative sample of Yugoslavs to examine their political culture and value orientations. By means of factor analysis, he discovered five clusters of attitudes; employing anxious-pessimistic, parochial-traditional, egalitarian-allocative, socialist-patriotic, and state-rationalistic dimensions. Zaninovich concluded that the greatest value difference between the elite (officials and professionals) and the masses (workers and peasants) was manifested along a modernism-traditionalism axis. What was important was the discovery that the elite group was much more homogeneous with regard to values (preferring modernism, decentralism, and atheism) than the workers and peasants, who reflected predominant traditional, egalitarian, state-rational, and anxious-pessimistic orientations.

Zaninovich also identified three types of political culture. One culture was a central type which was closest to the Communist ideology of the day and was in evidence in the Serb-Croat regions of the country (exhibiting a dominant modernist, collectivist, and moderate centralist trait). The other two peripheral political cultures included a northwestern type (Slovenia) characterized by modernism, individualism, and decentralism, and a southeastern one (Macedonia), in which traditionalism, collectivism and state-rational orientations were evident. He found that the Communist party in Yugoslavia (later the League of Communists of Yugoslavia) performed two value-related functions: a cohesive function and a modernist one. These were also manifested in the consciousness of members of the League of Communists. Using the same empirical material, Barč (1970) showed that the growing social mobility of the population at the time was accompanied by an erosion of traditionalism and particularism.

A comparative study of local leaders was carried out between 1966 and 1969 in four countries: the United States, India, Poland, and Yugoslavia (Jacob et al., 1971). The researchers evaluated the following value orientations: proclivity toward innovation and change (modernism), enterprise, activism (in contrast to the avoidance of risks), concern for economic development, concern for economic equality, participation, the avoidance of conflicts, national identification, unselfishness (the readiness to subordinate one's own interest to higher ones), and honesty in public affairs. It was found, among other things, that there was a similarity between the profile of the typical Yugoslav local leader and those of his typical Indian and Polish counterparts. Unlike them, however, and in common with American leaders, Yugoslav leaders attached greater significance to worker participation.

Of theoretical importance was the discovery that values can be of nearly identical importance for the behavior of local leaders, irrespective of differences of a political, economic, or cultural nature. What is more, the differences in values were found to be greater within the countries themselves than between them. This points to the existence of a transnational political culture, but to an even greater extent, it emphasizes the significance of the professional role (of leaders) which transcends national differences. The authors' conclusion was that in each country, there are at work numerous specific factors of value formation, and that in general, personal factors prevail over those of the social environment.

Studies of Yugoslav opinion makers, which polled national political, economic, and intellectual leaders (Barton, Denitch, and Kadushin, 1973; Pantić, 1969) portrayed them as being markedly modernistically oriented, disinclined toward egalitarianism, and more liberal than the population at large. There were, nevertheless, certain ideological differences among the leaders: the businesspersons insisted mostly on economic development objectives; the politicians, on keeping things under control and avoiding conflicts; and the intellectuals, on the freedom of expression and the need for ample opportunities for criticism.

In the late 1960s, a time when various obstacles were raised to the first serious Yugoslav economic reform conceived upon Western models, the conclusion was drawn (Županov, 1970), though it was only in part grounded in empirical research (Županov and Tadić, 1969), that the Yugoslav society is, to a high degree, egalitarian. Egalitarianism slows down the growth of economic aspirations, regardless of whether or not it is internalized. Županov presupposed that egalitarianism is often manifested through the following components: limited goods, the redistributive ethic, egalitarian distribution, opposition to private ownership, antiprofessionalism, intellectual egalitarianism, and anti-intellectualism. Several researchers actually identified egalitarianism as the relatively most widespread value orientation in the population (e.g., Šiber, 1974; Zaninovich, 1973; Jacob et al., 1971; Pantić, 1974, 1977, 1981, 1990a; Kuzmanović, 1987). However, no confirmation was found for the thesis of the universality of this value or for the belief that is has the force of an obligatory norm in some social strata. The structure of egalitarianism was also disputed.

The main findings at least in my research studies, are that egalitarianism has been on a constant downward trend over two decades, that it was rooted mainly in the materially endangered social strata, and that it expressed a defensive mechanism. It is interesting to note that egalitarianism was not manifested as an aspiration toward total equality, but only appeared in the sphere of allocation of material goods. Županov's basic conclusion that egalitarianism is disfunctional to industrialism could, however, stand in light of the results obtained by empirical research. Several of my studies showed that egalitarianism is part of a broader ideological cluster, identified on the basis of factor analysis as statism. Statism, contrasts to liberalism, in the framework of which nonegalitarianism appears.

In the early 1970s, Šiber (1974) selected a representative sample of citizens of Croatia to study the relationship between social structure and political attitudes and orientations. Using factor analysis, he isolated three ideological factors: prosystem versus antisystem, egalitarianism, and centralism versus decentralism. Attitudes toward self-management, the League of Communists, and the working class were the variables that were found to correlate positively with the first, most important factor, in contrast to bourgeois values, religiousness, and inclination to criticize the system. The second factor-egalitarianism, though not so ideologically relevant, represented a projection of economic interests of members of social classes (above all, a feeling of being materially deprived) and of an inertia of a social consciousness (owing to the rural origin of a part of the population). In the framework of the socialized sector, there was the trend that the higher a respondent stood on the social scale, the more firmly he or she embraced the prosystem values. On the other hand, the small private owners grouped themselves on the antisystem pole of factors.

A 1974 study encompassing members of 10 social classes and strata in Serbia (Pantić, 1977) covered the following ideological dimensions: traditionalism versus modernism, individualism versus collectivism, egalitarianism versus nonegalitarianism, openness to the world versus insularity or localism, ownership dimension (orientation toward private property versus orientation to socially owned property), orientation to self-management versus orientation to decision making by political authority, material versus nonmaterial orientation (similar to "hedonism-asceticism"), religiousness versus irreligiousness, and humanitarianism versus repressive orientation. Also included were, the individual's personal characteristics referring to the activity syndrome (including ambitiousness or achievement motivation and a striving for leadership) and the intolerance syndrom. As for the descriptive level, a number of findings were attained, only some of the most important ones will be mentioned here.

There exists a significant ideological differentiation depending on the stratum. As far as I know, no research carried out in Yugoslavia thus far has shown such great differences between individual strata with regard to certain ideological dimensions. As an illustration, I would stress just the following: only 8 percent of peasants displayed modernism, compared with as much as 81 percent of political and business leaders; only 19 percent of small business owners, compared to almost 81 percent of leaders, displayed collectivism as a political orientation; 90 percent of leaders and 14 percent of small business owners displayed an orientation toward socially owned property; a self-management orientation was displayed by one-third of peasants but nearly all leaders; and so on.

Interstratum differences with regard to the acceptance of particular ideological contents were far greater than intrastratum differences, which are determined by similar needs and interests. The stratum of political leaders was the most homogeneous ideologically. The differences with regard to the extent and intensity of orientations grew proportionately greater as the social distance between strata became more distinct by objective criteria. While the value profiles of peasants and small business owners do differ from one another, together they contrast in quality to the strata profiles of those employed in the social sector. For example, as supporters of traditional and early bourgeois value systems, respectively, the other strata differs only in the intensity of their commitment to the self-management ideological system. Using factor analysis in all strata, the basic ideological factor self-management versus traditionalism was isolated, but its structure was found to vary somewhat. In some strata it approximates to the hypothetical ideal type structure, while in others, it involves only major or core dimensions. A second isolated factor was statism versus liberalism (which was found to be somewhat eroded), and a third factor (a completely psychological one) was tolerance versus intolerance. The main research finding is that elements of the ruling self-management ideology in higher social strata are possible to explain by understanding ideology as an instrumentality and by using the principles of utilitarianism.

Recent Research (A Selection)

Recent research coincides with a period of manifest social crisis in Yugoslavia which began in 1979, enabling us to keep track of its effects on preferred values. However, a global economic crisis inevitably brings on a moral crisis. The latter, in turn, cannot be considered without a reference to the system of values. For this reason, values are at the core of the universal crisis in Yugoslavia (i.e., they actually reflect the crisis severity). What is more, the persistence of certain values in changed social circumstances can be looked upon, even partially, as an independent cause of social crisis.

A common feature of recent Yugoslav value research, compared with the early studies, is that it relies more heavily on theory and methodology. In their research projects, the majority of authors take into account at least a number of theoretically relevant issues such as the nature of values, the problems of definition, the significance of human dispositions, the classification and contents of values, and so forth. Of the major methodological topics, the authors concern themselves with the choice of evaluation indexes, the construction of complex instruments (such as scales, indexes, semantic differentials, and hypothetical situations), the characteristics of research techniques (observation, interviews, and questionnaires), and problems related to the employment of sophisticated methods of data processing (factor analysis, etc.). They also pay considerable attention to the problems of sampling, evaluating especially to what degree a sample is representative of the whole (probability) and analyzing the range of the quota sample models.

A series of studies of children, young people, and their parents in Vojvodina (Đurić, 1980, 1987), ascertained the presence of a majority internationalist orientation and of the presence of similar images of each other on the part of members of different nations (Serbs feelings about Hungarians, and vice versa). It was found that the general affective attitude of a respondent toward other nations was dictated by the selection of the contents of his or her ethnic stereotypes. Prejudices were not pronounced but rather, latent, and they were in greater evidence among children than among adults. This can be explained by children's greater spontaneity and insufficient experience with members of other nations (the contact hypothesis).

Research into national attitudes of young people in an ethnically highly homogeneous environment (Serbia proper) showed that until recently, the majority of young people found the nation too narrow a framework for their identification (Pantić, 1987). Many of them manifested a multiple loyalty, identifying themselves with their own nation, Yugoslavia, and with Europe simultaneously. At the same time, they advocated personalistic beliefs (i.e., that people should be regarded as persons rather than members of nations). This attitude was in line with the finding that only 39 percent of the sample considered one's national background as being of personal importance. On the whole, national background was regarded as less important than one's profession, circle of friends, generation, family, class, sex, political views, and even regional background. National background was put in ninth place on the list, and was listed as more important only than one's favorite sport or religion. Similar tendencies were also found among pupils in Croatia (Jerbić and Lukić, 1982). For example, ethnocentrism was discovered among only 15 percent of the respondents, whereas the majority (59 percent) felt drawn toward humankind as a whole. The correlates of ethnocentrism were authoritarianism, anomy, anxiety, and a lower cognitive and socioeconomic status.

Later research into youth values in Croatia (Radin et al., 1988) confirmed a low rating for national background (occupying the 11th and last place on the list), the first five preferences being privacy, leisure, professional success, material status, and selfhood. Nevertheless, a contradiction in the national consciousness of young people in Serbia and Croatia was manifested in a considerable ethnic distance from members of other races and non-Christian faiths. Admittedly, this was chiefly the case with regard to a hypothetical question about interethnic marriage (the most intimate social relationship on the Bogardus scale).

In Yugoslavia, authoritarianism remains a rather widespread personality syndrome. It should not be equated with an undemocratic orientation because authoritarianism is only one of the potential conditions of this orientation (Pantić, 1981, 1985, 1988, 1990a; Jerbić and Lukić, 1982; Hrnjica, 1982; Kuzmanović, 1987; Katunarić, 1987; Bojanović, 1989). The large measure of authoritarianism cannot be interpreted entirely by means of the consciousness inertia model (i.e., the persistence of traditional patriarchy as a result of the rural background of a part of the urban population). This is because in Serbia, young people were found to be more authoritarian even than members of the older generation with the same level of education (Pantić, 1981).

There is no doubt that during the 1980s, authoritarianism was influenced by the political system, ideology, and educational system, as well as by the social crisis, which hit the young generation hardest (through economic frustration and lack of opportunities). All research, here as well as elsewhere abroad, shows authoritarianism to be the least pronounced among the educated population strata. Among persons with university degrees, both in Belgrade and in Ljubljana, authoritarianism was considerably lower among professionals than among political and business executives (Pantić, 1985). As a rule, authoritarianism has a positive correlation with religiousness and a negative correlation with a self-management orientation (Kuzmanović, 1987; Pantić, 1988, 1990a,e).

It has been established that authoritarianism tends to link up with similar phenomena, forming a wider category of consciousness and behavior (Bojanović, 1989). However, the question remains as to whether this involves a personality type or an outlook on the world at large. In young people in Yugoslavia (Pantić, 1990e), it is possible to discern three authoritarian "cultural zones": a low-intensity zone to the northwest, an intermediate-intensity zone spreading in a southwest-northeast direction, and a region of heightened authoritarianism in the southeast (Kosovo, Macedonia, and southern Serbia). Authoritarianism is also considerable in Greece (Stankov, 1977).

It is possible that religion has played a part in the origin and survival of authoritarianism. As a rule, the trait is higher among a population living outside its country of origin or that is surrounded by another larger nation (e.g., Serbs in Kosovo, Moslems outside Bosnia, Croats outside Croatia, and Hungarians in Vojvodina). A number of research studies indicate that authoritarianism and the political engagement of citizens are in a curvilinear correlation, which means that the most politically active persons are to be found among the most authoritarian persons as well as among the nonauthoritarian (tolerant) ones.

In conditions of a deepening social crisis, the young people in Serbia, as well as older workers, have increasingly come to look upon work first as a means of ensuring their bare existence, next as a duty, and only then as an opportunity for self-actualization (Ničić et al., 1987). A shift toward an utilitarian attitude to work was also perceived in Croatia (Jerbić and Lukić, 1982), and especially, a strong tendency among young people to seek security in work (Čulig, Fanuko, and Jerbić, 1982). These trends also apply to the unemployed, who are somewhat more passive than their working peers, feel more cold toward the system and more prone to anomy (Pantić, 1981), and more authoritarian (Kuzmanović, 1987).

A self-management orientation reached a climax in all social strata and generations at the end of the 1970s. By that time, this major systemic value-and specific Yugoslav experiment-had been embraced by nearly two-thirds of the population. The rule that the higher a person stood on the social scale, the more highly he or she would value self-management as a method of social organization and decision making held true until the mid-1980s. The social crisis proved to be a reliable indicator of the erosion of the self-management orientation. Among young people, its popularity fell from 62 percent in 1979 to only 35 percent in 1989 (Pantić, 1990e). In addition to the influence of the social crisis itself on the erosion of the self-management orientation in Yugoslavia, one should keep in mind the fact that self-management in Yugoslavia was long a substitute for democracy (especially for democracy at work), with the result that it sometimes bordered on anarchy. With the emergence of the first signs of multipartyism and political democracy in general, self-management ceased to perform this substitutive function, and its ideological importance began to decrease.

By the 1980s, religiousness had steadily been on the decline in Yugoslavia, though not to the same extent in all regions. The largest drop was registered in traditionally Orthodox Christian areas and among those with transnational preferences (who declared themselves Yugoslavs). On the other hand, the decline was slower in traditionally Islamic and Roman Catholic regions of the country. Since 1968, the least fluctuation in religiousness has been registered in Slovenia (Roter, 1986; Toš, Roter, et al., 1987). At the beginning of the 1980s, religiousness began to spread again, especially among young people in traditionally Roman Catholic areas (Vrcan, et al., 1986; Vušković, et al., 1987; Pantić, 1990e, Marinović, 1988) and those experiencing a social crisis, but also as a part of international trends (i.e., a revival of religiousness). The return of religiousness was in evidence until the advent of the process of political democratization toward the end of the decade. There is no doubt that many people went back to religion in protest against the manifestations of national homogenization and in search for a substitute of nonexistent political pluralism.

At this time, the average number of Yugoslav religious persons is 43 percent (Pantić, 1991), but there are considerable differences between one region and nationality and another. For example, there are 70 percent of ethnic Albanians, 60 percent of Slovenes, 53 percent of Croats, 45 percent of Macedonians, 37 percent among ethnic Moslems, and 35 percent among Serbs and among Montenegrins. About one-half the Orthodox Christians and about one-third of the Roman Catholics and Moslems are not religious, and even for many religious-oriented persons, religion is of primary importance only for cultural, national, and traditional reasons. Religiousness continues to be concentrated in rural areas and among the older and less educated population segments. However, one should not ignore urban religiousness, especially among the young (Pantić, 1990e).

Also of political relevance is so-called secular religiousness, which may theoretically be viewed as a functional equivalent to classic religiousness. The former is manifested in tendencies toward idolizing political leaders, events, and symbols and turning the nation-and even personalities from the sphere of contemporary mass culture-into fetishes. The distribution of secular religiousness in regional and national terms is similar to that of authoritarianism, thus these two phenomena can not be treated as equal. The relationship between classic and secular religiousness is highly complex, and the available empirical evidence does not fully support either of the following three hypotheses: (1) secular religion is a substitute for classic religiousness, (2) the two are completely independent, or (3) the two are merely different manifestations of a wider, more general kind of religiousness. Nevertheless, empirical findings (Pantić, 1988, 1990a) are mostly in disagreement with the first hypothesis which claims that there is a reciprocal relationship between the two types of religiousness.

The presumption that there exist coherent value structures (i.e., materialist and postmaterialist values), which was verified by Inglehart (1977, 1990) in many industrialized countries and includes the assumption that younger and better educated people are changing over from the former to latter values, has not been clearly confirmed in Yugoslavia (Vasović, 1988, 1991). As a result of the deep social crisis, even the critical groups encompassed by the hypothesis attach priority to economic prosperity and personal living standards. In addition, the sharp political divisions, the clashes of interests, and the specific status of certain categories of the population have caused considerable national and regional differences in the hierarchy of objectives, which are, at times, unexpected and contradictory to the expectations based on Inglehart's theory. One such finding is that ethnic Albanians in Kosovo have postmaterialist preferences in spite of their evident material poverty.

A comprehensive study of youth values in Croatia (Čulig et al., 1982) used eight large value-normative systems of Western civilization. The authors set apart typical claims which the respondents evaluated on five-point scales. Taken as a whole, they embraced an intellectual (chosen by the students in particular) and a hedonistic system. They were indifferent or ambivalent toward a cynical and relativistic system, and they mostly rejected the contents of a utilitarian, stoic, pessimistic and Christian system. Nevertheless, the last system was found attractive by certain categories such as younger respondents, women, and those with a lower social status. The factor analysis showed that the young respondents reduced these systems to five independent groups (combining the stoical-cynical and utilitarian-pessimistic-relativistic systems). For a value-related differentiation of young people, their intellectual capacity and the educational status of their parents proved most important.

One of the rare studies of political culture shows that shortly before the changeover to multi-party democracy, there existed among young people in Serbia all six kinds of ideal type: self-management (50 percent), humanistic (49 percent), participative (38 percent), alienated (34 percent), traditional (30 percent), and subject political culture (22 percent). It is obvious that these kinds of political culture overlap, and that on average, there are two kinds evident in each respondent. The factor analysis showed that the first three kinds of ideal type combined to form a second-order cluster of dispositions which might be identified as democratic political culture, especially as it encompasses the variable critical orientation. The more emancipated among the young generation are characterized by a combination of these features, whereas the socially deprived strata tend toward an alienated, traditional, and subject political culture. The large heterogeneity of the political culture of young people is also reflected in the finding that only 6 percent of the respondents could be classified exclusively under one of the six above-mentioned types.

On the basis of the development of three components of political culture-cognitive, value-oriented and action-oriented, it was possible to devise an eight-element typology which is empirically dominated by the following types: outsiders (22 percent), meaning those who were below the average in relation to all three components; conformists (18 percent), meaning those in whom only the value-related component was developed; and all-rounders (17 percent), in whom all three components were developed above the average. The uncommon types included negativists, ideologues, opponents, a practical-political types, and a theoretical type (Pantić, 1990b).

Changes in value orientations (see Table 9.1) can be substantial, as show particularly by research among young people in Serbia proper before the outbreak of the crisis (1979) and again nearly a decade later (1988), after the crisis had considerably deepened and had lasted long enough for distinct changes in values to be manifested in the young generation (Pantić, 1981, 1990a).

Table 9.1

Changes in the Distribution of Selected Value Orientations among Young People in Serbia during the Crisis Period

Value orientations (%)	I (1979)	II (1988)	Change
anomy	24	75	+51
openness to the world	70	73	+3
humanism	66	65	-1
hedonism	51	61	+10
ambition/			
achievement motive	69	57	-8
solidarity	71	55	-16
modernism	52	55	+3
individualism	37	41	+4
authoritarianism	50	40	-10
self-management			
orientation	62	37	-25
political potency	74	36	-38
Promethean activism	52	32	-20
material orientation	28	32	+4
egalitarianism	35	21	-14
religiousness	7	17	+10

There is no doubt that the long-standing social crisis effected enormous changes in the values held by youth. Above all, there was a tripling of anomy, which is manifested as a value conflict or, from a structural point of view, as disorientation, anhedonia, and withdrawal. The distribution of all components of the activist syndrome diminished substantially, which can also be attributed to the discouraging effect of the crisis on youth. The extent of hedonism increased, whereas solidarity (the concrete level) declined perceptibly, though the extent of humanism (the declarative, general level) was preserved. The once-important ideological values-self-management orientation and egalitarianism-were also on the decline, but a number of others retained their high ratings (including openness to the world and modernism), which is of significance for the coming unavoidable process of value reorientation in line with the advent of a market economy and political democracy. The chief value characteristic, high anomy, was also perceived among young people in other parts of the country (Pantić, 1990c).

In the mid-1980s, egalitarian-statist consciousness and preference for an authoritarian and centralized state were quite widespread in the lower social strata in Slovenia. By contrast, university graduates, especially business executives and politicians, were opposed to these orientations (M. Hafner-Fink, 1989). However, a strong ideological orthodoxy prevailed among the Slovenian leaders of that time, which was expressed in the broad-based acceptance of the monopoly and leading role of the League of Communists, whereby this ideology, in fact, functioned as civil religiousness. Only three years later, a rejection of the role of the League of Communists was dominant in all segments of the Slovenian population, a part of the general changes in Central and Eastern Europe.

In a critical review of research into modernism and modern personality, prompted mainly by the works of A. Inkeles (1983, as well as Inkeles and Smith, 1974), I concluded that in Yugoslav society, the values of modernism do not exist in the consciousness and behavior of a population isolated from other values, but that they rather appear in the framework of broader systems that are characteristic of the then ruling self-management ideology, as well as the activism syndrome, and the tolerant type of personality. Two decades ago, the term *modern personality* may have seemed appropriate for describing a modal personality in societies of forced and even delayed modernization, a group to which the Yugoslav society on the whole belongs.

However, the results of research conducted in this country do not provide sufficient confirmation for the retention of the term *modern personality*, and it is therefore more useful to use the less binding concept of modernism as a value orientation (Pantić, 1990d). It is logical that there are still fewer signs of the existence of postmodern personality in a developing country (i.e., a society of the transitional type), but this term is controversial in many aspects, even with regard to the situation in the developed, postindustrial societies.

It has been established that some value orientations are quite well formed among students toward the end of junior high school (15-year-olds) but that, when viewed as a whole, their value systems are less structured than those of adults (Kuzmanović, 1990). A characteristic of these young people is that they embrace constrasted orientations; for instance, they simultaneously hold considerable authoritarian and some democratic values (equality of the sexes, etc.) or also believe at the same time in conformism and activism. Children of parents with a lower socioeconomic status are more inclined to adopt the traditional values, while better and more intelligent students and children of more educated parents tend toward socially more desirable and progressive goals. Students of this age group prefer several life-styles simultaneously (Popadić, 1990). They especially appreciate values of their intimate family group, followed by altruism and an orientation toward intellectual acquirement and popularity. After these come the utilitarian, individualist, hedonist, and Promethean orientations, while the least accepted were the religious and power orientations.

One of the most important conclusions of this study is that the socialization effect of elementary school is more pronounced than its educational effects, as measured by the criteria of knowledge tests (Havelka, et al., 1990). The forms of socialization of values are obviously complex, and it has been observed in Yugoslavia that an individual's values take a long time to form, sometimes solidifying as late as postadolescence or even later, which means that school is just one of many agents in the socialization of values.

SYNTHESIS AND CONCLUSIONS

Early research into the values of the Yugoslav population afforded a rather unconflicting picture which was mostly the result of ideological homogenization and indoctrination. These values of the Yugoslav population were, of course, formed by other factors too: efforts to forget and overcome the consequences of World War II in this country (especially the effects of the civil war), stable economic development assisted by the West, the significant role played by Yugoslavia during the Cold War through the Nonaligned Movement, endeavors to neutralize industrial conflicts with the practice of self-management, and recourse in all serious conflicts to political arbitration by the League of Communists.

Nevertheless, value research conducted in the 1970s brought to light certain contradictions in values that are not unusual in a developing country (i.e., a society of a transitional type in which there are also major religious disparities). For instance, there was an obvious inharmony between the considerable authoritarianism, which in some parts of the country is ingrained in members of the society and serves as an expression of cultural patterns, and, on the other hand, the declared humanistic goals and quasi-democratic values. I use the word *quasi* because the purported global self-management was, in fact, merely participation in the labor process brought to the point of absurdity (that is, anarchy), while at the same time, classic political democracy was absent. Empirical value research at the time also pointed up the discordance between modernism and traditionalism, collectivism and individualism, egalitarianism and nonegalitarianism, and similar trends.

Up to the mid-1980s, the main line of value divisions was social, and not ethnic, religious, or territorial. In terms of values, the most homogenous were held by business executives and politicians, followed by other university graduates. Administrative and clerical workers were around the middle of the scale, while workers, particularly the semi- or and unskilled, and traditional farmers, as a rule, comprised the most heterogenous social stratum. Elite social groups differed from the mass strata in their greater acceptance of the values of the ruling ideology, which were chiefly, modernism, the self-management orientation, openness to the world, collectivism, orientation to social ownership, atheism, humanism, and the achievement motive.

This system of values was made up of a mixture of classic Socialist utopias, some liberal goals, and certain specifically Yugoslav ideological characteristics. As a rule, the higher a group stood on the social ladder, the more eagerly and firmly its members espoused the above mentioned values. Among the multiple explanations for this which, generally speaking, are not mutually exclusive, the most important involve the interests and privileges secured for themselves by the leading strata of society through imposing such an ideology, which they did primarily in order to retain their dominant positions.

Changes in the system of values were gradual in the post-Tito period (i.e., in the early 1980s) and were characterized by a long-lasting economic crisis as well as political and social strifes of which values themselves are part (the moral crisis). These changes began to accelerate in the second half of the decade, particularly after the collapse of socialism in Eastern Europe. The first changes were observed among young people in the sphere of religion (including a reawakening of religiousness as a form of political protest) and in connection with the leading role of the League of Communists. These changes started in the northwest of the country and soon spread into the southeast. With time, other systemic values eroded, too, including the self-management orientation and the syndrome of activism values. In recent years, widespread anomy has emerged among young people in the entire country as an expression of the general conflict of values, the breakdown of old standards, and various false stares in the search for new values appropriate to pluralism. Values like openness to the world, modernism, and humanism proved to be the most resilient, perhaps because they correspond to the system of values of the future societies of civil democracy in these parts.

Apart from anomy, the change in values did not indicate the possibility of open conflicts and civil war breaking out in Croatia in the middle of 1991. Until very recently, nationalist and chauvinist values in all the Yugoslav republics, and especially among young people, were limited to a negligible minority (around 15 percent of the population), existing mainly on the margins of society. However, the power struggles of the newly established civic elites (predominantly former Communist leaders) were waged in an area in which the Yugoslav society, which is the ethnically most heterogenous in Europe, was the most vulnerable. In place of the obsolete self-management ideology, these elites, as a rule, offered equally anachronistic and, in addition, aggresive nationalist projects which could not but clash and lead to separatist tendencies and the use of force.

In order to thrust their nationalist values into the forefront, the elites in all parts of Yugoslavia unleashed a media war and propaganda campaigns such as the world had not witnessed since Nazi and Stalinist times. This was understandable in view of the fact that as late as 1986, membership of a national group among young people in Croatia and Serbia was at the very bottom of the list of potentially important affiliations, ranked at the ninth place or even lower (and followed only by religious affiliation). The elites resorted to violence, manipulation, and indoctrination to homogenize their subjects and, at the same time, suppress the mounting social tension and retain their power. Labeling their critics and the opposition as national traitors, these elites used neither the liberal nor the conservative values of civil societies, but instead employed naked nationalism; by applying the four classic mechanisms of power which have been known since ancient times: social demagoguery, scapegoating, the method of divide and conquer, and the use of bread and circuses.

With the breakdown of the old system of values, and despite the above-mentioned retrogressive processes, a silent revolution started in

Yugoslavia, just as it did everywhere in Central and Eastern Europe. The emergence of new values, such as preference for private ownership, individualism, the private initiative, nonegalitarianism, material orientation, and so on, is linked with the budding of a market economy. Civil liberties have been formally introduced and guaranteed, but they can be exercised only to the extent that people are not reduced to mere members of an ethnic group, or subjects. These new values, when coupled with modernism, openness to the world, and the preserved declarative humanism and achievement motive, might prove to be the nucleus of a future system of values of a civil society, although, naturally, this will be possible only after the current populist and nationalist deviations have been expended.

At present, humankind is going through a period of abrupt change of values, that is, it is in a state of *culture shock* or *future shock* (Toffler, 1970), which assumes different forms. Some authors even claim that what we are experiencing now is a real and permanent value revolution initiated by the technological changes (an information society and the postindustrial era) and the culture of postmodernism. There are also different assessments of the system of values in the contemporary world, especially in its developed part, which represent variations on both the subject matter of A. Maslow (1962, 1964), who was concerned about the spiritual state of American youth, and the conclusions of other authors who claim that the modern age is characterized by a perfection of means and a confusion of ends.

An extensive discussion, which includes the contradictory results of empirical research, is being conducted and concerns claims that materialist values are being replaced by postmaterialist values of growth, or goals that stress freedom, the spirit of democracy, humane living, an unpolluted environment, solidarity, the development of personality, and self-actualization (Inglehart, 1977, 1981, 1985, 1990; Inglehart and Flanagan, 1987; Harding and Phillips, 1986; Vasović 1988, 1991). One debatable question is the nature of the modern Western world's culture, in which the central dilemma relates to the crisis and change in values (Gibbins, 1989). Namely, to what extent is the classic urban culture being replaced by late-modernist and postmodernist political culture? The latter concept has been defined by some authors (whether or not justifiably as pluralistic, anarchic, disorganized, rhetorical, stylistic, ironic, and blurred (Gibbins, 1989).

It is important to determine, both theoretically and practically, the change in the values of the coming generations. Is it typical of these changes that traditional values coexist with the new, modernist, and, in certain aspects, postmodernist values, producing a dominant mixed type dominant. To what extent does the mixing of values occur and give rise to a new quality: a hybrid value system or some as yet unknown combination of elements in which the original values may cancel each other out, or, perhaps, produce a synergic effect? Is the successful breakthrough of modernist values due to their initial force or to the erosion of traditionalism? Has, as Toffler prophesied two decades ago, the process of creation of clusters of values already started in the industrialized countries, or is a reverse process-the formation of a new comprehensive system of values with chances of becoming a neo-ideology-under way? Are there signs that postmaterialist values are spreading even in countries that are not leaders in economic growth, or are only aquisitive values typical of societies that are still tackling problems of bare existence emerging. These are only some of the questions relating to the values situation in present-day Yugoslavia that are still awaiting to be answered by value research in the period ahead.

10

A Survey of Value Priorities Among the Yugoslav Public

Mirjana Vasović

Of the theoretical models of political behavior relating to political culture and cultural changes, the materialist-postmaterialist value syndrome has attracted considerable attention among social researchers during the last two decades. The American author Ronald Inglehart (1977), who developed this theory, has put forward the thesis that there has been a gradual change of value priorities of people in advanced industrial countries based on the influence of the economic, technological, and sociopolitical changes since World War II. These changes have exerted considerable influence on shifts in the predominant basic values relating to politics and certain major social issues (i.e., on changes in political culture in advanced industrial countries as a whole).

Inglehart looked upon these changes, which have taken place quite gradually, as a "silent revolution," reflecting the formative experiences that have shaped, in various ways, the social consciousness of successive generations. The essence of these changes, in Inglehart's view, is that the emphasis has shifted away from economic well-being and physical security (the major societal goals of the wartime and postwar generations) to quality of life as the major societal goal. It is for this reason that the prevailing outlook on life in a society changes as one generation succeeds another. This, in turn, results in the adoption of a whole series of different attitudes and beliefs in regard to various social and political issues and different forms of political engagement (i.e., the emergence of new types of political culture).

There is a psychological explanation for the concept of the materialist-postmaterialist value syndrome. Inglehart proceeded from Maslow's theory of a hierarchy of the basic human needs, according to which priority is always given to the fulfillment of the "more basic" among them (the needs for material security and physical survival). It is only after these needs have been satisfied that the individual turns to other, nonmaterial needs (such as the need for love, belonging, and esteem). Next come even "higher," intellectual and aesthetic, pursuits, and finally, on the top of the scale, is the need for "self-actualization," namely, to realize all one's potentials and abilities.

The key assumption of this theory is that in adulthood, the individual strives to retain that pattern of priority needs (and the resulting value priorities) that was established during his or her formative years. Following this analogy, Inglehart assumed that, on a macro plane as well, individuals and social groups with different socialization histories of needs satisfaction will fundamentally differ from one another in their choice of social values and the priority of societal goals.

Inglehart categorized individuals of different generational, ethnic, and status backgrounds according to materialist or postmaterialist value types on the basis of the importance they attached to certain societal and political goals. The choice of goals associated with ensuring the material and political stability of society (a strong economy, rising living standards, powerful defense forces, and a vigorous fight against crime) represented an indicator of a "materialistic orientation". Giving priority to goals such as a more humane environment and political rights and liberties served as an indicator of a nonmaterialist or postmaterialist orientation.

On the basis of his comparative research, which was carried out in the West between 1970 and 1988, Inglehart set out to prove the existence of a global shift in the value priorities of members of older generations, who had grown up in conditions of economic crisis and war, and those members of younger generations who had enjoyed periods of peace and economic prosperity in the West. Indeed, comparative research has confirmed that different societies are characterized by a widely differing distribution of these specific syndromes of political-cultural attitudes and that they are primarily associated with one's generation. These cultural differences are, according to Inglehart, relatively permanent in nature (though not immutable) and, most important, they exert considerable influence on the political and social life of these societies. Above all, they are important factors for the development and preservation of democratic institutions.

The author regards the shift from materialistic to postmaterialist values as only one aspect of a far more widespread syndrome of cultural changes. These changes reflect a decline in traditional religious orientations and in conventional social and sexual norms and are manifested as different aspects of economic and political behavior.

SURVEY DESCRIPTION AND DESIGN

The theoretical assumptions described above were taken as the basis for our survey of value priorities among the Yugoslav public. The survey was conducted as part of a public opinion survey in Yugoslavia. It was carried out in May-June 1990 on a sample of 4,230 citizens over 18 years old from all republics and provinces. We looked upon Inglehart's idea as a fitting and economical framework for tapping the global value orientations of Yugoslavs and, at the same time, as a tool for comparing our findings with the strategic goals of the economic and political program offered by the Yugoslav government.

We evaluated the choice of priority of social goals on two levels: one, as a simple ranking according to the importance that a respondent attached to different global aims that "this society is to attain in the next ten years"; and two, as a consistent pattern of selection of specific goals associated with the materialist or postmaterialist value syndrome. Unlike Inglehart, however, we did not concern ourselves primarily with determining the structure and distribution of certain value types in society as a whole, nor with the changing trends in value priorities. Since our survey was of a pragmatic nature, our chief aim was to ascertain differences between certain segments of the society in their outlook on priorities of social development and to analyze the factors influencing these differences. Only then were the researchers interested in determining, at least approximately, the correlation between members of individual groups of society and the above-mentioned value types so that they could analyze (and predict) attitudes and convictions that would be applicable to a far greater number of specific social problems and issues.

The researchers used a somewhat modified version of Inglehart's battery of items. Respondents were presented with three groups of items, each of which was designed to tap four global social goals which were to be ranked in terms of importance. The items were formulated as follows:

"There is a lot of talk these days about what the aims of this country should be for the next ten years. Which of the following aims do you, yourself, consider most important?" The respondents were presented with the following groups of objectives:

I. 1. Maintaining a high rate of economic growth.
   2. Maintaining a strong government (defense forces, law and order, etc.)
   3. More respect for the will of the people and public opinion in deciding things at work and in people's communities.
   4. Trying to make our cities and countryside cleaner and more beautiful.
II. 1. Maintaining order in society.
   2. Giving people more say in important government decisions.
   3. Fighting rising prices.
   4. Protecting freedom of speech.
III. 1. Maintain a stable and sound economy.
   2. Progress toward a more humane and less alienated society, a society with a "human face."
   3. Progress toward a society where ideas are more important than money.
   4. The fight against crime.

The introductory sentence was formulated to place the goals in a long-term perspective so that they might encompass global value preferences rather than the immediate needs of individuals. To conform with our theoretical expectations, two items in each group were designed to tap materialist priorities (the value attached to one's economic stability and physical security), while the other two related to postmaterialist priorities (rights and liberties and aesthetic and ecological needs). The respondents were allowed to make two choices within each group of goals and were requested to rank their priorities.[1]

In the original version of the survey, the three groups of questions were projected in such a way as to provide a basis for determining the value types by a computation of the index of materialist/postmaterialist value priorities. However, this time we were chiefly interested in making a comparative analysis of the frequency of choice of individual groups in Yugoslavia. For a comprehensive analysis of the value priorities of the Yugoslav public (the incidence of certain value types), the reader is referred to Bačević, et al. (1991).

The theoretical model that we adopted suggested three basic hypotheses with regard to the choice of priority goals by members of the Yugoslav society. First, we hypothesized that there would be significant differences in the choice of materialistic/postmaterialist goals between

Yugoslav society. First, we hypothesized that there would be significant differences in the choice of materialistic/postmaterialist goals between regions with different economic development. Since the boundaries of such regions largely coincide with republican and/or provincial borders, we assumed that on average, the inhabitants of Kosovo, Macedonia, Montenegro, Bosnia-Herzegovina, and, to a certain extent, Serbia proper would be more inclined to chose goals associated with economic and physical security, and that the respondents from the two most economically advanced republics-Croatia and Slovenia-would be more interested in postmaterialist goals.

A second hypothesis pertained to the effect of generational changes on the value priorities of the population as a whole. In other words, it was expected that the older respondents would be more inclined toward materialist goals than the younger ones, while the latter group would tend to attach priority to postmaterialist goals. Such a pattern may be attributed to the influence of changes in an individual's attitudes, and preferences that are typical of the different phases of his or her life cycle. Individual psychology has proved that old age brings resistance to change, increasingly conservative political attitudes, and a feeling of uncertainty. However, Inglehart predicted the same effects as a result of changes in intergenerational value priorities based on different formative experiences of different age groups.

On the basis of these two premises, it should be possible to determine the true meaning of eventual differences between age groups. The effect of the life cycle is no doubt the same for the Yugoslav population in general, although some of its national-regional segments differ markedly from one another in terms of their economic and political histories. A comparison of regional and intergenerational differences as an indirect test should help dispel any doubts in this connection.

The third hypothesis that we tested does not stem from the theory itself. It assumes that there is a linkage between the choice of societal goals and certain situational and contextual factors that are not part of the history of the individual, nor of generational experience. Instead, they are part of the current social and intergroup situation in which one exists as an individual, but especially as a member of a certain group as well. Here we are referring to the specific characteristics of a given political and economic situation to develop a collective idea of the causes of shared problems and difficulties.

Stable societies are characterized by relatively stable values. In such societies, value changes may be observed as part of long-term culture and the preponderant values, which sooner or later results either in the breakdown of the norms or a change of the priorities (i.e., in a complete redefinition of the system of values). The meaning and direction of these changes are not necessarily the same in respect to all social groups. Their interpretation and acceptance (or nonacceptance) are influenced by the position that a group occupies in the structure of intergroup relations and by the nature of these relations itself.

COMPARISON OF REGIONAL GOAL PRIORITIES

A respondent's republican or provincial background was a singularly important and powerful determinant of the social mind in a series of surveys conducted in Yugoslavia over the last 15 years or so.[2] It has proven to be responsible for the most distinctive and theoretically most challenging differences in the choice of priority of societal goals.

Although the methodology that we employed does not fully justify a cross-comparison of the choices of all the 12 goals offered, from the data in Table 10.1 it is possible to conclude with certainty that the goal of "maintaining a stable and sound economy" is the prevalent priority of the Yugoslav public.[3] Taken as a whole, in the greatest number of cases (77 percent), a societal goal formulated in this way was chosen as first or second most important. If we bear in mind that "maintaining a high rate of economic growth" was the second most frequently preferred choice (62 percent), we can say with confidence that the Yugoslav public is interested primarily in the fulfillment of those social goals that ensure the economic stability of the society. The least frequently chosen goals were "progress toward a society where ideals are more important than money" (17 percent) and "trying to make our cities and countryside cleaner and more beautiful" (32 percent).[4]

This prevalent national picture is different from the choices of inhabitants of some of the federal units within each of the group of goals. If we adhere to the model of materialist and postmaterialist priority values, we may note that the population in two federal units-Serbia (without Kosovo) and Montenegro-came out overwhelmingly in favor of materialist goals. Of the four goals in each group, citizens from these two republics most frequently chose two that imply economic security and political (social) stability. As to the first group of goals, a special

Table 10.1
Priorities of the Yugoslav Public

Goal	Republics/Provinces								
	BH	MO	CR	MA	SL	SE	KO	VO	Tot
Group I									
Economic growth	66	63	67	54	68	61	45	71	62
Strong state	53	75	25	35	12	63	22	59	44
Will of the people	53	35	64	55	50	44	81	40	53
Beautiful cities	23	24	41	39	54	22	39	26	32
Group II									
Order in Society	67	70	46	47	42	66	19	68	55
More say in gov't	39	34	38	43	42	38	72	30	41
Fight rising prices	57	56	60	59	49	54	28	65	55
Protect free speech	31	32	51	35	40	32	72	32	40
Group III									
Stable economy	83	76	78	68	78	82	64	82	77
More human society	58	46	62	57	56	50	74	51	57
Ideas count	12	16	12	21	21	13	36	13	17
Fight crime	39	56	42	37	33	44	21	45	40

BH - Bosnia-Herzegovina; MO - Montenegro; CR - Croatia;
MA - Macedonia; SL - Slovenia; SE - Serbia; KO - Kosovo;
VO - Vojvodina; Tot - Total

Note: Shown are the percentages choosing the given goals as the first or second most important out of the four in the given group. Because the table presents cumulative data (the sum of percentages for I and II choices), the figures do not relate to the percentage of respondents but rather to the percentage of cases in which the goals were chosen. Replies such as "don't know" and "undecided were omitted.

preference was given to "strong government"; on the other hand, the population of these two republics chose less frequently (less than average) the goals of "more respect for the will of the people" and "trying to make our cities and countryside cleaner and more beautiful."

Already at this point we can emphasize something that will be substantiated later, namely, that more than the other items, the choice of the goal, "maintaining a strong government" was influenced by the different connotations attached to it by different social (ethnic) groups within the context of the current political relations among them. Whereas for some individuals who viewed a "strong government" in a positive light, this meant maintaining the status quo, others regarded it as an obstacle to desirable and expected changes. The strengthening of the state and of state power was viewed and evaluated, at least partially, through the prism of a belief in the legitimacy of that power and of state order in general. The population of those federal units in which separatist aspirations are in evidence looked on a strong state as the strengthening of unitarism (i.e., as a threat to its own goals). In other parts of the country which oppose disintegration of the federation, however, there was a tendency to stress the importance of this goal.

Response differences were especially marked between these two republics (Serbia and Montenegro), on the one hand, and Kosovo, Croatia, and Slovenia, on the other. A characteristic feature of Croatia is that its population preferred "the will of the people" at the expense of a "strong government." (The example of Kosovo is highly specific and calls for special consideration.)

In the second group of goals, materialist goals were emphasized over nonmaterialist goals in most federal units. In nearly all regions, "fighting rising prices" was given nearly equal importance, which is to be expected in a country which, only a year before, had experienced four-digit inflation and falling real incomes.

Differences may be perceived in the ranking of the goal, "maintaining order in society." The populations of Montenegro, Vojvodina, Bosnia-Herzegovina, and Serbia without the provinces chose this goal more frequently than those of Croatia, Slovenia, and Macedonia. It seems that "maintaining order in society" produced different associations in different social groups. In common with "a strong government," this phrase may have been associated with efforts to preserve the status quo in society. On the other hand, it appears that to certain ethnic groups, this meant the prevention of social conflicts.

Differences with regard to such postmaterialist goals as "giving people more say in important government decisions" and "protecting freedom of speech" were not so marked except, of course, in Kosovo. There was some departure from the average in Vojvodina, where the former goal appeared somewhat less popular, and in Croatia, whose population attached more importance to the latter goal.

Finally, in the third group of goals, "maintain a stable economy" was ranked as most important in all federal units except Kosovo. In Bosnia-Herzegovina, Serbia, and Vojvodina, this was preferred by more than 80 percent of respondents. On the other hand, "progress toward a society where ideas are more important than money" was chosen with the least frequency. (Kosovo again was an exception, as we shall see later.) Most of the differences appeared in regard to "the fight against crime." In Montenegro, in more than 50 percent of cases, this goal was denoted as the first or second value priority in its group. In Slovenia, it was accorded such a ranking in nearly one-third of cases, and in Kosovo, in one-fifth of cases.

IMPACT OF SITUATIONAL CIRCUMSTANCES

Generally speaking, situational circumstances have played a major part in influencing and determining the current value priorities of the Yugoslav public. Unless we take account of the social and political relations prevailing at the time of the survey between certain regions, republics, and provinces in Yugoslavia and the political objectives that were being openly stated and propagated, the choice of the most prominent goals of social development will remain unexplained and obscure.

This is best substantiated by the choices made by the population of Kosovo, in which Albanians are in the majority. In other words, in contrast with all other segments of the Yugoslav public, the population of Kosovo overwhelmingly chose the so-called postmaterialist goals in all three groups of goals, as follows: "more respect for the will of the people" (81 percent); "progress toward a more humane society" (74 percent); "giving people more say in important government decisions" (72 percent); and "protecting freedom of speech" (72 percent).

This is the least economically developed region, with the lowest income level and the highest recent population increase in the country (a region having all the prerequisites for a high "index of poverty"). However, the goals reflecting a preference for economic development and prosperity were chosen far less frequently than in other, economically more developed parts of the country, and even less frequently than in the most affluent republic. In a province that has for years been afflicted by a striking absence of rights, judicial protection and state efficiency, the majority rejected the prospects of a more powerful state, order in society, and the fight against crime, giving preference instead to goals promoting political emancipation and political liberties and rights.

It is obvious that for different social groups with different political objectives, a specific political status, a specific attitude toward Yugoslavia as a political community, and a characteristic history of intergroup relations, social goals formulated in this way have an altered meaning. Such goals are not, as Inglehart hypothesized, of universal importance, but rather are understood and interpreted according to the context of the given social and political situation. "Maintaining order in society" has an entirely different meaning for a group with separatist aspirations that adopts civil disobedience as the basic strategy of its struggle than for a group that is bent on preserving the status quo. A strong government in conditions of an emergency state has one meaning for members of the majority group imposing that state and quite a different meaning for the minority group against which it is imposed (on account, for example, of its political activities and aspirations). In other words, for the former group it connotes a juridical state; for the latter, however, it implies repression.

At the moment, the main social conflicts in Yugoslavia are not taking place on the political-territorial (republican and/or provincial) borders, but on ethnic intergroup boundaries. For this reason, an additional validation of our hypothesis would call for a comparison of the responses (choices) of members of different ethnic groups, irrespective of their republican/provincial background. In order to sharpen our discussion, we considered differences in the choice of the first value priority in each group of items only. In this way, the comparison findings could be rendered more distinct and illustrative. In this connection, there are certain "critical" ethnic groups (from the point of view of the actual political situation and intergroup relations) with which our arguments are most easily proved.

We began by analyzing differences in goal preference between the two most characteristic groups, the Albanians and the Serbs. These groups are characterized by pronounced ethnic and political antagonisms. At the same time, segments of both peoples live in an ethnic, political, and economic environment that is very different from that prevailing in their "home" territories. This fact enabled us to study the influence of a specific political climate and examine the definition of a social and political situation as opposed to long-term cultural factors.

Table 10.2 points to differences in the responses of Albanians and Serbs as homogeneous ethnic groups and as parts of ethnic groups inhabiting different regions in Yugoslavia. Several figures in the table strike the eye as particularly important for a sociopsychological analysis. First, there are marked differences in goal preferences between Albanians from Kosovo (and Macedonia) and Albanians from other parts of Yugoslavia. Second, there were differences in the responses of Albanians and Serbs from Kosovo. Third, differences in the frequency of economic growth preferences occured between Serbs from Serbia proper (without the provinces) and Serbs from Kosovo. Fourth, differences in preferences occured between Serbs from Croatia and Serbs from Kosovo.

The differences between the responses of Albanians from Kosovo (and partly Macedonia) and those living in other parts of Yugoslavia leave no room for doubt that the influence of actual sociopolitical circumstances has greater weight than that of cultural ones. Those goals that emphasize a strong government and the enforcement of law and order, calling up images of state violence even in relation to the fight against crime, were rejected almost totally by the Albanian population in Kosovo (they were chosen by only 5 to 7 percent of respondents). This state of affairs is attributed to the specific connotation imparted on these goals by the state of emergency imposed by Serbia's state authorities at the time of the survey.

The resistance of the Albanian population in Kosovo to state control, which was reflected in emphasis on certain societal goals and the rejection of others, is an immediate reaction to the current political situation. The current preferences of this minority group are incompatible with its long-term aspirations for a sovereign state (republic) of its own within a Yugoslav framework or, in more extreme cases, with its open separatism. Thus, in the final analysis, the choice of goals under the circumstances by this ethnic group makes sense only if it is viewed as a challenge to the legitimacy of the actual government. Albanians outside Kosovo, however, were far less troubled by the drama of the present political context; in far greater numbers, they placed an emphasis on goals associated with economic development, which brought them, in this respect, much closer to the average of the majority population in whose midst they live.

Table 10.2
Goal Distributions of Albanians and Serbs

Goals	Albanians				Serbs						
	KO	MA	O	T	SE	BH	CR	KO	VO	O	T
Group I											
Economic growth	34	27	52	35	46	51	67	16	47	29	47
Strong gov't	6	6	29	8	34	33	15	59	42	40	34
Will of the people	48	52	11	44	12	12	10	16	7	16	11
Beautiful cities	7	9	0	7	4	2	1	3	2	13	3
Group II											
Maintain order	7	25	34	13	49	61	60	29	55	53	52
More say in gov't.	50	23	18	42	15	12	15	22	10	16	14
Fight rising prices	11	27	30	15	22	18	15	22	24	18	21
Protect free speech 30	22	11	27	10	3	1	19	8	11	8	
Group III											
Strong economy	48	52	61	50	63	67	74	31	65	53	63
Humane society	33	31	9	30	15	16	10	26	14	18	15
Ideas count	12	3	2	10	3	5	5	9	2	9	4

BH - Bosnia-Herzegovina; CR - Croatia; KO - Kosovo; MA - Macedonia; SE - Serbia; VO - Vojvodina; O - others; T - total

Note: Shown are percentage choosing as first importance among Albanians and Serbs by ethnic and regional critiera. Percentages do not add up to 100% because "don't know" answers are omitted for greater clarity.

The comparison of the preferences of Albanians and Serbs in Kosovo is a good illustration of how a social situation may be differently interpreted by social groups guided by different, political goals. The distribution of value priorities among these two ethnic groups leads to the conclusion that the respective social action goals are not only different, but incompatible. Put another way, the goals of one group can only be fulfilled at the expense (i.e., the sacrifice or suspension) of the goals of the other.

This incompatibility provides a rich seedbed for social conflicts, which is amply illustrated by the responses to the goal, "a strong government." Nearly 60 percent of the Serb population in Kosovo (10 times as many as members of the Albanian minority) gave priority to this goal above all others. On the other hand, three times as many Albanians as Serbs pitted "the will of the people" against this goal. Further, in the eyes of the Serb population, which is steadily emigrating from Kosovo, either because of real pressure from the Albanian majority or because it perceives and experiences the intergroup situation as being insufficiently safe, the prospect of a strong government and the maintenance of law and order may appear as a compensation for the lack of security.

A linkage between the perceived illegitimacy of the relationship between power and domination, on one hand, and the choice of "a strong government," on the other, was also in evidence among Serbs in Croatia, where this ethnic group is a minority that challenges the legitimacy of the newly elected authorities and calls for autonomy. In comparison with Serbs in other parts of the country, Serbs in Croatia attached priority to "a strong government" far less frequently. In this respect, striking differences were found between Serbs in Croatia and Serbs in Kosovo, the latter being in quite an opposite social situation. The majority of Serbs in Croatia gave priority to economic goals (economic growth), in common with other inhabitants of that republic. Serbs living outside their "home" republic (in Croatia and in Bosnia-Herzegovina) character-istically stood out for their preference of "order in society" (60 percent). Such a priority may be associated with historical events (the experience of genocide), as well as with a feeling of immediate insecurity associated with a (real or imagined) threat of civil war.

The differences in the preferences of goals between Serbs in Kosovo and those in Serbia proper were due to the fact that Serbs in Kosovo stressed far less frequently needs bound up with economic development and stability, and far more frequently those associated with "a strong government." These differences essentially point to the possibility that in the social mind, the two basic indicators of materialist values-striving after economic security and political stability-may be separated. At the same time, these differences support the hypothesis that a real or imagined dangerous situation in the present can have a greater influence on one's preference of societal goals and values than his or her formative experience. The example of Serbs and Albanians has shown that psychological factors, whether in the form of a feeling of immediate threats to one's needs or a collective perception and interpretation of an intergroup situation, have a considerable influence on the choice of goals of social action.

A further analysis of the choice of goals by different ethnic groups in Yugoslavia shows that those groups that had experienced civil war or genocide were more inclined to stress goals that, according to Inglehart, are associated with the need for security and safety and that may be interpreted as an advocacy of the prevention of social conflicts. As a rule, all groups living in multinational environments burdened with the past experience of ethnic conflict-especially the Hungarians in Vojvodina, Serbs in Croatia, Moslems in Bosnia-Herzegovina, and Serbs in Bosnia-Herzegovina-give preference (60 percent) to "order in society" over goals associated with political rights and liberties and higher living standards.[5] As stated earlier, the population of Kosovo is an exception in this regard: Albanians chose this goal in only 7 percent of cases, and Serbs, in 29 percent of cases. The Slovenes, too, were below the Yugoslav average in this respect.

GENERATIONAL GOAL PRIORITIES

Up to now, our analysis of societal goals among the Yugoslav public has dwelt primarily on the plane of macro groups. It was logical to assume that these choices can not be explained by the formative experiences of groups of individuals alone (i.e., by differences in their present economic status). It was felt that the specific context of an intergroup situation is of crucial importance. Nevertheless, one may wonder whether intergenerational shifts in value priorities, as postulated by Inglehart's theory, are occurring independently of the actual political situation. In what way does a respondent's age (i.e., his or her generational background), influence the choice of goals irrespective, of his or her national and/or republican background? Do the present material status and educational level of members of this society narrow or widen differences in the choice of goals of social development throughout Yugoslavia, and does the character of this choice fit into our theory?

If we analyze the choice of the first priority in the group of items containing "a strong government," "the will of the people," and "a more beautiful environment" by members of different age cohorts, we can notice two main tendencies. Older age cohorts (over 5 to 6 years of age) were somewhat more inclined toward "a strong government," whereas younger age cohorts (under 35) prefered "more respect for the will of the people". In both cases, the ratio of the percentages of given responses among the oldest and youngest respondents was roughly one-to-two. There were no differences in the frequency of choice of "maintaining a high rate of economic growth." In the second group of items, there were no differences with regard to the choice of "fighting rising prices" (i.e., higher cost of living). However, the older age cohorts were more inclined towards "maintaining order in society" (49 percent) than the younger ones (31 percent). On the other hand, the younger age cohorts showed a greater preference for postmaterialist goals. "Giving people more say in important government decisions" was chosen by nearly 30 percent of the youngest age cohort but by only 12 percent among the oldest. "Protecting freedom of speech" was prefered by 15 percent of the former and 5 percent of the latter group. In the last group of items, however, the preponderant orientation was toward a stable and strong economy, so the differences in the frequency of choice of the remaining three goals ("a more humane society," "ideas count more than money," and "fight against crime") were minimal.

It should be noted that even where differences were perceived we can only speak in generalities since the coefficients of contingency (reflecting the relationship between two variables), though statistically significant, were relatively small. When we later analyzed the correlation between the index of materialist/postmaterialist values and age, we shall show that these tendencies were even less pronounced, first and foremost as a result of a general agreement regarding the choice of goals pertaining to the economic development of society. The presumed regularity was "disturbed" by the Albanian population in Kosovo, which was overwhelmingly in favor of the (specifically interpreted) postmaterialist goals, irrespective of age.

The assumption that the formative experience of the older generations in Yugoslavia is one of destitution while the younger generations grew up in periods of prosperity is only conditionally correct. The youngest age cohort encompassed by the survey spent more than half its life in a period of serious economic crisis. The middle-age cohort can boast only some 10 years of relative economic prosperity, though it could not fully benefit even from that period since at that point it was only beginning to assume its proper place on the social stage. Since the beginning of the 1980s, no generation has associated its future with economic improvement. For this reason, our endeavor to prove intergenerational shifts in value priorities resulting from assumed progressive economic trends in society rests on a rather shaky premise.

The situation in Yugoslavia still does not present an adequate experiential basis for verifying Inglehart's thesis. However, if we are unable to prove a linkage between preferences for certain types of societal goals and the history of economic needs satisfaction of the Yugoslav public, we may nonetheless ask ourselves whether it is at all possible to determine their relationship with the present level of individuals' material well-being. Do differences in one's material status have a bearing on one's choice of goals between the materialist and the postmaterialist poles?

MATERIAL STATUS AND GOAL PRIORITIES

In order to verify the existence of such a correlation, we analyzed the level of current material well-being as indicated by the respondents themselves, with the choice of individual goals as the choice evaluated as most important in their respective groups.[6] Our intention was to test the assumption that respondents with a lower material status will more frequently choose materialist goals while those above the average in this respect opt for postmaterialist goals. In this respect, too, the results proved us wrong. The resulting correlation coefficients were very low, although the differences in choice percentages were statistically significant.[7]

The only goal that did live up to our expectations involved the choice, "fighting rising prices." The respondents whose material situation was below the average opted for this goal more frequently in the same cohort than those who were better off. These differences persisted when the factor of education was also taken into account. In all education cohorts, the poorer individuals attached greater importance to "fighting rising prices" than the more well-to-do. Although we are dealing with a goal belonging in the materialist group, it is obvious that here we have an attitude that results from a direct deprivation of material needs and not a general value orientation.

There are several reasons why education is considered a very important factor of differences in the acceptance of social values and goals. It has a bearing on differences in mastering certain cognitive skills and in the volume of acquired knowledge, and it influences accessibility to various kinds of information. Moreover, it determines the network of communication and, thus, one's exposure to different ideological and value-related projects. Education is bound up with different interests stemming from differences in the social status of individuals, and so forth.

In the context of the discussion of materialist-postmaterialist value priorities, the role of education is associated with the formative experience of affluence since, in Western societies, it is a relatively reliable indicator of a family's material status. It is, therefore, considered that the choice of priorities can more easily be predicted on the basis of an individual's level of education than on the basis of a profession. In Yugoslav society, the link between the educational level and the material status of a family is not all that straightforward. However, according to a number of authors, there is reason enough to look upon this as a "closed society." At any rate, our findings do not indicate that higher education is a precondition for preference for goals from the nonmaterialist sphere. Advocacy for ensuring a high rate of economic growth and a stable and healthy economy, is for the most part, a characteristic of the more educated strata of the society.

On the other hand, such goals as "a strong government" and "fighting against crime" were characteristic of the less educated strata. However, these tendencies are not consistent. In certain cases, as we have shown before, the regularity was seriously disturbed by national background. With respect to profession, certain differences can be more clearly perceived. Goals associated with commercial (economic) prosperity were most frequently emphasized by highly educated professionals. "A more humane society," "ideas count," and "the will of the people" were emphasized by secondary school pupils and students. "Fighting against crime" was important to farmers, unskilled and semiskilled workers, and housewives. "More say in important government decisions" was emphasized by private businesspersons and freelancers.

It was also shown that the choice of goal is not appreciably influenced by a respondent's sex, except (to a degree) when the goal involves the overall economic development of society (preferred by men) and fighting rising prices and crime (preferred by women). These results support Inglehart's conclusion based on his own research that such preferences are in line with the respondents' traditionally different roles: thus, men have the task of providing for their families on a long-term basis, and women of doing so on a daily basis. If we look at things in this way, it appears that the choice of goals is determined, not only be material and educational differences, but also by differences in the life styles of individuals and/or of the groups to which they belong.

We examined the influence of a more generalized worldview on the choice of social development priorities by including the respondents' confessional affiliation in our analysis. At first, the differences were manifested in such a way that the Roman Catholics more readily opted for goals associated with the improvement of the overall economic condition of the society, whereas the Orthodox Christians (along with the atheists) showed a preference for goals associated with social stability and security. Among the adherents to Islam there was a preponderance of nonmaterialist goals. However, these differences in response were obliterated by the factor of national background. As far as the Yugoslav public is concerned, nationality has obviously proved to be the most powerful determinant of the choice of basic goals of social development.

MATERIALIST AND POSTMATERIALIST VALUE TYPES

In the preceding analysis we have already shown that the terms materialist and postmaterialist are quite relative, however, the theoretical concept on which they are based does not fully correspond to what which has been taking place in the Yugoslav society. We retain these terms, however, as mere references to certain kinds of value priorities-the one is associated with the advocacy of economic prosperity and (political) security of the society, and the other, with political liberties and rights (i.e., with a more humane society). We arrived at the value priorities index by weighing the first two preferences within each of the three groups of items and by disposing the resultant scores into seven categories representing a continuum from marked materialist priorities (with three intensity grades), through a mixed type, and down to marked nonmaterialist priorities (also differently graded). The scores within this index ranged from 6 (marked materialism) to 12 (marked postmaterialism).

In what way are these two value types distributed in the consciousness of the Yugoslav public and what is their chief determinant? A general distribution of value types in the Yugoslav public yields the following percentages: materialists (56 percent), ambivalents (28 percent), and postmaterialists (16 percent). In common with the choice of individual goals, it turned out that regional (i.e., republican/provincial) background was rather closely associated with the type of value priorities but did not fully conform to the regularity envisaged in our hypothesis. In all regions with the exception of Kosovo, the percentage of the materialist value type prevailed over the postmaterialist. The percentage of materialists was greatest in Montenegro (76 percent), Vojvodina (70 percent) and Serbia proper (69 percent), where the highest percentage of marked materialist orientation (roughly one-seventh of the number of respondents) was registered. These regions were followed by Bosnia-Herzegovina, with 62 percent of materialists, 9 percent of whom were of the most pronounced type. In these parts, the percentage of respondents opting for postmaterialist values ranged from 6 to 10 percent (with most evincing only a mild type of postmaterialism).

In the remaining republics, the percentage of materialist-oriented respondents was under 50. In Macedonia, one of the underdeveloped regions, it was 49 percent, whereas in Slovenia and Croatia, the most prosperous regions, it was 47 and 44 percent, respectively. In all three republics, postmaterialism was in evidence in about one-fifth of the cases. Kosovo, which is the least economically developed region in the country, had only 23 percent materialists and as many as 57 percent postmaterialists. It appears that the inconsistency in the relationship between a region's level of economic development and the incidence of value types indicates that the group history of materialist needs satisfaction (as well as the satisfaction of security needs) is neither the only, nor a sufficient, determinant of this consciousness.

We have already pointed to a number of possible interpretations of these findings. We assume that the chosen goals, which enter into the materialist/postmaterialist index, are given various meanings depending on the given social and political situation. They are also characteristic of individual ethnic (national) groups which have varied levels of status in the existing system of intergroup relations, above all with regard to the degree of their domination and political power.

The correlation between national (ethnic) background and a value priority type indicates that materialism was most pronounced among

Montenegrins, both in terms of frequency and intensity, followed by Serbs. Next on the list were those who declared themselves as Yugoslavs and Moslems. Postmaterialism was most widespread among Albanians (strong intensity in 5 percent, medium in 15 percent, and weak intensity in 26 percent). This is the only ethnic group in Yugoslavia in which this value type prevailed, according to our findings. Among Croats, Slovenes, and Macedonians, who were also somewhat distinguished by the percentage of postmaterialists, this kind of priority was almost equally distributed, affecting roughly one-fifth of the population. In common with our conclusion regarding the choice of individual goals, segments of certain ethnic groups inhabiting different regions (republics and provinces) differed to a degree in terms of the incidence of the two value types.

This difference was especially true of the Albanians and Serbs, and partly true of the Croats. As a rule, in this respect Croats were closer to the rest of the population of the region in which they live than of members of their nationality elsewhere. For example, Albanians outside Kosovo and Macedonia exhibited a far stronger materialist orientation than the rest of Albanians. Similarly, Croats in Vojvodina were also closer to other inhabitants of Vojvodina than to Croats in Croatia. Moslems in Montenegro had a much stronger materialist orientation than those in Bosnia-Herzegovina, who represented, the majority population there. However, Serbs in Croatia were much more materialistic than Croats, though they not quite as materialistic as Serbs living in Kosovo or in Serbia proper. One of their characteristic features was that, in relation to the rest of the Serb population, they were more frequently ambivalent in this respect. These data may indicate the degree to which certain ethnic groups have been assimilated, in terms of a political and value preferences, into their domicile regions.

If the degree of economic development and similar collective formative experience are not what binds together those regions in Yugoslavia whose populations contain the largest percentage of ambivalent (i.e., nonmaterialist) orientations on our value priorities index, how can one account for these similarities? Whereas the republics of Slovenia, Croatia, and Macedonia and the province of Kosovo cannot be compared in terms of economic development, a common link may be found in the field of politics.

All these regions are characterized by open political aspirations toward national states (which have already been fulfilled in these republics) and toward the decentralization of political power (federal power in the case of the republics, and republican power in the case of Kosovo). These aspirations are increasingly being manifested as claims for secession (i.e., the disintegration of the Yugoslav federation).

We are not going to consider the political reasons behind these claims or their justifiability. What is important for us is that, from the point of view of the social psychology of ethnic groups, aspirations for decentralization are a manifestation of the efforts of those social entities who perceive themselves as being different and, at the same time, socially and politically suboriented to preserve their social identity and make their own decisions. In a social and political sense, this tendency toward differentiation from other groups implies a rejection of the status quo. It is, therefore, possible to understand why all social goals implying a stronger government or the preservation of the existing relations in society will to be rejected in favor of those implying the consummation of the group's will.

The resultant polarization into materialist and postmaterialist value priorities might have been different had we asked our respondents about personal rather than societal goals. The relationship between the socioeconomic status of the individual and his or her choice of material goals might have been more direct. As it turned out, the so-called index of materialist-postmaterialist values was not appreciably connected either with a respondent's educational level or with his or her (subjectively evaluated) material status.

As for the differences between generations, they may eventually be perceived only as mere hints on a global plane and then only in extreme categories. These differences conform to an expected pattern: compared with the older age cohorts, the youngest age cohorts manifested, materialism of a strong or medium intensity in a smaller number of cases and postmaterialism (though only of small intensity) in a larger number of cases. Within these intensity categories, too, it is possible to observe in respect to each age cohort that the number of materialists diminished and that of postmaterialists increased with the respondents' educational level. We therefore think that the verification of Inglehart's premise about gradual and long-term intergenerational shifts in value priorities with reference to the Yugoslav public, irrespective of whether we agree with its psychological propositions, should be postponed until a time of greater peace and stability.

CONCLUSIONS

Our analysis of the choice of social development goals preferred by the Yugoslav public was based on the theoretical concept of so-called materialistpostmaterialist value priorities. Our findings showed, however, that for Yugoslav conditions, the choices did not support the assumptions of the theory and that the value profile of the Yugoslav public does not correspond to the profile that has been registered in Western industrialized countries. Taken as a whole, the Yugoslav public is oriented primarily toward goals associated with economic growth and stability. Thus, against the backdrop of the grave economic crisis besetting their country, the respondents gave priority to all goals pertaining to the economic prosperity of their society and to personal living standards, almost without exception.

The problem that has divided the public and is preventing us from speaking of a coherent materialist value syndrome is the gap between economic and political goals (i.e., those goals that according to our theory, result from the deprivation of "material" needs and from a thwarted need for security). During conditions of major political rifts and sharply opposed interests of certain social groups, those groups having a specific social status, a specific attitude toward Yugoslavia as a political community, and a characteristic history of intergroup relations. They also attach different meanings to goals that have been operationalized as "maintaining a strong government (strong defense forces, law and order, etc.)" and "maintaining order in society." Their preferences are, therefore, strongly influenced by their republican/provincial and/or ethnic background, which currently coincides with the boundaries of the major political divisions. On average, the populations of Serbia (without Kosovo), Montenegro, and, partly, Bosnia-Herzegovina opt for such goals in appreciably greater numbers than the populations of Slovenia, Croatia, Macedonia, and, particularly, Kosovo.

A more detailed analysis shows that differences do not appear only on the level of global sociopolitical communities, but that specific features can also be discerned in the preferences of certain ethnic groups within such communities. Such features were especially prominent among Albanians, who have a specific political status in Yugoslavia. This group represents a minority in the republic of Serbia but also represents the majority in Serbia's province of Kosovo. Their political demands are incompatible with the current state of political domination, and their value preferences have been overshadowed by the state of emergency imposed in the province at the time of the survey. This group showed a much greater preference for goals placing emphasis on "the will of the people," "giving people more say in important government decisions," and on political rights and liberties than the average sample. These goals were not only given priority, but were chosen as antipodes to what was interpreted as power. It should be stressed as very significant that in Kosovo, the most impoverished part of the country, these goals were chosen at the expense of goals associated with strengthening the economic base of society and economic prosperity.

Our findings contain indications that, irrespective of their ethnic background, the younger generations and the population of the developed parts of the country prefer nonmaterialist goals in somewhat greater measure than the other respondents, but such tendencies are clouded by the common consent that the economic stability of the society should be given priority. Further, these regularities cannot be associated with respondents' history of "material" needs deprivation, but they possibly correlate with a higher average level of education and better access to information (i.e., with one's life-style). All other differences influencing the choice of goals at the individual level, which can only barely be discerned as tendencies that are seriously threatened by the national and regional background, are determined, above all, by the given situation.

A prototypical model of value priorities may not be suitable for describing the political culture of societies going through serious economic and political crises or changes. Instead, it is possible that the model may apply only to relatively stable societies and to predicting long-term cultural shifts. The incidence of certain types of value in the consciousness of the Yugoslav public obviously cannot be understood if one lacks insight into the connotations of individual goals contained in the materialist-postmaterialist values index. In the final analysis, these connotations are determined by the overall social, economic, and political situation, the analysis of which is beyond the scope of our discussion. In this primarily sociopsychological analysis, our chief concern was to clarify the meaning of our findings in the context of the given intergroup situation, as perceived and defined on the part of different national groups. We have seen that the goals determining the materialist value type are not associated with economic improvement. Instead, the purely economic goals are relatively evenly distributed among the population because, in the context of a deep economic crisis, they assume almost universal priority.

It is obvious that here we have a clash of two demands of a more general nature: a demand for supporting and maintaining the authority of the state (government) and a demand for democratization of the society. The data that tell us that the adoption of these two demands is primarily determined by one's republican/provincial and ethnic background (and not one's membership in any definite social, educational, or age group) indicate that they are adopted or rejected within the framework of people's images about the balance of power between the macropolitical communities and the principal ethnic groups in Yugoslavia. In this context, the demands (goals) assume a different meaning since they are looked upon and interpreted from the point of view of whether the relations of domination between these groups will be accepted as legitimate or rejected.

The explosive situation that exists today in the regions of former Yugoslavia reflects the conflicting social, economic, and political priorities that have emerged over time. These priorities may be similar for some ethnic groups, however, the ethnicity factor dominates all initiatives for change. This is why the meaning of the materialist/post-materialist value syndrome in Yugoslav conditions is substantially different from that attributed by Inglehart to the publics of Western industrial countries.

NOTES

1. In this survey, relative ranking of all 12 goals was not our objective; the battery had primarily been designed to make it possible to compute a materialist/postmaterialist syndrome index.

2. One's national and republican background has proved to be a more important determinant of his or her consciousness than the "classic" sociodemographic variables.

3. The respondents were allowed to choose 2 (of the 4) goals in each group, but they were not asked to make any relative comparison (ranking) of all 12 goals grouped together.

4. It must not be overlooked that each goal was chosen only in competition with the remaining three goals in the same group. For this reason, these conclusions, which were made on the basis of frequency of choice, are only of relative importance and serve merely as illustrations.

5. Such choices are also characteristic of respondents declaring themselves as Yugoslavs. Earlier surveys show that the majority of those who give this label to their nationality are in fact Serbs.

6. Respondents were asked to compare the material status of their households with those of others from their milieu in terms of "considerably better," "somewhat better," "same," "somewhat worse," and "considerably worse."

7. In such large samples, even small percentage differences in contingency tables prove, as a rule, to be of statistical significance.

11

Constitutional-Legal Reform in Yugoslavia

Aleksandar Fira

BACKGROUND

Yugoslavia has been experiencing a crisis for nearly a decade. At the beginning of the 1980s it started as an economic crisis which was initially thought to be the direct result of the large external debt of the country, which exceeded $20 billion U.S. The most direct consequence of the crisis manifested itself in the second half of the 1980s in the form of soaring inflation, which in 1989 turned into genuine hyperinflation, reaching a monthly rate of about 30 percent. All this was accompanied by a drop in production, which led to stagflation.

For quite a long period of time, the official leadership of the country, in spite of serious warnings from both the domestic and international publics, asserted that the crisis was exclusively an economic one and that the political situation was good. However, increasing numbers contradicted this assessment. As early as 1981 there was a nationalist-separatist insurrection by the Albanians under the guise of the demand for a "Kosovo Republic." This movement toward nationalism and separation has been going on in spite of political, and even coercive, measures taken during that period today, primarily by the Republic of Serbia, but also, to a much lesser extent, by the Russian Federation. In all the republics there emerged a wave of nationalism, which was initially concealed, but then rapidly became increasingly overt, assuming separatist connotations.

Such developments were primarily caused by the crisis in the League of Communists of Yugoslavia. It was actually a crisis of the one-party political monopoly which has been assessed by the majority of the society as the main obstacle to overcoming the social crisis befalling the whole system, including both the political and the economic structures. The League of Communists of Yugoslavia or, more precisely, its leadership, really bears full responsibility for establishing a genuine political monopoly, which was the main cause of the collapse of the concept of direct self-management democracy. However, in all fairness, we must admit that in the League of Communists of Yugoslavia, albeit with a long delay, forces arose that were strong enough to face this unpleasant truth and take decisive steps for overcoming their own political monopoly.

These developments in Yugoslavia became more frequent because of the collapse of political systems based on one-party monopolies in East European countries. In a certain respect, we may say that the processes in Yugoslavia are a part of that, but we must not lose sight of the important difference that existed, and still exists, between those countries and Yugoslavia. Although this is a subject in its own right, I shall mention two factors. Yugoslavia was permanently an independent country and it had self-management, which, irrespective of how deformed it may have been, posed an obstacle to absolute bureaucratic power. That is why the level of personal freedoms in Yugoslavia, as well as the nation's openness toward the world, were always substantially higher than in the other East European countries.

Under the circumstances I have just briefly outlined, in the second half of the 1980s, there began another process of constitutional reform in Yugoslavia. I would like to mention in passing that Yugoslavia's postwar constitutional development was very turbulent. In that period of just over four decades, three completely new constitutions were passed in the federation and in the republics, and three profound constitutional revisions were made. We could even say that as a rule, after any major political event in the country, and particularly after a crisis, Yugoslavia underwent a constitutional change.

In the situation we are considering, the ruling circles first advanced the thesis that a constitutional revision was not necessary, but rather, that the constitution was not being properly implemented. This initiated the first large polarization between those who accepted such a thesis and those proceeding from its counterthesis: namely, that the constitution itself was the cause of its lack of implementation, as it was not being applied and was not suited to social needs. This, like all the previous polarizations, ignited the already existing national contradictions between those who saw a way out of the crisis in the strengthening of centralism with a view to a higher level of social integration and those who demanded fuller independence extending to separatism. However, both factions tacitly agreed, after a temporary conflict, that it was indispensable to change the constitutional system.

The only point on which genuine agreement was reached was that all citizens were entitled to democracy and the protection of the rights of their nation. Nevertheless, even that was sufficient to initiate the process of changing the constitutional system. Even though the process has been going on for more than three years during the latter part of the 1980s, it is by no means certain when it will be completed, while its final outcome is even less certain. However, we can say something about this only after we provide a picture of the situation in the autumn months of 1990. I shall confine myself to the legal-constitutional situation in narrower terms, which, it goes without saying, does not answer every question, but, on the contrary, postulates frameworks for possible solutions to the dilemmas which appear to be increasing geometrically.

ANALYSIS OF CONSTITUTIONAL CHANGES

When adopting the 1974 Constitution, it was officially emphasized that it was a question of providing constitutional documents, which, contrary to the previous ones, should last for a longer period of time as the main law of the country and the charter of socialist self-management. I wish to add that in a number of works, I have warned of the harmful interpretations and overly extensive wording of certain constitutional provisions as the possible source of necessary constitutional changes, and to assert that I was not alone in this endeavor. However, even more important was the concern that the fate of the constitution would primarily depend on the situation in the economy and the actions of people or, as commonly phrased then; on subjective forces. I consider this warning topical even today, although for a long time it had no adequate impact on social policy, or in particular, on the behavior of the leadership of the League of Communists of Yugoslavia.

Constitutional changes that ensued soon thereafter increasingly denied the thesis of the lasting nature of the 1974 constitutional documents. First, amendments were made to some republican constitutions (in Bosnia-Herzegovina in 1976 and in Montenegro in 1978). In 1981 the first eight amendments to the Socialist Federation of Republic of Yugoslavia (SFRY) Constitution and appropriate amendments to the constitutions of the republics were adopted. These amendments made no substantive changes in the economic and political systems, but only further elaborated some of the already existing features. This could not be said of the 1988 and 1989 amendments, which meant the beginning of a global revision of the constitutional system. At the beginning of 1990, the Presidency of the SFRY launched a formal proposal to start work on a new constitution. Some time after that, the Federal Executive Council proposed another group of constitutional amendments whose adoption it deemed crucial for implementing the economic reform.

Processes in the republics unfolded even faster, and the 1989 and 1990 constitutional amendments marked the beginning of a new stage of republican constitutionality, which brought into question the relations still in effect between the SFRY Constitution and the republican documents. This was, in fact, officially stated only in respect to a relatively small number of provisions of the 1989 republican constitutional amendments, in the opinion of the Constitutional Court of Yugoslavia. They had no impact on the actual constitutional situation. After the adoption of some republican constitutions (e.g., the Constitution of the Republic of Serbia was proclaimed on September 28, 1990, new amendments to the Constitution of Slovenia were adopted on September 27, 1990, and some constitutional amendments were passed later in the other republics) it became clear that their enactment meant the practical suspension of the largest part of the Constitution of the SFRY which was still in force. All this is taking place in conditions in which all issues boil down to a single question: will Yugoslavia exist at all in the future, and if so, will it continue to be a federation, will it be a confederation, or will it be some sui generis complex community?

CURRENT STATUS OF THE CONSTITUTION

Leaving aside the political aspect of all those processes, I shall attempt to outline the constitutional provisions that are currently valid under these circumstances, which border on nearly total unconstitutionality. At the federal level, in addition to the changes formally made by Amendments I-48 and the changes that will possibly be carried out in the near future, an additional number of constitutional provisions have been changed in another manner. Thus, although the 1988 amendments explicitly changed only certain provisions in the normative part of the

SFRY Constitution, their contents, in constitutional-legal terms, meant a much broader change of the constitution. The pluralism of ownership sanctioned by the 1988 amendments actually suspended all those provisions that had constitutionally founded the socioeconomic order on "social ownership and freely associated labour."

Proof of the advanced thesis can be found even in a casual comparative analysis of the texts of Amendments 10-23 and the texts of Sections 2 and 3 of the Basic Principles. It can also be found in the second part, and particularly in Chapter 1, "Socio-Economic Order, Articles 10-87 of the Constitution of the SFRY." Similar analyses have already been made in our literature, and I myself have made some partial ones. In view of this fact, it now seems possible and suitable, on the basis of those studies, to try to answer at least partially what parts of the SFRY Constitution are still operating as a constitutional norm in practice. Understandably, this cannot be fully elaborated given the restricted space, but it will at least encourage further, more precise, research and may serve as a provisional orientation. I am convinced that this is indispensable, for regrettably, the competent state bodies are not only not contributing to clarifying the existing confusion, they are increasingly succumbing to it.

In all this, I am trying to avoid value judgments, not only because I consider them unimportant or because I wish to retain the pleasant position of an uninterested observer, but because I am convinced that they cannot be of help in this analysis. Thus, without putting into question one of the common aspirations towards a "legal state," (which I prefer to call the "rule of law"), I would like to state that the first prerequisite for the struggle for constitutionality and legality is the clarification of the confusion that has come to pass in the constitutional system.

The Basic Principles of the SFRY Constitution were not changed by the explicit provisions of the 1988 Amendments, and at the time of their adoption it was adduced that this was not a change of the constitutional system, but rather a change in certain of its provisions. That seemed true at first glance, but the first analysis in which this author drew attention to that in relation to the position of a basic organization of association labour proved this incorrect. Later developments revealed rather that this was a step inspired by daily politics and was aimed at ensuring political agreement between various factors in the adoption of the constitution.

After all the events I have already mentioned, analyses today give quite a different picture. We can say that really very few of the Basic Principles have not been actually suspended, either by federal or republican amendments or by republican constitutions. Let us once again direct our attention to the already mentioned complex of the socioeconomic order. After introducing the full pluralism of ownership forms, the largest part of Section 2 and all of Section 3 of the Basic Principles of the SFRY Constitution must be considered suspended, in particular the function of the Basic Principles that was defined as "the basis and guidelines for interpreting the Constitution and law and the action of every and all."

In the already mentioned provisions of the normative part (Arts. 10-87 of the SFRY Constitution), numerous changes have also been made formally by the amendments. Over 40 articles underwent formal substantial changes, and several new provisions have been added which are technically related to various sections of that chapter. However, the remainder has also, for the most part, been suspended in practice, by virtue of the changes made. I shall mention just the provisions of Articles 10, 11, and 20-22 concerning the position of workers under conditions of social ownership as the ruling ownership form of self-management and as the basic socioeconomic relationship. Under question, not expressly but at least under question in constitutional-legal terms, is the operation of the unchanged constitutional provisions on the pooling of labour and resources of social reproduction (Arts. 44-50), as well as some 1988 amendments. The latter is raised as a question after the Law on Enterprises and some other laws and after republican amendments, (i.e., constitutions), that no longer recognize the category of work organization, which is in the amendments as a generic concept of workers' organization and association.

Although I am aware that this part of the analysis is incomplete and deficient, I am nevertheless convinced that, speaking in constitutional-legal terms, in Yugoslavia, we already have a socioeconomic order that differs from the order mandated in the Constitution of the SFRY, which is still in force. That order has still not been developed, nor has its full physiognomy been given; that is why, at the moment, I shall colloquially term it, "a mixed economy of a transitional nature." Without going into forecasts of the constitutional future of this model, I think that it is a transitional stage toward more stable socioeconomic categories. At the moment, the label is the least important matter (i.e., it is hardly critical to decide which ideological term should be used to denote what will be created). It is only certain that history cannot simply repeat itself, just as it cannot be improved, and that no society, including the one in which we are living, has a permanent guarantee that it will not disappear in one of the variety of catastrophes that have been known in the course of history to date.

INTERPRETATIONS AND CONCLUSIONS

In conclusion, I am sure that the currently existing situation in the socioeconomic order cannot be considered a Socialist one in neither a statist nor a quasi-self-management sense. Moreover, I am not convinced either that the attribute *Capitalist* adequately reflects the essence, (i.e., the direction it is taking). I doubt if a way out of this antinomy should be sought in the application of fashionable names. That is why I shall describe the situation as a mixed economy in which there are elements of different epochs and in which, since it is full of internal contradictions, there are still so many intangibles that its movement cannot be exactly perceived.

No simpler is the situation with regard to the political system, although the changes there are more radical and more evident, and they yield larger consequences more rapidly. After the establishment of party pluralism in the whole country (and that process has indisputably been finished in the first months of this year) Sections 7 and 8, as well as some substantial paragraphs of Sections 2 and 4, of the Basic Principles of the SFRY Constitution, stopped operating in a specific way. The provisions on the constitutional position of the League of Communists of Yugoslavia and the Socialist Alliance of the Working People of Yugoslavia, which have ceased to exist, have also disappeared from the constitutional order along with the disappearance of the subject of their regulation. This manner of repeal of certain legal regulations is rather rare, but it was also encountered in earlier constitutional history. Some provisions of the 1946 Constitution of the Federal People's Republic of Yugoslavia stopped existing in the legal order after nationalization measures (i.e., when the subject they regulated had disappeared), although that was not explicitly stated by later constitutional acts.

This, however, is only the first constitutional-legal consequence of the effected political changes. Much larger changes have been made by the 1989 and 1990 republican constitutional amendments and by the 1990 republican constitutions. These changes, first of all, suspended most of the common principles of the political system that were determined by the SFRY Constitution, and particularly by Sections 1, 2, 4, 5 and 6 of the Basic Principles. They also suspended the remaining provisions of Part 2 of the normative part of the Constitution of the SFRY (i.e., those that have not yet been mentioned in connection with the socioeconomic order). A certain exception to this type of suspension of the SFRY Constitution are the provisions on the freedoms, rights and duties of humanity and of the citizen, which have, for the most part, been "taken over" by the republican constitutions but have also been considerably changed, particularly in the part related to self-management. In this manner, the provision relating to the political system as a system of "socialist self-management democracy as a special form of the dictatorship of the proletariat" has disappeared from the Yugoslav constitutional order, at least as a common basis of the political system. If we take this primarily as a change of ideological impact, which is only partly true, the other changes have a direct institutional effect.

The most important of these changes is the definite abandonment of the delegate system. It is not popular now to mention the really noble motivation that was used as a motto in advocating the delegate system as the "finally discovered form" that would overcome the logical and practical antinomy between direct and indirect democracy, but this should nonetheless not be neglected. Irrespective of the basic belief in delegate institutionalization which stemmed from the common basis of the political system, however, that concept has been irrevocably suspended by party pluralism in favor of representative democracy. Some republican constitutions have done this explicitly, and all have done so tacitly (i.e., on the basis of new arrangements). The question of what this means from the standpoint of the full emancipation of the human personality in the future goes beyond the topic I am discussing, but it is certain that such developments today suit the will of a convincing majority of the society and that they enjoy indisputable democratic legitimacy.

An analogous situation to that which I described in connection with the delegate system exists with regard to the attitude toward the assembly system, to the extent that it is regulated by the constitution as an element of the common principles of the political system. Here, too, some constitutional changes made in the republics have suspended the corresponding provisions of the federal constitution. Instead of the principle of unity of power, for example, the principle of the division of power has been introduced, with some variants. However, in all places there is a strongly pronounced role for the executive. Some of the arrangements are actually typical of a presidential variant of the division of power.

We can say that abandoning the delegate system has democratic legitimacy at the start, (i.e., that it has been adopted by the social majority. The demand for a more efficient state, which, in Yugoslavia as in all cases in history, usually includes a preference for a strong executive and president. This also is true of some other democratic connotations, primarily those for reinforcing the independence of the judiciary, which traditionally accompany strivings for the division of power. However, we must not forget that the principle of the unity of power also had a democratic source. In any case, only the future will show to the extent to which the new arrangement is in keeping with true democracy and progress.

A situation similar to the one discussed here exists in respect to other constitutional elements, such as the common grounds of the political system, constitutionality and legality, courts, and the public prosecutor's office. Thus, we can conclude that the majority of those provisions of the SFRY Constitution are actually not being applied. In constitutional-legal terms, a certain exception relates to the provisions of the SFRY Constitution on the freedoms, rights, and duties of humanity and of the citizen. However, in that set of provisions there are some that have also been suspended, (e.g., the right to self-management).

Nevertheless, the highest degree of constitutional uncertainly relates to the genuine confusion that exists with regard to the relations in federalism. Here, the situation is such that actually everything appears to be open to question. Although federal organs still exist and function as determined by the Constitution of the SFRY, the discharge of their rights and duties, and to an even greater extent, all the "vertical" relations in Yugoslav federalism, have been profoundly disrupted. In other words, that part of the Constitution that extends from the contents and manner of exercising joint interests in the SFRY through relations in legislation, execution, and economic functions have, both normatively and practically, been completely suspended. That is why this survey will not dwell on the subject.

All in all, from the standpoint of constitutional rights, the situation in Yugoslavia, reflects a deep disruption in the constitutional order which is so serious that it borders on complete unconstitutionality. The experience of the whole world, and that of the Yugoslavia citizens as well, has many times confirmed the fact that this never leads to democracy but instead brings about total anarchy which leads to tyranny and catastrophe. The current socioeconomic, political, and military events attest to this fact.

12

An Analysis of Values Throughout the History of Venezuela

Rosalind Greaves de Pulido and
Yolette Ramirez

This chapter describes and analyzes the values present in Venezuelan society throughout its existence as a nation. We have chosen the historical perspective because it serves as a frame of reference for understanding and explaining prevailing values along with the rise of attitudes and their permanence over time. In this regard, facts have been chosen and interpretations made from the available literature. This review provides revealing elements of Venezuelan's aspirations, our motivations, and vision as a country. It also provides insights into the way in which we interpret events and how we think success can be achieved. The bibliographic review that has been made is biased toward those authors who are oriented to analyzing the country, not only in terms of happenings and events that have taken place, but also in terms of perceiving historical personalities as acting on the basis of their motivations toward certain objectives, conceptualizations of certain projects, and the exercise of power and influence over others.

For these reasons, this chapter does not attempt to provide an exhaustive description of the periods that have given rise to our nationality, since instead it concentrates on those periods that especially highlight a particular ethos. As a consequence, it is divided into the following parts:

- Venezuela before 1810: Prehispanic and Colonial Period,
- Toward an Integrated Venezuela (1810-1958),
- Modern Venezuela (1958-1983),
- The New Venezuelan Reality (1983-1991), and
- Conclusions.

The selected bibliographic review provides the basic theme for this chapter. This review was assembled through interviews with qualified persons who are connected with different sectors of Venezuelan society.

VENEZUELA BEFORE 1810: PREHISPANIC AND COLONIAL PERIOD

Very little is known about the historical past of Venezuela prior to the European discovery of America. Its inhabitants did not know how to write, and consequently, the available information comes from references and interpretations of chronicles and stories of the conquest, along with archeological investigations from the few material remains of Indian cultures and from knowledge of the few Indian groups that survived the process of conquest and colonization of the country. The European who reached America held the perspective that humans are the center of the world, which was in direct contrast with the Indian perspective that humans simply form a part of the world. Both civilizations acted in accordance with these considerations, which gradually changed with the incorporation and integration of new beliefs.

Venezuela was discovered in 1498 during Columbus's third trip. At the time of its discovery the Indian population located in the territory that is now Venezuela is estimated to have been no larger than 120,000. It was made up of nomadic tribes with an economy based on fishing, hunting, and collecting, and in some sedentary tribes, rudimentary agriculture subsistence was evident. The first Spanish settlements were established in the Eastern part of Venezuela in the islands of Cubagua and Margarita. The Spanish were attracted by the abundance of pearls in both islands. In order to guarantee a stock of water, firewood, and Indians to obtain the pearls, the Spaniards carried out raids in the mainland, where they captured Indians and took them as slaves to Cubagua. This practice of enslaving Indians produced the first fights.

In 1510 the conquistadors began to establish themselves on the mainland, starting with the western coast of Venezuela. Through the Agreement of 1528, Charles V (Emperor Charles V of Rome and King Charles I of Spain) created the Province of Venezuela and assigned its conquest and colonizing to the Welsers, a company of German bankers with whom Charles V had assumed economic obligations. As they were a commercial enterprise, the Welsers were interested, above all, in obtaining gold and slaves, and they did not found towns or exploit mines. Instead, they enslaved the Indians and speculated commercially with the Spaniards of Coro, to whom they sold imported articles at very high prices. They were credited for having explored for the first time a large part of what today is Venezuela, and to have done so in a relatively short time (18 years, until 1546).

In 1545, Tocuyo was founded in the midwestern region of Venezuela. This city soon became the center for the conquest and colonizing of the territory. From here, diverse expeditions departed to conquer the north-central and western parts of Venezuela. Barquisimeto was founded in 1552, Valencia in 1555, Trujillo in 1557, Merida in 1558, San Cristobal in 1561, Caracas in 1567, Maracaibo in 1569, Barinas in 1577, and Guanare in 1591. These cities arose to the degree that the territory was conquered, in some cases only after overcoming the resistance of the Indians. The Jirahara and Caribe tribes of Los Teques and Caracas most fiercely resisted the advance of the conquistadors.

As opposed to the conquest and colonization of North America by the English, in Central and South America, the Spaniards and Portuguese who came to the continent were principally interested in becoming rich. As a consequence, their behavior revolved around extracting wealth, sacking the Indian population, and forcing the Indians to submit to them if they opposed the invaders. This important difference has had important social and idiosyncratic consequences.

In the second half of the eighteenth century, the territory of Venezuela was politically organized into six provinces. Each was run by an official with the title of Governor and Captain General, who was directly appointed by the King, and each province has an existence separate from the others. They depended politically on different colonial authorities, some on the Audience of Santo Domingo and others on the Viceroy of Nueva Granada. During the latter part of the eighteenth century, King Charles III ordered that the six provinces of the Captaincy General of Venezuela were to be put under the authority of the Governor and Captain General of the Province of Caracas. As a consequence, the territory was unified from a political and administrative point of view.

The colonial economy of Venezuela was formed throughout the sixteenth, seventeenth, and eighteenth centuries, and its fundamental activities were agriculture, cattle, and commerce, although pearls and mining continued to interest the Spaniards. The exploitation of the pearls of Cubagua was under the control of the Spanish authorities of Santo Domingo, starting at the beginning of the sixteenth century. For manual labor, Indians and imported black slaves were used. Thanks to the pearls, Cubagua, a small arid and deserted island, became the center of colonization during these first years. Mining did not have great importance in colonial Venezuela, especially due to the low productivity of the gold deposits that were found. However, it did serve to stimulate the first activities of the conquest, exploration, and colonization of the country. In general, mining in Venezuela was characterized by its transitory and accelerated nature.

Agriculture and livestock were the basis of the economic activity of the colony. This was principally because of the availability of Indian and black labor and because some varieties of native plants were in demand in Europe. These plants became the basis of exports (including tobacco, cacao, and indigo, among others), while other varieties, such as corn, potatoes, and beans, constituted the basis of subsistence for the colonial population.

Colonial agriculture adopted two principal forms. One was subsistence agriculture, based on the traditional Indian farm in existence in the sixteenth century, with the crops destined for direct consumption. The second was plantation agriculture, based on farming large colonial tracts of land (haciendas) principally with slave labor, with the harvests destined for export and internal trade, which began to develop starting in the seventeenth century. Breeding of domesticated animals which was nonexistent in periods prior to the discovery of the country, developed as a consequence of the Spanish colonization. The products of breeding constituted an important category of the colonial economy (butter, cheese, and milk) along with raw material (hides) for the production of leather and other goods produced on farms and ranches. Moreover, these animals were used in transportation and in agricultural activities.

The colonial population was the result of the mixture of Indians with whites and blacks. As the product of this union, the mestizos grew in number. Racial mixing constitutes a typical feature of Spanish colonization, in contrast with the British colonization, that took place in America during the same period. The principal reasons for this difference were:

- The predomination of male elements among the Spanish conquistadors and colonizers. Spanish females came late to America, and, moreover, only in small numbers.
- Spanish law prohibited single Spanish women from coming to America. Only married women could come, and only if accompanied by their husbands or coming to the colonies to live with them. The union of Spaniards with Indian women and, later, with black women was a necessity, and racial mixture was

inevitable. Nevertheless, these unions were, with some exceptions, illegal.

At the end of the sixteenth century, when the conquest and foundation of the first cities took place, Venezuelan society included the following groups: Spanish whites, Indians, and blacks. Spanish whites formed part of the conquering group, and all were equal under the laws decreed on their behalf as the first inhabitants. The number of whites that emigrated from Spain to Venezuela during the conquest of the colony is unknown. The Indians, with a population of 100,000 to 150,000, were submitted to the condition of exploited labor by the whites, under the legal system of the *encomienda* (a form of ownership of property). Approximately 120,000 blacks, who were brought from Africa as slaves, constituted the most oppressed sector of the population and worked on cacao and sugar cane plantations.

The social evolution of these groups gave rise to the interracial mixing mentioned above, from which the following distinctions arose:

- Mestizos: from the union of white and Indian.
- Zambos: from the union of black and Indian.
- Mulatoes: from the union of white and black.
- Cuarterones: from the union of white and mulato.
- Quinterones: from the union of white and cuarterone.

To the degree that these mixed groups grew, the differences between them disappeared, and the previous denomination was substituted by the name of *Pardos*, which was defined by the greater or lesser quantity of black blood of the individual. At the end of the colonial period, the population of Venezuela reached some 900,000 persons and was classified as follows:

- Whites.................. 200,000
- Indians................. 160,000
- Blacks.................. 150,000
- Pardos.................. 400,000

At the end of the eighteenth century and as of the beginning of the Independence movement (1810), colonial society was characterized by its growth and dynamism and also by its heterogeneity and complexity, both in respect to the different groups that comprised it and its economic, social, and political interests. The principal social groups further evolved as follows:

- The Spanish whites (about 12,000 in 1810), born in Spain, who were recruited from the ruined nobility and the courtesans. They held the important public posts and were employed by the

Crown. They did not own large properties. The Crown was interested in maintaining the predominance of the white conquistadors and their descendants in order to guarantee their control over these lands.

- White Creoles and "coastal whites" make up about 173,000) in population. Creoles, descending from the conquistadors and encomenderos, who were born in Venezuela, were large landowners and slaveholders. They made up the educated and leadership class of the colonial economy and acquired nobility based on wealth. They discriminated against the persons from the other groups, especially those of black origin. They occupied the lesser positions in the political and administrative organization. Conscious of their economic power and their capacity, they aspired to run the colonial government, and thus formed a true oligarchy. The coastal whites were either of Creole and Indian origin or they were whites who had become established in the colony only after the distributions and encomiendas had been carried out. They held subordinate political posts. In general, they worked as craftspersons, small businesspersons, and laborers. The laws guaranteed whites the ownership of the land, slaves, and the encomiendas, the exercise of the municipal government, a monopoly over learning, noble titles, and social privileges.
- Indians (approximately 160,000) had no political activity. They provided free personal services to the encomenderos (owners of the encomiendos) and the missionaries. About half the Indians lived in the forest, making up a marginal population.
- Blacks were without political rights. They came from the lowest section of the society and were victims of white disdain. Most worked as slaves on the cacao and sugar cane plantations, although others worked as unskilled laborers and small tenants.
- Pardos were the most numerous group, but lacked any political right or influence. They worked as craftspersons, laborers, retail merchants, grocers, and small shop owners. Personally free, they lived in the cities. Pardos aspried to become the equal of the Creole whites in the social and political spheres.

The particular dynamic that was established among the above groups reveals that the interest of the Creole whites was to maintain the economic and social structure of the colony and to continue to the wealth and conserve social privileges to themselves. In this regard, they were opposed to the Spanish whites who held political power and represented Spain, the "Metropolis."

The greatest antagonism, nevertheless, was between the Creole whites and the pardos. The latter, together with the other nonwhite groups, hoped to rise in the area of social and political rights and to improve their inferior situation. In effect, the laws prohibited the pardos from marrying whites. They could not hold public positions, nor could they be members of the Municipal Councils or Ecclesiastical Courts. They could not enter any center of learning. Pardos were prohibited from using pistols, swords, or umbrellas. Women were not allowed to wear gold jewelry, silk, or precious stones. They could not use rugs to kneel or sit on in the churches. Moreover, they could only attend certain churches, and the certificates of baptism of their children were registered in separate books. As these class and group antagonisms grew, they had a significant influence over the struggle for independence.

TOWARD AN INTEGRATED VENEZUELA (1810-1958)

The year 1810 was of fundamental importance for the existence of the country in later times. It was the year when the idea of independence began to form in the wealthy class of Creole whites. This idea was inspired by the models of coexistence and political relations that the European and North American examples had provided (Soriano, 1988). The period of 1810-1830 covers the struggles for independence from Spain and the creation and existence of Gran Colombia (a state created by Simon Bolivar that integrated the province of Quito, Nueva Granada or Viceroy of Santa Fe, and the Captaincy General of Venezuela). Nevertheless, this period is overvalued in the history of the country. It is presented in the collective consciousness as a series of events produced by human beings whose characteristics make them superhuman, and the common citizen is thus needlessly diminished in the face of these feats.

The South American emancipation, and of course that of Venezuela, was related to the movements of the French Revolution and of U.S. independence, by the following bonds:
- By the ideas or principles of equality, liberty, property, security, federalism, republic, and alterability.
- By human models: behaviors, habits, ethical values, and the lexicon and forms of language.
- By institutional models (in the constitutions, and in the proce-

dures and objectives of political, administrative, and military actions).

Nevertheless, the emancipation of the colonies from Spain has a very characteristic specificity in relation to the nonhomogeneity of interests, forms, and resources (Soriano, 1988). For this reason, one of the principal points submitted for discussion, from the perspective of a social history, is the inconsistent nature of the Venezuelan emancipation project.

The society of 1810 had little demographic development. It was rural, isolated from the world, and politically dependent, and it had a mixed and complex social structure. Venezuelan society presents a paradoxical situation: the contradiction between evidently caste-like social structure (hermetism, rigidity, and endogamy) and the physical evidence that the mixture between the races was not only possible, but also real, as the presence of numerous pardos showed the interaction between the original groups. Nevertheless, there were specific legal regulations that interfered with mixed marriages, and in practice, there was a real exogamy. The pardos were limited in their political practice. Nevertheless, because of their numbers, they were a sector to be gained by the Creole whites to achieve their independence. To gain their support was not easy since the Creole whites represented the sector most opposed to recognizing the rights of the pardos.

In 1811, the same persons, members of an elite group, who before had rejected any possibility to interrelate on a factual or formal basis, drew up a constitution that proclaimed in its "Declaration of Rights," "that the Law must be the same for everyone" and that it was the obligation of the society "to make education available to everyone." The lower levels of society, whose members had struggled for social mobility and freedom, saw their aspirations now supported by Creole whites. This support suggested that those sectors that traditionally had not been allowed to pass through the doors to mobility and a new social recognition might be given opportunities to do so in the future (Soriano, 1988). The egalitarian discourse that the white Creoles pronounced, while it did not result in fully gaining the support of the lower levels, at least neutralized them and thus guaranteed for the white Creoles their predomination and political power, which was in the hands of the Spanish Crown.

Moreover, the civic values that were proclaimed were not rooted, and were shattered in the absence of shared and assumed interests (Soriano, 1988). Each social group was centered on its own interests and looked jealously toward its opposites. This situation was not overcome by the War of Independence because the conflict did not satisfy the aspirations of the diverse sectors of the society. It did not satisfy the slaves because slavery was maintained, and the Law of Emancipation placed them under a system of custody. It did not satisfy the slaveowners who considered it too liberal. Finally, the pardos resented the continued limitations on their political participation.

The Declaration of Independence of Venezuela was issued without overcoming the internal problems. Throughout the country's history, these coexisting inequalities will be seen to appear time and again. When Venezuela was declared to be an independent republic, noble titles were formally abolished and equality between citizens was decreed. In this way, the republic intended to satisfy the aspirations of the two groups: the Creoles now had the right to political direction; and the pardos obtained the same rights as other citizens. However, a new political inequality was established, based on property. In the constitution of the new republic, political rights to elect and to be elected were conceded to those free men who were property owners and had income. These circumstances meant that the Creoles would come out of the war as the governing class, since they were the only ones who satisfied these conditions.

The Creoles continued as landowners and slaveowners, and they were involved in commerce and finance. In the congresses of the new republic there was not a single representative of the pardos. Moreover, when, for political reasons, any form of representation was given to them, whites were designated to exercise it. The social struggle of the pardos was limited because of their economic weakness.

The royalist side wanted to exploit the antagonisms demagogically, advocating offering the pardos the distribution of the land and properties of the Creoles. In that attempt, the royalists obtained only transitory successes due to the inconsistencies of their leaders. In effect, the royalist leaders, particularly Boves (the one most identified with this concept of distribution of properties), could guarantee no more than a return to the colonial regime. Moreover, when they were successful, they placed at the head of the government white elements from the old Creole oligarchy.

Independence began to be formulated, not as a strictly or an exclusively political objective, but as the expression of a global aspiration for a new and different society, in which the negative values of the colony would be transformed into positive ones. The effort for independence was centered on finding a platform that allowed the conjunction of all the struggles. Nevertheless, for some sectors, the rupture of the colonial bond meant the almost automatic overcoming of the structural crisis of the society (Carrera Damas, 1991). The leadership class resulting from the war was small and weak in regard to internal coherence, which made articulation for the control of society difficult. Venezuelan population, in large part, was decimated and suffered a persecution syndrome that was produced by the confrontation.

In 1830, Venezuela separated from the Gran Colombia. This created a problem: the organization of a much more reduced geographic area in the form of a state of law (Urbaneja, 1988). In international terms, Venezuela abandoned its pretensions of hegemony and limited itself to aspiring for the recognition of other nations and establishing modest relations with the most important ones. At this time, little more than 25 percent of the territory was still to be penetrated. The agricultural base had been dislocated by the war, which had caused the loss or the destruction of the scarce infrastructure that had been built in the eighteenth century. The few more-or-less urban nuclei presented a desolate aspect (Carrera Damas, 1991).

Between 1830 and 1870, diverse forms, modes, and levels of consciousness were perceived in respect to the malaise of the society, and this was translated into an incessant effort to produce a diagnosis and to formulate solutions to the problems. In this period, the two constants in Venezuelan thinking materialized, which were defined as "lyrical optimism" and "systematic pessimism." The opposition between these tendencies brought forth a crisis of national consciousness, which put into doubt the feasibility of Venezuelan society (Carrera Damas, 1991).

The crisis of Venezuelan society of the period was expressed in economic terms with the incapacity of the *hacienda* (large estate) as an economic entity, to evolve and generate dynamic growth and development. It was expressed in reference to the changes taking place in the labor force. The continual use of slavery and the increase in the sector of wage workers created difficulties in the economic structure for the incorporation of free labor (Carrera Damas, 1991).

The crisis was also occurring in technology due to the difficulty of operating in the Venezuelan environment. Venezuela lacked roads and ports, and had no real way in which to change this situation. There was a crisis in the social structure manifested by the struggle of the slaves for freedom and the pardos for equality (which would subsequently be expressed in the Federal War). There was a problem of territorial integration, since local autonomous movements had not been eliminated. Moreover, Venezuela did not at this time produce any of the principal inputs to the process of industrialization that was developing in Europe. While Venezuela did continue to produce cacao and coffee, these products were not competitive due to their high prices.

The leadership class attempted to react in two directions: fomenting the rise and development of dynamic factors in the area of the economy and formulating a "national project." In the economic sphere, plans were considered to stimulate agriculture by means of loans. A policy of renting and selling lands took place, the formation of "societies of friends of the country" (associations of economic advisors) occurred, and immigration was promoted. This national project was based on defining the difference between independence and freedom, independence and equality, and independence and progress. Independence then appeared as a compensatory good: it was so important to be independent that it compensated the absence of liberty, equality, and welfare. In this context of grandeur, the cult of Simon Bolivar was formed, which was understood as a factor of government and a stimulus for national progress.

In the Venezuelan consciousness, what has been central is the figure of Bolivar of the Independence War. The lesson of history has been totally centered around the figure of a Bolivar, artificially constructed, in which the image of a classical hero is exacerbated. Insecurities and frustrations have created this mythical Bolivar, thus preventing a comprehension of the historical personality in its real dimension. The importance of the propagandist Bolivar has been forgotten, the man who was able to create a favorable opinion to convince and persuade all of his correspondents, internal and external, telling each one what he wanted to be said at the right time (Soriano, 1988).

In this national project the idea of the country was formulated jurisdictionally and liberally. This meant that the state must regulate its own conduct and that of its citizens through laws. Governmental action must be reduced to creating the legal and physical infrastructure that facilitates the unfurling of the initiative of individuals, in the form of channels and laws that protect the certainty of contracts. All this was necessary for Venezuelans to enjoy liberty and equality before the law, the supreme values of liberal thinking. The law could also regulate relations between nonequals, as with slaves and unskilled workers. Emphasis was placed on the level of legal seriousness, and not on economic progress (Carrera Damas, 1991). Venezuelan thinking in this period suffered a tremendous concentration on what Venezuela must be, and not on what it was. For example, there are repetitive texts in which it is assured that Venezuelans have been chosen for a great future.

In 1830, the Congress gave the country its new constitution as a sovereign State. Jose Antonio Paez was elected as the first president of the republic, and exercised a regulating function in the government that succeeded until 1846, thus prolonging his political and military influence.

In 1847, Jose Tadeo Monagas rose to power. He was succeeded by his brother, Jose Gregorio, who governed under the shadow of the former and under whose government the Law of Abolition of Slavery was decreed. However, some historians indicate that this law's impact was not significant.

Between 1858 and 1868, a harsh political situation occurred with the Federal War. Aspirations of regional autonomy were old and strong in this country with its acute problems of communication (Urbaneja, 1988). One of the desired political aspects was to substitute centralization for the adequate distribution of power between the central government and the regional governments (Urbaneja, 1988).

The period from 1870 to 1899 was one of political instability, with continual changes in government and uprisings in different parts of the country. It was the dictatorship of Antonio Guzman Blanco that initiated this period, which was marked by repression, the disregard of human rights, and administrative corruption. However, it was also a period of prosperity and economic growth. Gusman Blanco's government was followed by political disorder, country-wide confusion, and economic recession, which led to international conflict.

President Antonio Guzman Blanco wanted the dominant class to enter into a phase of development growth and consolidation. For this, an effort would be directed to the modernization of the state and the government and to the development of the infrastructure. These were viewed as basic conditions for international investors to become interested in Venezuela and to produce in it what at the time was the image of progress. Nevertheless, this attempt did not manage to unchain a self-sustained process of articulation with the international capitalist system (Carrera Damas, 1991). The failure was due, in part, to the fact that Venezuela at that time had a market with a very low consumer capacity. Moreover, as a provider of raw material, it was not offering what international trade required. The individual system of governing dating from 1870 had been weakened during three decades of business and political differences and skirmishes. As such, the country continued to be divided into a multitude of regions that did not render obedience to the central power. Eventually, the government was overthrown by a revolution, turning the power over to Caudilles from the Andes.

Two Emerging Currents of Values

Part of the period described up to now has been analyzed from a political-historical perspective. Maritza Montero (1987) studied the sociopolitical literature from 1890 to 1982 to provide information on the self-perceptions of Venezuelans. In parallel fashion, she contrasted that image with the results of studies carried out between 1968 and 1982 on different samples of the Venezuelan population by the Department of Social Psychology of the Central University. The author analyzed a total of 117 books, texts, essays, political speeches, and sociological, historical, and journalistic interpretations of political leaders, intellectuals, and historians, as well as pioneers of the social sciences. She utilized content analysis as her method of analysis. As historical events are presented, references will be made to the Montero study.

Her study observed the existence of two currents of values in regard to the self-image and the features of the Venezuelan: One positive current refers to paragraphs, phrases, descriptions and qualifying adjectives that describe good aspects of Venezuelans. There is also a second, negative, current which presents two subtendencies, one explicitly negative and the other pseudo-positive. The pseudo-positive one is positive only in appearance, since it employs ambiguous expressions that hide, as the author demonstrates, a negation, and therefore are implicitly negative. In regard to the explanations that are presented in regard to the origin of these characteristics, both positive and negative, they are based on:

- The concept of race and the mixture of the three races that make up the Venezuelan population: autochthonous Indians, African blacks, and Spanish whites.
- Explanations based on the impact of the geographic environment, including climate.
- Explanations based on the economic and sociopolitical conditions of the country, its governments, and, in particular, the situation of dependence and underdevelopment.
- Explanations based on the characteristics of the educational system.

The analysis that was performed established historical periods in which one or the other current of values predominated. Through references to the sociopolitical situation and to the principal events occurring in these periods, an attempt was made to consider some reasons that could explain the characteristics of the predominant self-concept in the literature under examination.

The first period, 1890 to 1900, was a pseudo-positive period, and it coincides almost exactly with the government of Guzman Blanco, who was in power until 1887. He had prepared the first national project of modernization, which was closely related to the development of capitalism in the country. Blanco introduced new technology and constructed a physical infrastructure (including roads, ports, railways, and public buildings). He also changed the infrastructure at the legal and educational levels. In this period, strong foreign investments were made with government protection. This period was also characterized by political instability, uprisings, and civil wars.

In this period, the pseudo-positive descriptions predominate. It is indicated that while the Venezuelans may be moderates, lovers of country and family, austere, restrained, loyal, and magnanimous at times to the extreme, the influence of dictatorial governments has made them corrupt and immoderate, with excessive desire for luxury and little interest in education. In effect, after the emancipating activities, which were a motive for genuine pride, a series of shameful governments follow. The arguments presented to explain the behavior of the Venezuelan and the characteristics described are based both on racial issues and on the corrupt actions of the government. (This point will be treated again later.)

Coming back to the historical description, in 1901, President Cipriano Castro proposed the creation of the military career. He purchased a new park for officials and troops, and later announced the creation of a naval war college. His government is no more than a new authoritarianism whose advent, in good measure, was due to the defeat of the elements being displaced, which he defeated during several episodes (Pino Iturrieta, 1988). This period is characterized by a popular ferment against foreign intervention, and it is centered around a sentiment of the country that was never developed. Nevertheless, parallel to this and at the cost of the public treasury, a series of fraudulent businesses developed. Ideas that would strengthen the political sphere were lacking (Pino Iturrieta, 1988).

In this scene, the secession of 1908 took place. It was led by Juan

Vicente Gomez, the vice president until that time, who capitalized on the discontent felt in the country and abroad. With Gomez in power, the regional strongmen disappeared, interference in the exercise of command ceased, and centralization became a reality. Nevertheless, in the handling of the public affairs, a system that conserves many ties particular to the past predominated, that is, in relations based on friendship and others that depend on direct contact between persons. A personalistic style continued, and the will of the leader was imposed without the intervention of laws or regulations.

Within the economy, measures to revive material activity were undertaken. The development of the essential elements for the centralization of authority were promoted: a road plan and the modification of the militias. In 1914, the first commercial oil well was drilled. The exploitation of petroleum permitted Venezuela to interact with the world capitalistic system. In Venezuela, cities had not been founded since the end of the eighteenth century. The cities founded starting at this time were the product of petroleum activity. With the movement of the population and an accelerated process of formation of infrastructures, the Venezuelan state, for the first time in history had attained the means to become national in the sense of its coverage. In this way, Venezuela was incorporated into the group of countries that possess capital. It had direct contact with new technological developments, a class was strengthened that was dedicated to consumption and the comfortable life, an unprecedented financial movement developed, and tastes changed (Carrera Damas, 1991).

In a recent article, Arturo Uslar Pietri (1991) indicated that it is still necessary to delve more deeply in what the government of Gomez represented for the country. In this period, the channels were established for the installation of the petroleum industry in Venezuela, a national government was was established, a network of highways was built to integrate the country, local strongmen were eliminated, and a national army was created.

The end of the Gomez dictatorship occured by his death. His demise was only a natural event, in which the nation had no input. Gomez was only attacked by a small group led by betrayed Castro followers and involving students born in the same period of the dictatorship. A group of these students constituted what has been called the "generation of the 28." Having had a great influence on Venezuelan politics, some of the students established political parties that are still being led by them or by people belonging to their generation.

Returning to the Maritza Montero's study, we see that the period from 1901 to 1935 is an explicitly negative period, and it corresponds to the stages of the dictatorships of Cipriano Castro and Juan Vicente Gomez. In this period, petroleum exploration and exploitation were initiated by the foreign companies acting under concessions that were extremely advantageous to them and unjust for the country. Petroleum exploitation favored the progressive rise of a modern bourgeoisie and an incipient working class.

The author's analysis, in the majority of cases, responds to the thesis of racist positivism which explains the nature of the Venezuelan through two groups of factors: racial inheritance and the influence of the geographical environment. In this stage, "the plainsman" (an inhabitant of the Plains) appears as the national prototype. In spite of the diversity of highly differentiated geographic regions and environments, the Venezuelan was identified with the plainsman: unstable, nomadic, individualistic, lacking a sense of community, valiant, fierce, suspicious, audacious, voluptuous but without tenderness, undisciplined, and heroic. Given this predominating character, the Venezuelan people are disorganized and difficult to govern. As a consequence their progress requires an authoritarian leader with a strong hand, the "necessary policeman." This is a formulation that is reconciled with, and justifies and reinforces, the dictatorships that predominated during this period.

The positive reasons that are indicated with greater frequency are egalitarianism, the fruit of the struggles and wars in which owners and slaves struggled side by side and that destroyed hierarchies, and personal courage and valor.

The principal political parties, which are still in effect, arose during the term of General Lopez Contreras, in 1936. In this same period, a process of modernization began in the country with the creation of ministries of labor, communications, agriculture and livestock, and other offices. In Venezuela, some situations were modified at this time, and there was a renovation of intellectual life. Nevertheless, the fear of and lack of confidence toward the political parties persisted, and there was a lack of confidence that they would change.

The presidential succession was again decided in military circles, and thus, in 1941, Congress voted for General Isaisas Medina Angarita as president. He, in turn, selected the most eminent civilians as his advisors. In this period, much leeway was given to participation. Social and economic problems were treated more seriously (Pino Iturrieta, 1988). However, these initiatives were not solidified and a system of thought susceptible to distinguishing and orienting the regime in terms of the political definitions remained unelaborated.

In spite of this, in Medina Angarita's government there were numerous innovations and changes in official attitudes designed to introduce the country to a different scenario. Nevertheless, the president and his cabinet did not realize that the problem of succession was taking other directions, and that in the political sphere the idea of universal suffrage had been created. They underestimated a proposal that was looked upon positively by the majority (Pino Iturriza, 1988). Moreover, they underestimated the discontent of the young military officers, and as a result, a coup d'état took place in 1946.

In that year, Venezuela was politically more uniform, cohesive, and bound together in its various components. In the period from 1948 to 1958, the expansion of the occupation of the territory was consolidated, the demographic revolution began, and the growth and diversification of economic life took place (Carrera Damas, 1988). In less than two decades, an infrastructure of a significant magnitude was provided which covered at least 40 percent of the national territory. The impact of the petroleum factor was essential in this. Nevertheless, some experts began to call attention to the disequilibrium of national development, with the predominance of the city of Caracas (Carrera Damas, 1991). The growth of the population and the inversion of the relationship between the urban and rural populations are elements that began to characterize the country. In the economic aspect, the state appeared to be the principal source of investment.

In the decade of the 1940s, an anxiety occured regarding the identity of the Venezuelan. Finding an answer to the question, "What is a Venezuelan?" became popular. From the magazine *Tierra Firme*, a survey was conducted on the theme, and it was responded to by a series of intellectuals. This generated in turn a series of round tables where the theme of the "Venezuelan" and typical characteristics were debated and this was echoed by the press. This search for identity and of definition appears to have evolved into a particular type of nationalism that utilized symbols such as folkloric music, using instruments such as the *cuatro* (a musical instrument with four strings) and the maracas. It put in vogue the use of the *liquilique* (a national suit for men made of white linen), as well as the orchid (the national flower).

The author suggested that this somewhat exalted and romantic nationalism which refers to the glorious past and its symbols, agrees well with the doctrine of the dictator, Perez Jimenez, of the "new national ideal," which is characterized by the construction of large public works. This type of folkloric nationalism coexists with cultural forms, uses, and customs, which have been increasingly affected by North American patterns brought by Venezuelan travelers, high-level employees of the petroleum companies, films, and the advent of television. No clear conclusions are drawn from the debate on Venezuelan identity, and again, reference is made to the racist argument to furnish explanations on this identity.

MODERN VENEZUELA (1958-1983)

An analysis of the period from 1958 to the present date, which coincides with an uninterrupted democratic system, reveals constant important growth and enormous changes which have taken place in the Venezuelan society in the last 40 years. Accelerated population growth (a rate that varies at from 3 percent to 4 percent per annum) occurred, along with rapid urbanization (in 1950, only 20 cities with more than 20,000 inhabitants existed, while in 1981, there were 65 such cities). During the period from 1958 to 1984, economic growth continued for 23 years at about 7 percent per annum (Naim and Pinango, 1986).

The infrastructure and social services multiplied, especially those related to education and health. M. Naim and R. Pinango (1986) reported that the number of institutions of higher education increased from 9 in 1960 to 80 in 1981, and the number of university students increased 11 times. The number of hospital beds increased from 15,000 in 1950 to 40,000 in 1980. The growth of the public sector is shown by the fact that in 1957 there were 20,000 employees, compared to 957,000 in 1981. In addition, the number of bank agencies increased from 80 in 1950 to 1,300 in 1981. The industrial sector multiplied in size between 1950 and 1978 by a factor of six. Moreover, the morbidity and mortality rates were dramatically reduced.

The petroleum income, which was administered by a strong and centralized state, contributed to these changes and, together with the large growth of all the parameters, the demands of the population also accelerated and the aspirations grew. In this regard, the party system, with its political clientelism, also had an effect through offers and demands of the diverse groups.

During this period, the process of modernization was reinforced. The middle class was strengthened, and the working class was further developed. An industrialized capitalist society linked with foreign capital and investments arose. From the beginning of petroleum exploitation to the decade of the 1970s, the Venezuelan economy had a relatively stable and continuous growth. Starting in 1974, petroleum prices rose rapidly. The important increase of the resulting petroleum income was translated into an increase of public spending. There was a significant increase of governmental bureaucracy, with the government assuming the provision of almost all public services as well as the development of different companies. The state assigned projects of great importance principally for the development of heavy industry. These "macroprojects" required large investments which, moreover, increased the public foreign debt. In general, an important increase in demand took place.

Although they do so to an unequal extent, all social layers benefited in some way from this economic bonanza. For all levels, consumption increased and aspirations of improvement rose. A climate of optimism and of hope grew, even among the most depressed groups. Expectations of social mobility became greater through the demonstration effect. The poorest saw the feasibility of overcoming the situation in which they found themselves. The middle class grew, and between 1977 and 1981, the distribution of income became more balanced. In spite of the authoritarian governments, a legalistic and civic tradition was always conserved.

From the analysis of the literature of this period carried out by Maritza Montero, the following may be concluded. The period of the 1950s initiated the appearance of some positive concepts of the Venezuelan: a happy person, an enemy of violence, tenacious, prudent and hardworking in spite of the authoritarian governments, due to legalistic and civic traditions which existed. Other features mentioned are generosity, love of freedom, egalitarianism, and intelligence. Moreover, negative opinions coexist that are based on the coincidence in the Venezuelan of the worst aspects of the three races and which are described as apathetic and distrustful (which comes from the Indians), superstitious and emotional (from the blacks), individualistic, bellicose, proud, gentlemanly, intuitive and lively (from the Spanish white). Toward the end of the period, typologies of Venezuelans, in which negative features predominate began to emerge.

At the end of the 1960s and during the 1970s, more systematic studies were initiated on the values and aspirations of Venezuelans, their psychosocial characteristics, and their self-concept. In 1968, an investigation performed in the Metropolitan Zone of Caracas was published, with 40 in-depth case studies based on an interdisciplinary approach (Abouhamad, 1970). The study involved the world of perceptions, values, needs, and expectations in relation to the self and the country. In addition, it examined the enormous changes recently occurring in the country, the persistence of traditional patterns coexisting with modern patterns, and the influence of the mass communications media, especially television, in the formation of models and stereotypes and in their power in shaping needs and aspirations.

In the same period, David C. McClelland (a psychologist in the United States), together with Venezuelan investigators, undertook studies on the achievement motive. The researchers found that the need to achieve of the Venezuelan was very low and that, in comparison, the needs for power and affiliation were very high. In the University of the Andes, on the basis of the theories of McClelland (1961), a series of investigations were carried out, with particular reference to the achievement motive.

Diverse components of the motive were measured, such as setting goals, instrumentality, achievement expectations, persistence of effort, deferral of rewards, perception and temporary orientation, and levels of internality and externality. These features were related to academic performance and the level of linguistic capacity. The majority of the investigations used university students and professors as their subjects. Nevertheless, the diversity of zones in which it was applied allowed the investigators to generalize the results with a level of reliability that was sufficient to refer to the social motivations of Venezuelans.

The investigations confirmed the findings of McClelland; in Venezuela, the highest motivation is that of affiliation, followed by that of power. Achievement motivation was very low. Other results obtained were the predominance of externality, the slight persistence in tasks, the difficulty to defer satisfactions and a high tolerance toward failure. It was found that expectations were not always the consequence of the association between "effort and result," since frequently, effort was not perceived as an instrumental factor associated with execution. The investigators hypothesized that possibly this was so because a negative conceptualization of effort exists since frequently it is associated with "sacrifice." In addition to effort, other cognitive factors were also rejected or were not very highly valued: the search for excellence, competitiveness, and persistent study.

The Venezuelan student was shown to be a person full of desires, hopes, and illusions, with high aspirations but little motivation to convert them into reality. Moreover, achievement itself is more associated with affiliative than with cognitive factors. The results point to the fact that the routes predominantly used to achieve objectives were less of a cognitive order (clear and realistic goals, adequate instruments, and persistence), and much more of an affiliative order (friendship, godfathers, and subservience) or involved with power (manipulation, imposition, authority, obedience, and command).

Between 1968 and 1982, a series of studies were carried out, connected with the Department of Social Psychology of the Central University of Venezuela, 10 of which are reviewed by Maritza Montero (1987). The studies largely dealt with nationalism and the stereotypes that Venezuelans have of themselves and of other nationalities. The results of the studies coincide in great part and reveal a self-image of the country and of Venezuelans that is devalued and negative, in comparison with the positive stereotypes of developed countries and their inhabitants. The United States, England, Spain, and Italy were the countries considered. Venezuelans prefer those countries to their own. Nevertheless, the order is inverted when Venezuela is compared with two other Latin American countries: Venezuelans prefer their own country to Colombia and Argentina.

One of the studies compared the self-images of Venezuelans and Colombians and their respective images of the other country. It revealed that the respective self-images were positive, while the images of the other country were negative. That is, Venezuelans and Colombians considered each other in a negative manner. To interpret these results, it is well to remember that Venezuela and Colombia, which are next to each other, have had border problems as well as an important illegal migratory movement from Colombia to Venezuela, so that these results could be influenced by ethnocentric attitudes.

Synthesizing the findings of these investigations, Venezuelans ascribed to themselves the following negative features: lazy, temperamental, impulsive, irresponsible, spendthrift, disorganized, uncultured, and disrespectful of the laws. As positive features, they considered themselves to be generous, hospitable, happy, intelligent, and nonexploitative. Evidently, the balance is inclined to the negative side, whose attributes have greater force and are more abundant.

The foregoing reveals a negative self-perception based on a hypercritical, deprecating, and depressed consideration of one's own group and an overvaluation that is made of almost all other countries. It is convenient to emphasize the fact that the overvaluation is related to the level of development of the country. According to Montero (1987), two valuative orders exist, one for "developed countries," the other for Latin American countries lumped together and called "developing countries" or simply underdeveloped countries. This negative image would appear to indicate not only national inferiority, but also perhaps at the same time, the current image of the individual Venezuelan. Venezuela is considered to be a beautiful and rich country, which in spite of its democracy and liberty, is backward, uncultured, and disorganized in respect to others that appear before Venezuelans as models.

Elements drawn from one of these studies allow drawing the conclusion that in relation to values, Venezuelans ascribe a high value to democracy and freedom, elements that they feel characterize Venezuela. That is, they describe it as a country that has many natural beauties, and is quite rich, democratic, and free. In regard to the characteristics of the national groups, Venezuelans value, in the following order, the eight attributes that are presented below:

1. To be responsible.
2. To be hard-working.
3. To be honest.
4. To be nonexploitative.
5. To be intelligent.
6. To be thrifty.
7. To be happy.
8. To be hospitable.

Nevertheless, when they describe themselves, Venezuelans consider that they do not have any of the first three attributes, which they ascribe instead to other national groups.

After the unexpected increase in petroleum prices in the 1970s, in the 1980s there was, on the other hand, a fall of petroleum prices (starting in 1982). This directly affected the volume of income that the state uses to deal with bloated public spending and high demand (products of the economic bonanza of the previous decade). With the restriction of petroleum income, together with the increasing foreign debt, inflation levels increased significantly, whereas previously they had not gone beyond the single digits.

THE NEW VENEZUELAN REALITIES (1983-1991)

In effect, from 1984 to 1986, a moderate inflationary outbreak, accompanied by recession took place. In the 1987-1988 period, there was inflation with growth, and in 1989, high inflation occurred. It reached an annual rate of 103 percent, accompanied by an economic contraction. In the face of these situations, the state adopted a series of policies and measures. In 1983, the first of several currency devaluations occurred. In 1989, a group of measures was applied for the corrective adjustment of macroeconomic disequilibria. These directly affected the population through the suspension of subsidies to a series of products, some of which were basic. Moreover, the measures provided for protectionist policies for the national industry, the freeing of prices, and giving incentives to foreign investments. All these measures raised inflation to unprecedented levels.

In synthesis, the 1981-1990 period, which was marked by the fall of real wages and economic contraction, has witnessed a more unequal distribution of income that in the previous decade. The evolution of the economy and the effect of inflation in the decade of the 1980s had made everyone (with the exception of a very small group) poorer. Studies performed by FUNDACREDESA indicate that between 1982 and 1988 families from stratum 1 (with high economic power) increased from 1.02 to 1.05 percent; those from stratum 2 increased from 4.46 to 6.5 percent; those from stratum 3 (Middle Class) dropped from 14.10 to 13.3 percent; those from stratum 4 (Working Class) dropped from 42.37 to 35.7 percent and those from stratum 5 (critical poverty) increased from 38 to 43.4 percent. The costs of the combination of inflation and recession have been unequally distributed. A disproportionate part of the load has fallen on the lowest income sectors. In effect, the percentage of households in a situation of poverty, which in 1981 was 37 percent, rose to 65 percent in 1989 (Marquez, 1990), and continued to increase through 1991.

Beyond the deterioration in the quality of life, particularly in the lowest income groups, the result of this whole process was an increase in the levels of dissatisfaction. This created a sentiment of frustration with a consciousness of the impossibility to materialize rising aspirations and expectations that had been formed as a product of the period of growth in the preceding decades, thus increasing the potential for social conflict. In fact, in February 1989, a popular outbreak occurred, the spark of which was the increase in the prices of public transport between a satellite city and the capital of Caracas. The disturbance left a balance of several hundred dead, thousands wounded, and thousands of businesses sacked (particularly small retail business). This popular reaction was unprecedented in Venezuelan history because of its violence and amplitude, and it revealed the accumulation of resentment and disappointment in the population.

Midway through this decade an investigation with a national scope was carried out, which covered four different areas of the country and involved 1,081 interviews (Briceno Leon, 1988a). The themes dealt with were: wealth, work, aspirations, the sense of a future, work as a means toward wealth and other goals different from wealth. The following are the principal results indicating the percentages of the most significant responses. In regard to wealth, the results reveal that approximately 60 percent of those interviewed desired to be rich, and that 40 percent were not interested in wealth and/or had other goals in life. In regard to moral judgments of wealth, 67 percent considered it good and 27 percent bad, because it was considered to be dangerous or because it was believed that poverty was good, valuable, or virtuous.

In respect to the utilitarian sense of wealth, 44 percent conceived it to be a means to invest and create more wealth, 26 percent considered it to be a means to do work that one likes and to have more freedom to choose it, and 28 percent saw it as a means to relax and enjoy it. To become rich, 37 percent believed that they will achieve it by working, 24 percent expressed the opinion that it could be achieved with luck or other factors beyond their effort, and 7 percent indicated that wealth was obtained by robbing or exploiting others. Of those interviewed, 46 percent believed that they could become rich while 52 percent did not think they could achieve this.

Among the responses in relation to work, the reasons for which they did or did not like to work, 28 percent engaged in it for the results obtained and for satisfaction, 23 percent, for benefits and remuneration; and 28 percent described work according to the human relations between workmates, clients, and the manager. It should be pointed out that among the reasons for dissatisfaction, 28 percent declared that what they most disliked was being ordered or controlled by others. When it was ascertained what individuals value most at work, it was found that among three alternatives, they chose human relations as a principal reason (52 percent) and put the pleasure of work itself in second place (29 percent).

The form in which respondents would distribute a large sum of money obtained by luck would be as follows: 47 percent would invest it in something related to their house, 24 percent would use it for making more money, and 13 percent would give it to needier persons. In the relationship of action to the achievement of objectives, the general attitude (72 percent) is that of activity, that is, to search for opportunities, versus 28 percent who present attitudes of passivity, awaiting for opportunities to arise.

When effort and achievement were related, it was observed that 55 percent prefered to work little and earn little. From the sample, 41 percent declared that they were not disposed to make an effort to be rich, including some who felt it would take away from their tranquility (35 percent), others who stated that it did not interest them (35 percent) or that they did not have it as a goal (31 percent), and still others because they did not relate the amount of effort with wealth (31 percent).

Of those interviewed, 65 percent had goals other than wealth. These goals referred to different aspects of their personal life or to goals related to their family life (the latter was 20 percent). Among those who had the goal of wealth, 45 percent were doing something to obtain it and 55 percent% were not doing anything.

It could be concluded that in regard to work and wealth there are differences of behavior among the diverse zones of the country and among different social groups. These differences seem to be associated with cultural differences principally due to different conceptions concerning the connection between work and wealth. In any case, the weight of the cultural variables and of the ideas in the population are dealt with beyond (or in addition to) objective conditions (Briceno Leon, 1988a).

From the results of the investigation, it can be deduced that in Venezuela, basically three groups coexist. There is a minority group, where a clear relationship is observed between ends, means and achievement expectations. This group has a capitalist conception of work and of wealth and in general work is viewed as the means to be rich. A second group, for which wealth is not an end, has other goals. Persons' views in this group are also consistent, but their conception of work and of wealth is not capitalistic. Their principal interest appears to be tranquility and personal and family welfare, and for this reason, they are not disposed to undertaking additional efforts to accumulate wealth. Finally, the third group is made up of those who are lost in the relationship between means and ends or between ends and achievement expectations. This is a quite large group and presents serious problems for any type of model of development that is to be implemented.

Examining the historical process of the last two decades, we see that Venezuela has experienced great contrasts. During the 1970s, economic expansion due to the increase of petroleum income, higher expectations and a climate of optimism occurred. The 1980s were a period of strong economic contraction, which required an important change in the economic policies of the state in favor of a general orientation toward the liberalization of the economy and a suspension of protectionist measures. Nevertheless, public spending continued to increase without budgetary equilibrium.

The measures mentioned produced an important increase in the inflation indices, which gave rise to serious social consequences: a generalized impoverishment, a collapse of expectations, and a climate of frustration, pessimism, and uncertainty. The compensatory measures adopted by the state to conceal the deterioration of the standard of living of the poorest classes did not manage to overcome the perverse effect of inflation and unemployment, considerably increasing the potential of social conflict and political instability. Moreover, there has been an attempt to redefine the role of the state, which from the beginning of the century has been increasing its power, accumulating functions that now, with a bloated bureaucracy, it is not able to carry out. A process of decentralization of power and functions toward the regions and the transfer of productive companies and services to the private sector is desired.

What is the perception that Venezuelans now have of these changes? What are the new realities that are affecting values, attitudes and behavior patterns? In October 1991, interviews were carried out of the following persons who occupy leadership positions in different sectors of Venezuelan society: Leopoldo Batista, civil engineer; Carlos Blanco, economist; Marcel Granier, economist; Ignacio Iribarren, doctor of mathematics; and Arturo Sosa, SJ, political scientist. These interviews reveal that while opinions differ in some aspects, they coincide in many important areas as discussed in the following paragraphs.

The 1983-1989 period was one of shock, stupor, and incredulity, which preceded the sudden change in the situation. A formation of consciousness on the need to undertake profound changes in national policies and in individual behaviors was initiated. Nevertheless, the direction of the change was still not consolidated, and both at the collective and the family levels, the same behavioral patterns from the previous decade continue to be maintained, with the hope that it was just a bad dream, a transitory phenomenon. Starting in 1989, the formation of a consciousness that this was a distinct country was formed, and processes of adjustment to the new reality were initiated. There is a coincidence in the appreciation that this juncture provides the chance to restructure the relations of power, and to permit new social sectors to arise. Moreover, the civil society should organize itself, and participate, assume responsibilities and play a more relevant role in the social life.

Individually, this is the occasion for Venezuelans to make the internal and conscious connection between work, progress and welfare. In effect, some symptoms of a greater consciousness, such as the increase of the capacity to protest, to dissent, to claim rights and a greater presence of neighborhood organizations were observed. On an individual and family basis, obligated by the economic situation, a greater discipline, anticipation, and assumption of consciousness of the future were attempted.

Nevertheless, the traditional political parties, Accion Democratica (Social Democratic) and Copei (Social Christian), which arose in the decade of the 1940s, still dominated the political scene and continued to invade practically all the areas of national activity. Their leadership, in the face of the deterioration of the ideologies, was based on political clientelism. They continued to be perceived as a mechanism for rapid socioeconomic mobility and as the only way to achieve power. In spite of the foregoing, these political parties every day proved to be more dissatisfying and less credible because they had lost their capacity to set a direction, their political programs had worn out, they were not in tune with the current situation and they had major internal disagreements.

A process of transition was being experienced with an uncertain future. Venezuela was still a society lacking integration and cohesion around a national project. Some asked about the elements around which this cohesion could be produced, since the ideologies had not responded to the concerns of today's citizen. What is required is a new proposal based on a concrete description of the country which is to be attained, and a recognition that the way out can be programmatic. It is necessary to mobilize the collective social energy as was done in 1936 and in 1958 upon the fall of the dictatorships of Gomez and of Perez Jimenez. Moreover, the lack of integration is due, not only to the lack of community of values, norms, and expectations but also to the fact that there are large sectors of the population that are far from having their basic needs satisfied.

Several persons interviewed want a distinct, non-sectarian leadership not subordinated to group conventions. They feel that in Venezuela there is a leadership outside the parties that must be grouped together, and a plan of action with a new direction must be presented. The role of the elite at this time must be to provide a purpose and a defined direction to the country. It is also affirmed that the problem of development is much less linked to the existence of an honest and effective leadership, and much more to the weakness and precariousness of our institutions. "The weakness of institutions makes men acquire an undue, excessive, and dangerous preponderance. Moreover, the search for leaders to direct us in this stage of crisis could be a way to avoid our own responsibilities, those of the civil society, those of private organizations, another symptom more of the culture of dependence," (Ignacio Iribarren, October 1991).

The changes stimulated by economic restriction have also brought negative effects; a notable increase of individualism, and an erosion in the area of values. "The first change in values is the loss of values." (Leopoldo Batista, October 1991). "An economic and political elite is emerging, devoid of scruples, whose only motivation is power and money" (Carlos Blanco, October 1991). "It is necessary to again inject hope and produce cohesion around a shared project that permits linking personal success to the success of the country" (Arturo Sosa, 1991).

The mass media have acquired a central role. On one hand they are an opening to the world and they permit knowing other conceptions, other forms of being and doing. Moreover, they have a negative role when they transmit life styles and motivate consumer patterns unattainable for the majority, and when they encourage the subordination of other values to individual success, and present an excess of violence. "Television exercises a great leadership, but it is a diffuse leadership and one that is not recognized or assumed as such by the owners of the media, but is perceived by them only as a personal business" (Arturo Sosa, November 1991).

What perception do Venezuelans now have of themselves? What are their principal values? How do they serve as advantages and limitations to overcome the current crisis of the country and what is the vision of the future? One interviewee states that there is not *one* Venezuelan, but rather many great regional differences in what Venezuelans are and how they feel, and in their motivations. Indeed, there is a great complexity. In spite of this, however, there is national identity. There is a consciousness that it forms part of the same administrative political unit, but this is a relatively recent sentiment that dates from this century. There is consensus on the Venezuelan being described as a "good person", simple, uncomplicated, healthy; with confidence, not jealous, with a mixture of docility and personal pride in the Hispanic style. Venezuelans are not cowards; they are valiant, and audacious, at times to excess. As a general rule, they are optimistic and able to be enthusiastic, amusing, and funny.

They tend not to be very analytical, somewhat superficial, and at times, not very serious. They like to put up a show, to pretend, to appear, and to impress. They are able to improvise and to escape from difficult situations gracefully. They associate roguishness and liveliness with intelligence. For Venezuelans, the connection between effort and achievement is weak, and they tend not to be very constant in their tasks. They are only slightly perseverant, they ignore and neglect details, "how to do things." They are is given to pleasure in the short run and center more on today than on tomorrow.

Venezuelans value shared efforts, friendship, and loyalty to family, to the group to which they belong, and to the party. "Who" is more important than "what" and "how" (Naim, 1989). Traditionally, they have been more closely connected with persons than with projects, and they are less concerned with rationality than with affection. Because of this same characteristic, they love peace, do not like to face open conflict, avoid confrontations, prefer to be liked by everyone, and search for harmony, which makes it difficult for them to face situations of competitiveness (Naim and Pinangro, 1986). They are a male chauvinists, placing excessive value on characteristics related to virility in spite of the fact that male chauvinism assumes distinct forms according to level of education.

Venezuelans, in general, are not closely attached to tradition and do not appear to be proud of a past that has been, in large part, painful. There is in the Venezuelans a weak emotion toward national identity, and patriotism is frequently reduced to a sentimentalism that is somewhat folkloric. There is a collective sentiment of low self-esteem. While it is less apparent at the individual level, collectively, there is an excessive valuation of other nationalities. This appreciation or collective image of inferiority constitutes a problem for progress.

The new situation doubtless makes up a challenge from which a more mature Venezuelan will emerge, one who is more conscious of the relationship between effort, achievement, and welfare, who is more diligent, and hard-working, and who, for this reason, has a sentiment of greater dignity, and self-esteem. In relation to the principal values, equality, democracy and solidarity persist, even though, as a consequence of the current context, individualism and the motivation for money have increased.

CONCLUSIONS

In this chapter an attempt has been made to summarize some moments of the historical past of Venezuela and to capture from them the elements that have contributed to the formation of a national ethos. Venezuela is a relatively young republic, when the fact is emphasized that only starting from 1920 has it had an integrated national territory. However, the history prior to this date is a sample of a fragmentation and political and economic opposition that has left a lasting mark on the Venezuelan idiosyncracy and in our appreciation of itself as a country.

The majority of the authors consulted emphasize the need and the urgency to develop in the country a group of common norms, values and expectations that give us coherence as a nation. The achievements that the country has attained in such a brief time are in danger of being lost to the skepticism present in many sectors of national life. What is a concern at this moment is the need for a national development plan that can consciously overcome cultural, economic, and political limitations which until now have impeded the development of long-term plans.

In a recent newspaper article published in the capital, the author gives an account of the fiftieth anniversary of a Venezuelan athletic victory. The author expresses the opinion that because the event mentioned is so far away the average citizen does not appreciate elements which are immediately at hand and that might make him also feel proud. For example, Venezuela in a very short period of its history has achieved democracy for more than 30 years in the middle of a region that historically favors dictators. It has a nationalized, efficiently managed petroleum industry with an international reputation, as well as other achievements that are not valued.

The challenge of this time is to achieve the transition of a culture of distribution to a culture of production. The current context indicates that it will no longer be possible to continue with a state model that, starting from the reception of the petroleum income, was responsible for distributing resources on a clientele basis. While the country until now has had a history that in some way has given rise to a low self-esteem as a nationality, there are also achievements that have the potential to produce important consequences. Most important, there is still a history to be written. What is said of Venezuela starting from this date is the responsibility of the men and women who daily commit themselve to the country.

13

A Profile of the Mexican

Alfonso Rodriguez-Coss
(Translated by Jorge Perez)

This chapter discusses the principal features of the Mexican idiosyncracy, such as the Mexican's temperament, values, traditions, customs, and attitudes in diverse circumstances. The essay uses as some of its primary references the concepts of Raúl Bejar Navarro, Fernando Díaz Guerrero, José Gómez Robleda, Jorge Castañeda, John Kenneth, Samuel Ramos, Francisco Javier Clavijero, and Jonathan I. Israel. I shall also include personal observations and experiences that, in retrospect, further elaborate on the different perspectives on being a Mexican and the evolution of the Mexican idiosyncracy.

To define an idiosyncracy of the Mexican in a strict sense today is perhaps more difficult than in the past. Today, more than 50 percent of the country's population is under 20 years old. Mexico is a country of young people in transformation and in search of an identity.

It should be noted that approximately 40 million Mexicans live in very precarious economic conditions, and they remain on the margin of scientific and technological progress. The values, aspirations, and habits of these Mexicans are quite different from those of the 17 million Mexicans who have secure jobs and salaries above the minimum subsistance level. However, we must also note that approximately 4 million Mexicans have not been incorporated into the Occidental culture. They continue to speak their native tongues, and they live isolated, in complete oppression. For example, these include the Lacandones, Tarahumaras, Huicholes, Tepehuanes, Otomís, and Mayas. A much smaller proportion of Mexicans have access to computers, travel, and education, and they celebrate their Independence Day with ardor and patriotism.

As one might imagine, there exist profound social, economic, geographic, and generational differences among Mexicans. The values and traditions of the youth of the 1950s seem antiquated to the youth of the 1990s. The majority of Mexicans were born at the end of the 1970s; thus, Mexico is indeed a nation of very young people. Notwithstanding, a great diversity of geographic, ethnic, cultural, socioeconomic, and generational factors have created profound differences in the attitudes of the Mexican. For example, a Mexican from the Federal District is very different from a Mexican from the forest, and a Mexican from the northern frontier is markedly different from one from the Yucatán peninsula. Such diversity makes it impossible to establish a specific idiosyncracy for one overall type of Mexican.

Nevertheless, in this chapter I shall try to draw general lines that will permit us to identify a profile or general identity of the Mexican. Although the task is not easy, there exists a historical tradition of identifying villages and cultures with respect to their values, customs and habits and that allows us to distinguish one village from another. The Mexican has been described effectively, but with little objectivity and scientific rigor, in films or novels that have traveled throughout almost the entire the world. This description uses the image of the Mexican from 40 or 50 years ago. It does not adequately reflect that Mexico has been transformed in the last 30 years, and the process of industrialization has attracted more than 70 percent of the population to live in urban areas. Fifty years ago, the majority of Mexicans lived in rural areas; to be precise, 65 percent lived in the open country.

The first part of this chapter discusses the pre-Hispanic influence, and the colonial epoch will be examined. In the second part, the Mexican of the nineteenth century and the Revolution of 1910 will be analyzed. The postrevolutionary Mexican (until 1968) is discussed in the third part, followed in the fourth part by a discussion of the Mexican of the last 25 years. The conclusion will integrate the characteristics that have emerged to endure over time as constants in the idiosyncracy of the Mexican.

Apart from the historical analysis, observations will also be made about the actual epoch observed in the press, in magazines, and in daily life.

PRE-HISPANIC AND COLONIAL INFLUENCES

The territories that comprise Mexico were once occupied by diverse cultures. When the Spanish arrived, the Olmecas, Toltecas, Teotihuacanos and Mayas had already practically disappeared. Only legends and archeological ruins remained as testimony to their existence. The influences of these disparate cultures in the Aztec villages and in the roughly 300 other indigenous villages that existed when the Spanish arrived are difficult to state precisely. It is certain, however, that the preceding cultures made deep impressions in the architecture, philosophy, and agriculture of the Aztecs, Tlaxcaltecas, and Chichimecas.

The indigenous peoples who survived the conquest were nearly exterminated by epidemics. Diseases such as chicken pox and a variety of venereal illnesses considerably reduced the indigenous population. These inhabitants were characterized by a profound religiousness and a rigid and disciplined conduct. Consequently, a stern education emerged, with a world vision that integrated them as citizens of the universe. Respect for the ancients, like a stoic sentiment in the face of life's misfortunes, was another characteristic of these peoples. Customs and values such as honesty, not imbibing in alcohol except on the dates preestablished as days of celebration, work starting in childhood, and helping, first, one's parents and, second, one's elders, made the Aztec society rigid and solidly stratified.

On the other hand, the Spanish conquerors were characterized by a high degree of cruelty and a covetousness toward riches, which contrasted with the true Spanish colonizers who, in spite of the propagation of faith and religion, were completing the conquest. That is, the process of the conquest requires two levels of analysis. The first is the violent conquest, and the second, the conquest by way of religion. Without this perspective, we cannot amply understand the process of the conquest of Mexico or the character of this country.

Spanish soldiers and public officials sent by the Crown to "New Spain" had as their principal purpose to avail themselves of sufficient riches and treasures of Mexico which would allow them to retire and live the rest of their lives peacefully in their native land. In other words, the conquistadors had no projected long-term plan to develop a great Mexican nation or consequently, to form an autonomous character. Thus, the Creoles (or natives) sought to identify themselves with Hispanic ways of being and customs. Only when those Creoles were rejected by the Spanish rulers did they attempt to develop their own idiosyncracy.

During the colonization period, New Spain suffered drastic changes in the population configuration. The figures are imprecise concerning how many and what classes of inhabitants existed in this period, or to their socioeconomic levels. What is certain is that epidemic illnesses assaulted and decimated the indigenous population. Millions of deaths are mentioned and it is estimated that by the year 1650, scarcely 1 million natives remained.

In addition to epidemics, there were other causes of mortality such as excessive hours of labor, poor nutrition, and insanitary conditions in mining. Moreover, the effects of the clash of cultures and the resulting social instability increased the natives' mortality rates. The demographic recuperation was slow. By the eighteenth century, the indigenous population had grown to approximately more than 2 million. With regard to the white population in New Spain, however, by the middle of the sixteenth century, it had grown to approximately 60,000 Spanish inhabitants. One century later there were more than half a million. The constant increase was due to immigration and better labor conditions, nutrition, and health in most of the territory. (It is important to note that the "white" population was not comprised solely of people of European origin as the children born of a legitimate union between a Spaniard and a native were considered "Spanish.")

The ethnic composition was quite varied and included Spaniards. Creoles, "mongrels," natives, Negroes, mulattoes, and zambos. The black population arrived with the conquerors and increased over the years. The trade in black slaves for New Spain, which was a common practice, also added to the manner in which the native population grew relatively smaller. For example, it is estimated that between the years 1615 and 1622, approximately 30,000 black slaves were legally introduced.

With time, the population that experienced the greatest growth was that of mongrels. This alarmed and preoccupied the Spanish authorities, who thought of mongrels as badly inclined people who had strong tendencies toward abuse and lack of discipline, took advantage of natives, and set a bad example. However, the caste that anchored the cultural base and the idiosyncracy in New Spain was the Creoles, who were not only the sons of Europeans, but also the grandsons and great-grandsons. The Creoles represented the impulse of a culture that adopted a baroque tendency with the aim of creating in the New Spain another Europe, but an "American" Europe, proper and proud. The

Creole culture was Americanized and differed in the way in which it captured a past, preHispanic tradition. The plan of the Creole culture, which was anchored in medieval times, did not survive to be incorporated into the renaissance, the Age of Reason and the scientific method, or the period of the Enlightenment. Instead, the Creole culture of the time of the colonization was trapped in a social, economic, and political structure that was semifeudal (Carlos Fuentes).

THE NINETEENTH CENTURY MEXICAN AND THE REVOLUTION OF 1910

The Mexican of the nineteenth century, following the country's independence, suffered a succession of historical accidents that have made life abnormal. Foreign invasions and civil wars spanned the nineteenth century. The absence of peace and tranquility confused the Mexicans of that epoch, who marched along disoriented, trying to find a course for existence and to fill the empty void they carried in their beings.

Another generic characteristic of the Mexican of the nineteenth century was a strong tendency on the part of the socially privileged to imitate the Europeans. The imitation was indiscriminate and there was no specific tendency that could lend a direction to the Mexican culture. In addition, the diversity of the European influence (which was principally French, German, English and traditional Hispanic) in the Mexican culture did not adapt well to the geographic, ethnic, or cultural context of Mexico. The dominant philosophy in Mexico at the end of the nineteenth century was positivism. Although interpreted differently for a person of the masses than for a scientist, it was fundamentally the same idea about life, in which the concepts of order and progress are the essential systems.

Eighty percent of the populace was illiterate while the enlightened individuals of the time had their eyes fixed on the thoughts of the French and the Germans of the nineteenth century. The difficulty in talking of a general idiosyncracy of the Mexican in that time is due to the fragmentation and absence of a central governing power. It was not until the arrival of Porfirio Dîaz that power was consolidated. Dîaz was the first governor to pacify, centralize, and govern such a bellicose country, and one so fiercely assaulted by foreign powers. Dîaz established standards in education, art, and in general in the life of Mexico. His principal task was to reunify Mexico and pacify those who did not accept his authority.

His enterprise included the leading classes and excluded the natives or those who, due to poverty or ignorance, could not avail themselves of the opportunities for progress and modernization. Thus, under Dîaz, order and progress were traditional and essential elements in the exercise of his paternal authority. According to him, Mexicans were children who were incapable of governing themselves, spent more than they earned, and were weak and disorderly (Enrique Krause).

THE POSTREVOLUTION MEXICAN

The Mexican after the Revolution of 1910 searched in the indigenous races for an explanation to his being. The postrevolutionary governors exalted nationalism and aggrandized the figure of the Mexican machismo, which projected to the world the figure of the Mexican as the defender of his soil and his identity, and possessed of a profound social vocation.

The attacks from outside had been made in 1914 and 1917. World War I was further proof of the necessity to heighten nationalism and machismo to defend the nation. World War II also strongly influenced the Mexican governors who, in art (Mexican muralism, music, novels and cinematographic productions) promoted the Mexican machismo and nationalism. In such a violent world, they tried at all costs to create in just a few years an identity that would respond to the political necessities of the epoch.

After World War II, Mexico reached for a greater degree of industrialization (a process that continues to this day). The Mexican has transformed himself, not by presidential decree or campaigns of persuasion, but by personal initiatives. Industrialization generated new attitudes and values about labor and life in society. Mexicans readily accepted technological advances and decided to make them a part of their lives. Naturally, the process has not been easy, yet no Mexican would resist and thus deny his child an education.

THE MEXICAN SINCE 1968

Approximately 54 percent of the total Mexican population was born in the last 25 years, and especially in the last half of the 1970s. The

Mexican is a direct product of the nation's economic and political structure, a person who is influenced more by mass communication media than by school or family values. The Mexican of the last quarter of this century can be depicted as a pragmatic person living in a syncretic, surrealistic, and chauvinistic atmosphere.

The pagan elements and religion continue to form part of the life of the Mexican. Attachment to the law is intermingled, when necessary with corruption or violation of the law. Fraternity and personal survivorship are confused in the daily struggle for life. Democracy is confounded with authoritarianism in political campaigns and on Election Day. Mexicans are either direct or indirect accomplices of their reality.

Surrealism stems from the difficulty in accepting reality, which is, on occasion, intolerable, crude, or irrational. Because there are vast cultural and economic differences among Mexicans, reality is interpreted, by each sector of the society. An example of this is the reality that drives the upper class of the nation. Another is the reality of the countrymen, and yet another, very different, reality is that of the *Chavos Banda* (Band of Youths). The Catholic Church administers still another interpretation of reality.

As a consequence, there does not exist a sole reality in Mexico, and Mexicans understand this. They do not believe the discourses of public officials, nor those in the newspapers. They do not believe anyone whom they suspect might ridicule or deceive them. Carlos Fuentes noted that there live in Mexico different epochs in one time (there are different concepts of time in Mexico). Similarly, there are different concepts of reality in Mexico. There are those who opine that there is poverty and misery in certain marginated sectors of Mexican society because that is how some people want to live and because the miserable are not interested in escaping misery. Thus, each Mexican gives his own interpretation of reality.

In 1988, government agencies estimated that the population of the country exceeded 87 million inhabitants, but the 1990 census and a 1991 presidential brief officially declared there to be 81 million inhabitants. Information is hidden, distorted, used as a weapon, and often masked or softened so as not to injure or offend. It is not customary for the Mexican to take statistics into account when making decisions or developing sales trends, and failures and accidents are ignored. Whoever has that information destroys it so it is not used against him and fabricates new information to suit his aims.

Surreality is more acceptable than reality. Mexicans do not accept their errors. There is always someone else to blame when something goes wrong. Instead of pointing out failures, reports, chronicles, and explications exhibit a series of excuses, pretexts, and imponderables. Mexicans believe what is false, and this is where surreality is initiated. They live in a fantastic world. Personal realization is seen in television comedies, the lives of actors and athletes, and in narcotics traffickers who, without education, make fortunes and gain power. For certain, more is said than is done.

In Mexico, machismo takes on a general connotation which stems from diverse sources ranging from sexuality to the worlds of business and politics. Suffice it to consider José López Portillo and Ronald Reagan and their interchange of gifts in Juárez City in 1979. The Mexican must be clever (Alan Rider) and must have connections, leverage and resources to get the better of others so as not to be had. There are no barriers and no scruples.

The economic crisis in Mexico, as reflected in the increase in inflation (from 26 pesos for one U.S. dollar in 1981 to 3,050 pesos for that same dollar in 1991), has degenerated the Mexican, not solely in things material, but also in his values, traditions, respect for others, and belief in human dignity. This crisis, which has reached 170 percent inflation in one year alone (1987), has morally affected the Mexicans, and the most affected and worst damaged are the young people. The youth live in a crisis of values and have a profound difficulty in defining their identity. The Mexican youth of today lack heroes. The concepts of nationality and patriotism have a great variety of connotations, spanning a Mexican night with English music and letters reflecting an ignorance of the country's history and appeals.

The characteristic of machismo is conventional, opportunistic, abusive, and destructive. It is devoid of identification with political or social ideals, and it is irrational, explosive, and absurd. In other words, machismo is not translated into attempts or demands to recover violated rights, abuses of power, corruption or poor administration, but it is rather an emotion without cause. Almost all Mexicans have the will (machismo) to interpret the law at their convenience, to fail to respect traffic signals, and to violate laws and rules established in factories, schools, and clubs. They do this to avoid being caught in line waiting for a bus, to arrive at the theater or movie box office on time, or buy a box of chocolates.

When rendering services, Mexicans will charge unjustly, usually more than what is owed. Often, the work completed is badly executed and quickly requires an "adjustment," which obviously represents an additional charge. This may occur with an electrician, plumber, automobile mechanic, attorney, architect, electrical appliance repairman, secretary for a tribunal, chauffeur, taxi driver, or other individual. The secret is to haggle a price and to supervise the work with previous recognition of the cause of the problem, having consulted other experts or those who have experienced a similar situation.

One Mexican does not believe another Mexican, and this has nothing to do with the cultural heritage. The lack of trust owes to each and every one's effort to reach a better position or at least to not lose what with many difficulties they have succeeded in obtaining. In a time of crisis, the law of the jungle is more crude. Trust is not the best virtue in a system in which the judicial order is unresponsive and the person with the most leverage is the one who imposes himself.

In the decade of the 1980s, one of the characteristics that openly manifested itself is a profound sentiment in the Mexican for speculation. This sentiment emerged from the crisis of 1982, in which banking was nationalized and the government was practically fractured, and the crisis of 1987, in which the monetary value collapsed, inflation reached 160 percent and the peso dropped more than 300 percent against the U.S. dollar. The Mexican is speculative in his language. He does not compromise himself, does not assume responsibilities, and plays with words to arrive at nothing. He speculates to speak, to buy dollars, to elect his political representatives, and to invest in the money market. Speculation is more accentuated in the conduct of the Mexican than is necessary to reach a result or to go directly to the point to affect what is necessary to resolve a problem. The Mexican values risks and speculates with possibilities in a search for something more, such as a personal advantage or an egoistic interest. This tendency complicates concrete action, and attempts at the satisfactory completion of a given task within a specific boundary.

CONCLUSION

In the decade of the 1990s, the Mexican sees the future with illusion. He prepares to accommodate himself to change and to supersede challenges. In a survey of 35 youths from different specialties, 95 percent manifested a disposition to transform and improve themselves in order to become more competitive. The difficulties and the crises that Mexicans have suffered in the last 20 years have awakened in them the necessity to change and assimilate themselves into a new horizon without frontiers and without economic, social, or political barriers. Mexicans of every creed and social position aspire to live better, to benefit from scientific and technological advances, to develop their creativity and imagination, to supersede obstacles that restrain their well-being, and to be highly competitive in all aspects of life.

14

Future Directions for Research

Dan Voich, Jr., Lee P. Stepina,
and Mijat Damjanović,

The International Consortium for Management Studies is expanding its research on comparative analysis of values and political economy issues. The chapters presented in this book mostly reflect historical surveys of the relevant literature or ideas in each of the participating countries. Thus, they somewhat reflect a mix of the applicable theories, concepts, and emerging trends concerning values and issues. The second book that is being developed involves an analysis of a large cross-cultural empirical sample of data compiled in eight countries throughout the world. These countries include three groups: (1) more market-oriented countries-Japan, Germany, and the United States; (2) more socialist-oriented countries-Peoples' Republic of China, Soviet Union (Russia), and Yugoslavia; and (3) Latin American countries-Chile and Venezuela.

Through a lengthy questionnaire translated in the applicable languages, empirical data about people's family and workplace values have been compiled for each of the participating countries. Additionally, people's attitudes and perceptions about various social, economic and political issues at the organizational, national, and international levels have been compiled.

The analysis currently underway includes several major thrusts using these empirical data. One major focus includes an analysis of a number of independent variables that portray an array of people's family, workplace, and cultural values, broadly grouped into (1) those that tend to favor or emphasize an individualistic ethic, and (2) those that tend to favor or emphasize a social ethic. A cross-cultural comparison will be made of similarities and differences of these independent variables by country and by other demographic attributes of the respondents. A general result of this analysis will be to develop an "individualism versus socialism profile" of family, workplace, and cultural values for each country.

A second major focus includes a similar analysis of a number of dependent variables that reflect people's attitudes and perceptions in dealing with social, economic, and political issues at the organizational, national, and international levels. A cross-cultural comparison will be made of similarities and differences of these dependent variables by country and by other demographic attributes of the respondents. This analysis will result in an "issues profile" for each country.

The third major focus of the analysis is to search for relationships between values, as independent variables, and perceptions of issues, as dependent variables. The values, as indicated above, will be grouped according to individualistic versus socialistic tendencies. These relationships will be analyzed for each country and comparisons of similarities and differences between countries will be explored.

The status of this empirical research project is as follows. All the empirical data (about 8,000 responses) have been compiled and entered into a computer data base. Consortium members in each respondent country have received this data base and they are currently analyzing these data along the general approach outlined above. Consortium members are faculty peers in universities in each of the above countries who represent a variety of disciplines, such as economics, human resource management, law, manaagement strategy, multinational business political science, risk management, marketing, psychology, and sociology. The International Consortium for Management Studies plans to develop a book manuscript on the overall empirical research results within a year, to be entitled *Empirical Cross-Cultural Analysis of Family and Workplace Values and Perceptions of Political Economy Issues.* Additionally, a series of independent articles will be developed by various members of the consortium on selected, and more specific, results.

The members of the consortium are also considering other collaborative research initiatives and activities. These include more specific explorations into some of the findings revealed in this study. In addition, several new areas of collaboration are being discussed in light of the major changes and developments that have occurred in recent years. The consortium's focus will continue to include research on basic values as well as on the relationships between values-needs-organizations and goods and services.

The format of collaboration used in the initial two projects of the consortium has been effective in that all participants share equally in the data that have been compiled and analyzed. Additionally, members of the consortium meet annually, in a different country each time, which helps to consolidate and clarify ideas, views, and developments in a more effective, timely, and enjoyable manner. We are optimistic that smaller groups of consortium members will begin to collaborate on smaller-scale projects which may involve only a few countries. At any rate, the consortium has opened up communication channels for various kinds of collaborative efforts.

We are optimistic that the extensive research presented in this book and in the companion volume will open new doors to the understanding of culture and how culture operates to influence actions. This under-standing is more crucial than ever. After years of studying Eastern versus Western cultures in order to determine and forecast future behaviors, researchers worldwide are redirecting their efforts to examine the diversity of the many cultures that shape our modern world and its future.

Bibliography

Abouhamad, Jeannette. 1970. "Los Hombres de Venezuela, sus necesidades, sus aspiraciones." Universidad Central de Venezuela, Consejo de Desarrollo Cientifico y Humanistico, Caracas.

Adler, N. J. 1986. *International Dimensions of Organizational Behavior*. Boston: Kent Publishing.

Adorno, T., et al. 1960. *The Authoritarian Personality*. New York: Macmillan.

Ali, A. 1988. "A Cross-National Perspective of Managerial Work Value Systems." In R. N. Farmer and E. G. McGoun, eds., *Advances in International Comparative Management*. (Vol. 3, pp. 151-170). Greenwich, CT: JAI Press.

Alisjahbana, S. 1966. *Values as Integrating Forces in Personality, Society, and Culture*. Kuala Lumpur: University of Malaya Press.

Allport, G. 1961. *Pattern and Growth in Personality*. New York: Holt, Rinehart and Winston.

Allport, G., Vernon, P. E., and Lindzey, G. 1931. *Study of Values*. Boston: Houghton Mifflin.

Andreenkova, N. V. 1971. "Socialization of the Individual at the Beginning of Work Activity," (in Russian). Ph.D. dissertation. University of Moscow.

_____. 1988. *A study of labor activity at the contemporary stage of the socio-economic development of the USSR*. Moscow: Work and society.

Aseyev, V. G. 1976. *The motivation of behavior and the forming of the individual* (in Russian). Moscow.

Attinger, Joelle. 1991. "Savoir-Vivre." *Time International* (Special issue: "The New France"), July 15, 48-49.

Bačević, Lj., et al. 1990. "Neposlusni medij" (Intractable media) *RTV* (Novi Sad, Yugoslavia).

_____. 1991. "Jugoslavija na kriznoj prekretnici" (Yugoslavia at a turning point in crisis; summary in English). Belgrade, Yugoslavia: Institut drustvenih nauka.

Baier, K., and Rescher, N., eds. 1969. *Values and the Future*. New York: Free Press.

Balakina, E. F. 1965. *Researchers Should Give Attention to the Problem of Values* (in Russian). Voprosi Filosofii, 9. Moscow.

Banning, T. 1987. *Lebensstilorientierte Marketing-Theorie*. Heidelberg, Germany.

Barč, G. 1970. "Social Mobility, Individual and Yugoslav Socialist Community," (in Serbo-Croatian). *Sociologija* 3-4: 399-411.

Barney, J. B. 1986. "Organization Culture: Can it Be a Source of Substantial Competitive Advantage?" *Academy of Management Review*. 11(3):656.

Barret, G. V., and Bass, B. M. 1976. "Cross-Cultural Issues in Industrial and Organizational Psychology." In M. Dunnette, ed., *Handbook of Industrial and Organizational Psychology* (pp. 1297-1350). Chicago: Rand McNally.

Barroso, Manuel. 1991. *Autoestima del venezolano, democracia o marginalidad*. Caracas: Editorial Galac.

Barton, A. 1963. *Measuring the Values of Individuals*. Columbia University, BASR. New York.

Barton, A., Denitch, B., and Kadushin, C. 1973. *Opinion-Making Elites in Yugoslavia*. New York: Praeger.

Bassoux, Jean Louis, and Lawrence, Peter. 1991. "The Making of a French Manager." *Harvard Business Review*. (July-August): 58-67.

Bastidas, Aristedes. 1991. "Existen cinco tipos de familias en el pais." *El Nacional*, November.

Baumann, E. J. 1990. "Produkte für Senioren-aber keine Seniorenprodukte." *Asw.* (1), 26-42.

Bbouhamad, Jeannette. 1970. "Los Hombres de Venezuela, sus necesidades, sus aspiraciones." Universidad Central de Venezuela. Consejo de Desarrollo Cientifico y Humanistico, Caracas.

Beliayeva, J. F., and Y. G. Kopnin. 1989. *Attitude toward Work of Young Workers: Value-motivational Aspect* (in Russian). Moscow: Scientific Research Institute of Work. Moscow, (in russ.).

Bertch, G. 1976. *Values and Community in Multinational Yugoslavia.* New York: Columbia University Press.

Bhagatt, R. S., and McQuaid, S. J. 1982. "Role of Subjective Culture in Organizations: A Review and Directions for Future Research." *Journal of Applied Psychology.* 67(5): 653-685.

Bojanović, R. 1989. "Authoritarianism and Youth", Belgrade (in Serbo-Croatian). Manuscript (Belgrade, Yugoslavia).

Briceno Leon, Roberto. 1988a. *El comportamiento social del venzolano ante el trabajo y la requeza.* Final report of the P.C. 012 project, Social Research Laboratory. Central University of Venezuela.

———. 1988b. *Los efectos perversos del Petroleo.* Caracas: Fondo Editorial Acta Cientifica Venezolana, Consorcio de Ediciones Capriles.

Bridgford, Jeff. 1987. "French Trade Unions: Crisis in the 1980s," *Industrial Relation Journal.* 126-134.

Brigham, J. C. 1986. *Social Psychology.* Boston, MA: Little and Brown.

Buchholz, R. A. 1976. "Measurement of Beliefs." *Human Relations.* 29(12): 1177-1188.

———. 1977. "The Belief Structure of Managers Relative to Work Concepts Measured by a Factor Analytic Model." *Personnel Psychology.* 30: 567-587.

———. 1978. "An Empirical Study of Contemporary Beliefs about Work in American Society." *Journal of Applied Psychology.* 63(2): 219-227.

Buyeva, L. P. 1968. *The Social Environment and the Consciousness of the Individual* (in Russian). Moscow.

———. 1978. *Man: Activity and Association* (in Russian). Moscow.

Carrera Damas, German. 1991. *Una Nacion llamada Venezuela*, 4th ed. Monte Avila Editores.

Castro Leiva, Luis. 1988. *El dilema octubrista 1945-1987.* Caracas: Cuadernos Lagoven, Serie Cuatro Republicas.

Chavchavadze, N. Z. 1984. *Culture and Values* (in Russian). Tbilisi, Georgia.

Chernovolenko, V. F., Ossovsky, V. L., and Paniotto, V. J. 1979.

   Prestige of Professions and Problems of the Social-Professional Orientation of Youth (in Russian). Keyev.

Chkhartishvili, S. N. 1958. *The Problem of the Willing Behavior Motivation* (in Russian). Tbilisi, Georgia.

Coates, J. F. 1986. *Issues Management: How You Can Plan, Organize, and Manage for the Future*. Mt. Airy, MD: Lamont Publications.

Cochrane, R., Billig, M., and Hogg, M. 1979. "British Politics and the Two-Value Model." In M. Rokeach, ed., *Understanding Human Values: Individual and Social* (pp. 122-142). New York: Free Press.

Čulig, B., Fanuko, N., and Jerbić, V. 1982. "Values and Value-Orientation of Youth" (in Serbo-Croatian). CDD. Zagreb, Yugoslavia.

Daft, R., Sormunen, J., and Parks, D. 1988. "Chief Executive Scanning, Environmental Characteristics and Company Performance: An Empirical Study." *Strategic Management Journal.* 9: 123-139.

Dennison, D. R. 1984. "Bringing Corporate Culture to the Bottom Line." *Organizational Dynamics.* 13(2): 4-22.

Dilić, E. 1971. *Social Structure and Orientation of the Rural Youth* (in Serbo-Croatian). Belgrade, Yugoslavia: Institute of Social Sciences.

Dilić, E., et al. 1977. *The Rural Youth Today* (in Serbo-Croatian). CDD Zagreb, Yugoslavia.

Diligensky, G. T. 1976. *Problems of Human Needs Theory* (in Russian). Voprosi Filosofii, no. 9.

_____. 1986. *In Search of Sense and Purpose* (in Russian). Moscow.

Dorfman, P. W., and Howell, J. P. 1988. "Dimensions of National Culture and Effective Leadership Patterns: Hofstede Revisited." In R. N. Farmer and E.G. McGoun, eds., *Advances in International Comparative Management* (Vol. 8, pp. 127-150. Greenwich, CT: JAI Press.

Dukes, W. 1955. "Psychological Studies of Values" *Psychology Bulletin.* 52: 24-50.

Đurić, Đ. 1980. *The Psychological Structure of Ethnic Attitudes in Youth* (in Serbo-Croatian). Novi Sad, Yugoslavia: J. Vukanović.

_____. 1987. *Socialization of the Young in a Multinational Society* (in Serbo-Croatian). Novi Sad, Yugoslavia: Pedagoški zavod Vojvodine.

Džinić, F. 1973. *Value-Orientations in Yugoslavia* (in Serbo-Croatian). Sarajevo, Yugoslavia: Pregled.

Džuverović, B. 1975. *Values and Rebellions in the Youth* (in Serbo-Croatian). Subotica, Yugoslavia: Radnički univerzitet.

England, G. W. 1975. *The Manager and His Values: An International Perspective*. Cambridge, MA: Ballinger Publishers.

Farr, R. M. and Moscovici, S. eds. *Social Representations*. Cambridge: Cambridge University Press.

Flanagan, S. 1980. "Value Change and Partisan Change in Japan: The Silent Revolution Revisited" *Comparative Politics*. 11: 253--278.

Frances, Antonio. 1990. "Viviendo en inflacion: El comportamiento del venezolano en una economia inestable." Paper presented in the IESA Conference on "Social Aspects of Inflation," March 1990. Caracas.

Fromm, E. 1941. *Escape from Freedom*. New York: Holt.

_____. 1947. *Man for Himself*. New York: Holt.

_____. 1955. *The Sane Society*. Greenwich, CT: Fawcett.

_____. 1959 "Value, Psychology and Human Existence" in A. Maslow, ed., *New Knowledge in Human Values*. New York: Harper.

Fulgosi, A., and Radin, F. 1988. "Lifestyles of Students in Zagreb" (in Serbo-Croatian). CDD SSOH, Zagreb, Yugoslavia.

Fürstenberg, F. 1987. "Wandel in der Einstellung zur Arbeit-Haben sich die Menschen oder hat sich die Arbeit verändert?" in L. V. Rosenstiel, H. E. Einsiedler, and R. K. Streich. eds, *Wertewandel als Herausforderung für die Unternehmenspolitik* (pp. 17-22). Stuttgart.

Gibbins, J., ed. 1989. *Contemporary Political Culture*. London: Sage.

Goati, V., et al. 1989. *Jugosloveni o drustvenoj krizi* (What Yugoslavs think about the social crisis). Belgrade, Yugoslavia: Izdavacki centar "Komunist".

Gomez, Edward M. 1991. "A Desert No More." *Time International*. (Special issue: "The New France" July 15: 22-26.

Gomez-Mejia, L. R., and McCann, J. D. 1986. "Assessing An International 'Issues Climate': Policy and Methodology Implications." INUBPRO Project unpublished report, Gainesville, FL.

_____. 1986. "Caribbean/Latin America Issues Survey Results." Unpublished report from the INUBPRO Project, Gainesville, FL.

Grimm, E. 1989. "Die Deutschen als Europäer." in *Planung und Analyse*. (11/12): 418-422.

Gross, B., and Springer, M., eds. 1970. "Political Intelligence for America's Future." *Annals of the American Academy of Political and Social Science*. 388.

Gurova, R. G. 1977. *The Secondary School Graduate* (in Russian). Moscow.

Gutenberg, E. 1951. *Grundlagen der Betriebswirtschaftslehre*. Berlin.

Hafner-Fink, M. 1989. "Ideology and Consciousness of Social Strata in Slovenia" (in Slovinian). Ljubljana, Yugoslavia.

Hahn, D. 1988. "Führung und Führungsorganisation." Zfbf 2, pp. 112-137.

Hambrick, D. C., and Lei, D. 1985. "Toward an Empirical Prioritization of Contingency Variables for Business Strategy." *Academy of Management Journal*. 28: 763-788.

Handy, R. 1970. *The Measurement of Values*. St. Louis, MO: Warren Green.

Harding, S., and Phillips, D. 1986. *Contrasting Values in Western Europe*. London: Macmillan.

Häusler, J. 1977. *Fuhrungssysteme und -modelle*. Koln.

Havelka, N. 1975. "Value Research in Yugoslavia" (in Serbo-Croatian, Summary in English) *Psihologija*. 3-4: 139-150.

Havelka, N., et al. 1990. *Educational and Developmental Achievements by Students at the End of Elementary Schooling*. Belgrade, Yugoslavia: Institute of Psychology, Faculty of Philosophy.

Himmelweit, H. T., and Gaskell, G., eds. 1990. *Societal Psychology*. London: Sage.

Hoffmann, F., and Rebstock, W. 1989. "Unternehmensethik-Eine Herausforderung an die Unternehmung" *ZfB* 59b: pp. 667-687.

Höfner, K. 1987. *Fünf neue, einkommensstarke Verbraucherzielgruppen in Westeuropa*, München.

Hofstede, G. 1980. *Culture's Consequences-International Differences in Work-Related Values*. Beverly Hills, CA: Sage.

_____. 1983. "The Cultural Relativity of Organizational Practices and Theories." *Journal of International Business Studies* 14(2): 75-90.

_____. 1985. "The Interaction Between National and Organizational Value Systems." *Journal of Management Studies* 22(4): 347-357.

Hofstede, G., and Bond, M. H. 1984. "Hofstede's Cultural Dimensions: An Independent Validation Using Rokeach's Value Survey." *Journal of Cross-Cultural Psychology* 15(4): 417-433.

Höhler, G. 1990. "Neue Führungsstrategien" in E. Zahn, ed., *Europa 1992 - Wettbewerbsstrategien auf dem Prüfstand* (pp. 187-199). Stuttgart.

Holzmüller, H. H. 1986. "Grenzüberschreitende Konsumentenforschung" in *Marketing* (1: 45-54).

Hopfenbeck, W. 1989. *Allgemeine Betriebswirtschafts-und Managementlehre*. 2d ed., Landsberg.

Hornblower, Margot. 1991a. "Foreign Overdose." *Time International* (Special issue: "The New France"). July 15, 44-45.

_____. 1991b. "Les Miserables." *Time International* (Special issue: "The New France"). July 15: 10.

Hrnjica, S. 1981. "Post-Materialism in an Environment of Insecurity." *American Political Science Review.* 75: 880-890.

_____. 1985. "Aggregate Stability and Individual-Level Flux in Mass Belief Systems" *American Political Science Review* 78: 97-116.

_____. 1990a. *Culture Shift in Advanced Industrial Society.* Princeton, NJ: Princeton University Press.

_____. 1990. *The Maturity of Personality* (in Serbo-Croatian, summary in English). Belgrade, Yugoslavia: Zavod za udžbenike.

Ikonnikova, S. N., and V. T. Lisovsky. 1969. *Youth on Themselves and Their Contemporaries* (in Russian). Leningrad.

Inglehart, R. 1977. *The Silent Revolution: Changing Values and Political Styles among Western Publics.* Princeton, N. J.: Princeton University Press.

_____. 1979. Wertwandel in den westlichen Gesellschaften: Politische Konsequenzen von materialistischen und postmaterialistischen Prioritäten, in H. Klages, and P. Kmieciak, eds., *Wertewandel und gessellschaftlicher Wandel* (pp. 279-316). Frankfurt.

_____. 1980. Zusammenhang zwischen sozio-okonomischen Bedingungen und individuellen Wertprioritaten, in *Kolner Zeitschrift fur Soziologie und Sozialpsychologie* 32: pp. 144-153.

_____. 1990. *Culture Shift in Advanced Industrial Society*. Princeton, NJ: Princeton University Press.

Inglehart, R., and Flanagan, S. 1987. Value Change in Industrial Societies *American Political Science Review*. 81: 1289-1319.

Inlow, G. 1972. *Values in Transition*. New York: Wiley.

International Monetary Fund. 1991. *World Competitiveness Report*. Washington, DC.

Jacob, P., et al. 1971. *Values and Active Community: A Cross-Cultural Study of the Influence of Local Leaders*. New York: Free Press.

Janićijević, M. et al. 1966. *Yugoslav Students and Socialism* (in Serbo-Croatian, summary in English). Belgrade, Yugoslavia: Institute of Social Sciences.

Jerbić, V., and Lukić, S. 1982. *Value Orientations of Pupils and Students in Croatia* (in Serbo-Croatian). Zagreb: Prosvjetno-pedagoški zavod (Manuscript).

Joksimović, S., et al. 1988. *Youth and Informal Groups* (in Serbo-Croatian). ICC SSOS (Belgrade, Yugoslavia).

Katunarić, V. 1987. "Authoritarianism-Ethnocentrism-Sexism" (in Serbo-Croatian, summary in English). *Sociologija* 3-4: 603-610.

Keegan, W. S. 1974. Multi-National Scanning: A Study of Information Sources Utilized by Headquarters Executives in Multinational Companies. *Administrative Science Quarterly*. 19: 411-421.

Kefalas, A. G. 1990. *Global Business Strategy: A Systems Approach*. Cincinnati, OH: South-Western Publishing.

Kelley, L., Whatley, A., and Worthley, R. 1987. Assessing the Effects of Culture on Managerial Attitudes: A Three Culture Test. *Journal of International Business Studies*. 18(3): 17-33.

Kelley, L., and Worthley, R. 1981. The Role of Culture in Comparative Management: A Cross-Cultural Perspective. *Academy of Management Journal*. 24(1): 164-173.

Kelly De Escobar, Janet. 1990. "Concertacion y Desconcierto: Aspectos politicos del fenomeno inflacionario." Paper presented in the IESA Conference on "Social Aspects of Inflation," March 1990. Caracas.

Kharkov University. 1977. *The Communistic Ideals and the Formation of the Student's Personality* (in Russian). Kharkov, Ukranian Republic.

_____. 1980. Problems and Results of Researches (in Russian). Moscow.

Klages, H. 1984. *Wertorientierungen im Wandel*. Frankfurt/New York.

Klein, H. E., and Linneman, R. E. 1984. Environmental Assessment: An International Study of Corporate Practice. *Journal of Business Strategy*. 5(1): 66-75.

Klineberg, O., et al. 1979. *Students, Values and Politics*. New York: Free Press.

Kluckhohn, C. 1952. "Values and Value Orientation in the Theory of Action." In T. Parsons, and E. Shils, eds.: *Toward a General Theory of Action*. Cambridge, MA: Harvard University Press.

Kluckhohn, F. 1953. "Dominant and Variant Value Orientations." In C. Kluckhohn, H. Murray, and D. Schneider, eds., *Personality in Society, Nature and Culture* (pp. 342-357). New York: Knopf.

Kluckhohn, F., and Strodtbeck, F. 1961 *Variations in Value Orientations*. Evanston, IL: Row, Peterson.

_____. 1980. "Zusammenhang zwischen sozio-ökonomischen Bedingungen und individuellen Wertprioritäten." *Kölner Zeitschrift für Soziologie und Sozialpsychologie* 32: 144-153.

Kotler, P. 1982. *Marketing Management* (in German). 4th ed. Stuttgart: Prentice Hall.

Kroeber, A. L, and Kluckhohn, C. 1952. "Culture: A Critical Review of Concepts and Definitions." *Peabody Museum Papers*. 47. Cambridge, Mass.: Harvard University.

Kuzmanović, B. 1987. *The Problems of Motivational Foundations of Self-Management* (in Serbo-Croatian). Belgrade, Yugoslavia: Filozofski fakultet, Doctoral dissertation.

_____. 1990. "Value Orientations of Students at the End of Elementary Schooling." In N. Havelka, et al., *Educational and Developmental Achievements by Students at the End of Elementary Schooling* (in Serbo-Croatian; summary in English; pp. 215-234). Belgrade, Yugoslavia: Institute of Psychology, Faculty of Philosophy.

Leontiev, A. N. 1976. *Activity, Consciousness, Personality* (in Russian). Moscow.

Locke, Edwin A. 1976. "The Nature and Causes of Job Satisfaction." In M. Dunnette, ed. *Handbook of Industrial and Organizational Psychology* (pp. 1297-1350). Chicago: Rand McNally.

McCann, J. E. 1983. "Design Guidelines for Social Problem Solving Interventions." *Journal of Applied Behavioral Science.* 19: 177-189.

McClelland, David. 1961. *The Achieving Society.* New York: Van Nostrand Rhinehold Company.

"Mafo-Instrumente für das Euromarketing" 1989. *Asw* (5): 84-87.

_____. 1985. "Analyzing Industrial Trends: A Collaborative Approach." *Long Range Planning.*

McClelland, David. 1961. The Achieving Society. New York: Van Nostrand Rhinehold Company.

Marinović, D. 1988. "Youth and Religion" (in Serbo-Croatian, summary in English). In F. Radin, et al. *The Fragments of Youth* (pp. 153-198). Zagreb, Yugoslavia: IDIS.

Marquez, Gustavo. 1990. "Escaleras y Ascensores: La distribucion del ingreso en la decada de los ochenta." Paper presented in the IESA Conference on "Social Aspects of Inflation." March 1990. Caracas.

Marx, K., and Engels, F. 1980. *Collected Works* (3) London: Lawrence Wishart, Ltd..

Maslow, A. H. 1954. *Motivation and Personality.* New York: Harper.

_____. *Toward a Psychology of Being.* New York: Van Nostrand.

_____. 1964. *Religions, Values and Peak Experiences.* New York, Viking Press.

Meissner, H. G. 1959. *Anthropologische Grundlagen der Exportmarktforschung.* Berlin.

_____. 1985. "Historical Development of Consumer Research: National and International Perspectives." *Proceedings of the Association for Consumer Research International Meeting in Singapore*, July 18-20.

_____. 1986. "Neuere Entwicklungen des Marketing-Konzeptes." In K. Homann, and H. G. Meissner, eds., *Schriftenreihe des Lehrstuhls für Marketing* (pp. 21-29). Dortmund.

_____. 1990a. "Marketing im Gemeinsamen Europäischen Markt." In H. Berg, H. G. Meissner, and W. B. Schünemann, eds., *Markte in Europe--Strategien fur das Marketing* (pp. 99-162). Stuttgart.

_____. 1990b. *Strategic International Marketing.* Berlin.

Mermet, Gerand. 1990. *Frances.* Paris: Librairie Larousse.

Mihailovic, S., et al. 1990. *Deca krize* (Children of crisis). Belgrade,

Yugoslavia: Institut drustvenih nauka.

_____. 1991. *Izmedju izbornih rituala i slobodnih izbora* (From election rights to the free elections). Belgrade, Yugoslavia: Institut drustvenih nauka.

Miočinović, Lj. 1988. *Cognitive and Affective Factors in Moral Development* (in Serbo-Croatian; summary in English). Belgrade, Yugoslavia: Institut za pedagoška istraživanja i Prosveta.

Mitchell, T. R., and James, L. R. 1989. "Situational Versus Dispositional Factors: Competing Explanations of Behavior." *Academy of Management Review.* 14(3): 330-331.

Momov, V. 1975. *Man, Morality, Education: Theoretical and Methodological Problems* (in Russian). Moscow.

Montero, Maritza. 1987. *Ideologies, Alienacion e Identidad Nacional.* Caracas: Central University of Venezuela, Ediciones de la Biblioteca.

Morris, C. 1956. *Varieties of Human Life.* Chicago: University of Chicago Press.

Müller-Böling, D., and Ramme, I. 1990. *Informations- und Kommunikationstechnologien für Führungskräfte.* München.

Naim, Moises. 1989. *Las Empresas Venezolanas: Su Gerencia.* Caracas: Ediciones IESA. Caracas.

Naim, Moises, and Pinangro, R. 1986. *El caso Venezuela, una ilusion de Armonia.* Caracas: Ediciones IESA.

Newgren, K., Rasher, A., and LaRoe, M. 1984. "An Empirical Investigation of the Relationship Between Environmental Assessment and Corporate Performance." *Proceedings of the Academy of Management,* 352-356.

Ničić, J., Bojanović, R., and Maksić, S. 1985. *Attitudes of Youth toward Work.* Belgrade, Yugoslavia: IIC SSOS (mimeo, in Serbo-Croatian).

Painton, Frederick. 1991. "The Great Malaise." *Time International* (Special issue: "The New France." July 15.

Pantić, D. 1969. *The Values and Attitudes of Opinion-Makers* (in Serbo-Croatian). Mimeograph. Belgrade, Yugoslavia: Institute of Social Sciences.

_____. 1974. "Some Value Orientations of the Youth" (in Serbo-Croatian). In S. Joksimović, ed., *Attitudes and Beliefs of Yugoslav Youth* (pp. 25-53). Belgrade, Yugoslavia: Mladost.

_____. 1977. "Social Strata's Values and Ideological Orientations" (in Serbo-Croatian, summary in English). In M. Popović, ed.,

Social Strata and Social Consciousness. Belgrade, Yugoslavia: Institute of Social Sciences.

_____. 1981. "Value Orientations of the Youth in Serbia" (in Serbo-Croatian). Belgrade, Yugoslavia: Institute of Social Sciences

_____. 1985. "Differentiation of Political Engagement Depending on Personal Traits." In V. Goati, ed., *Political Engagement in Yugoslav Society* (pp. 201-277). Belgrade, Yugoslavia: Mladost.

_____. 1987. "National Attitudes of the Youth in Serbia" (in Serbo-Croatian). Mimeograph. Belgrade, Yugoslavia: Institute of Social Sciences.

_____. 1988. *Classic and Secular Religiousness in Belgrade* (in Serbo-Croatian, summary in English). Belgrade, Yugoslavia: Institute of Social Sciences.

_____. 1990a. *Change in the Value-Orientations of the Young in Serbia* (in Serbo-Croatian, summary in English). Belgrade, Yugoslavia: Institute of Social Sciences.

_____. 1990b. "Political Culture of Youth in Serbia" (in Serbo-Croatian). In *The Young at the End of the Eighties*. Belgrade, Yugoslavia: IIC SSOS.

_____. 1990c. "Promene vrednosnih orijentacije mladih u Srbiji" (Changes in the value-orientations of the young in Serbia). Belgrade, Yugoslavia: Institut drustvenih nauka.

_____. 1990d. "The Psychological Structure of Modernism as a Value Orientation and the Characteristics of Modern Personality" (in Serbo-Croatian, summaries in English and Russian). *Psihologija*. 3-4: 5-25.

_____. 1990e. "Yugoslav Youth Values in the Age of Crisis: A Generation Characterized by Anomy and the Religiousness of the Yugoslav Youth: Cross-Cultural Diachronical and Social Coordinates" (in Serbo-Croatian, summary in English). In a S. Mihailović, ed., *The Children of the Crisis* (pp. 173-228). Belgrade, Yugoslavia: Institute of Social Sciences.

_____. 1991. "Religiousness of Citizens of Yugoslavia" (in Serbo-Croatian). In Lj. Baćević, ed., *Yugoslavia at a Turning Point* (pp. 241-257). Belgrade, Yugoslavia: Institute of Social Sciences.

Pešić, V. 1977. "Social Stratification and Lifestyles" (in Serbo-Croatian, summary in English). In M. Popović, ed., *Social Strata and Social Consciousness* (pp. 121-196). Belgrade,

Yugoslavia: Institute of Social Sciences
Petrazhitsky, L. J. 1904. *About the Motives of Human Actions Ethical Motives and Their Variety* (in Russian). St. Petersburg.
Petrović, M. 1973. "The Values of Delinquents and Non-Delinquents" (in Serbo-Croatian, summary in English). Belgrade, Yugoslavia: Institut za kriminološka i sociološka istraživanja.
Pettigrew, A. M. 1979. "On Studying Organizational Cultures." *Administrative Science Quarterly.* 24: 570-581.
Pigamiol, Claude. 1989. "Industrial Relations and Enterprise Restructuring in France." *International Labour Review.* 128(5): 621-631.
Pinango, Ramon. "El Peligro de Vacio de Autoestima." In *Diario de Caracas.* November 9.
Pino Iturrieta, Elias. 1988. *Venezuela metida en cintura: 1900-1945.* Cuadernos Lagoven, Serie cuatro Republicas.
Popadić, D. 1990. "Lifestyle Preferences of Students at the End of Elementary Schooling" (in Serbo-Croatian, summary in English). In N. Havelka, et al., eds., *Educational and Developmental Achievements by Students at the End of Elementary Schooling* (pp. 235-259). Belgrade, Yugoslavia: Belgrade: Institute of Psychology, Faculty of Philosophy.
Popović, B. 1973. *The Foundations of the Psychology of Morals* (in Serbo-Croatian, summary in English). Belgrade, Yugoslavia: Naučna knjiga.
Popović, B. and Miočinović, Lj., 1977. *The Moral Values of Children and Adolescents and Their Development* (in Serbo-Croatian, summary in English). Belgrade, Yugoslavia: Institut za pedagoška istraživanja i Prosveta.
Popović, B., Miočinović, Lj., and Ristić, Ž. 1981. *The Development of Moral Knowledge* (in Serbo-Croatian, summary in English). Belgrade, Yugoslavia: Institut za pedagoška istraživanja i Prosveta.
————. 1984. *Psychological Basis of Moral Thinking* (in Serbo-Croatian, summary in English). Belgrade, Yugoslavia: Institut za pedagoška istraživanja i Prosveta.
Preble, J. F., Rau, R. A., and Reichel, A. 1988. "The Environmental Scanning Practices of U.S. Multinationals in the Late 1980s." *Management International Review* 28(4): 4-14.
Prognos euroreport 1990. "Industrie-Länder in den 90er Jahren." In *Marketing-Journal* (2): 130-131.

Pugh, G. 1978. *Biological Origins of Human Values.* London: Routledge and Kegan Paul.

Rademaekers, William. 1991. "Grand Ambitions." *Time International* (Special issue: "The New France"). July 15: 30-35.

Radin, F. et al. 1988. *The Fragments of Youth* (in Serbo-Croatian, summary in English). Zagreb, Yugoslavia: IDIS.

Raffée, H., and Wiedmann, K.P. 1983. *Dialoge-Der Bürger als Partner: Das gesellschaftliche Bewußtsein.* Hamburg.

_____. 1985. Wertewandel und gesellschaftsorientiertes Marketing-Die Bewährungsprobe strategischer Unternehmensführung. In H. Raffée, and K. P. Wiedmann, eds., *Strategisches Marketing* (pp. 552-611). Stuttgart.

_____. 1988. "Der Wertewandel als Herausforderung für Marketing-forschung und Marketingpraxis." In *Marketing (ZFP).* 10(3): 198-210.

Rand, A. 1964. "The Objectivist Ethics." In A. Rand, ed., *The Virtue of Selfishness* (pp.13-35). New York: Signet.

Rivero, Manuel R. *La Republica en Venezuela. Pasion y Desencanto.* (Vol. 2) Cuardernos Lagoven, Serie Cuatro Republicas.

Rokeach, M. 1968. *Beliefs, Attitudes, and Values.* San Francisco: Jossey-Bass.

_____. 1973. *The Nature of Human Values.* New York: Free Press.

_____. 1979. *Understanding Human Values: Individual and Social.* New York: Free Press.

Romera, Garcia. 1985. *Motivando para el trabajo.* Caracas: Cuadernos Oswaldo Lagoven. Serie Siglo 21.

Ronen, S., and Shenkar, O. 1985. "Clustering Countries on Attitudinal Dimensions: A Review and Synthesis." *Academy of Management Review.* 3: 435-454.

Rosenstiel, L. V. 1987. "Wandel in der Karrieremotivation-Verfall oder Neuorientierung." In L. V. Rosenstiel, H. E. Einsiedler, and R. K. Streich, eds., *Wertewandel als Herausforderung für die Unternehmenspolitik* (pp. 35-52). Stuttgart.

_____. 1989. "Führungskräfte nach dem Wertewandel: Zielkonflikte und Identifikationskrisen?" In *ZfO.* (2): 89-96.

Rot, N., and Havelka, N. 1973. *Values and National Commitments in Youth* (in Serbo-Croatian, summary in English). Belgrade, Yugoslavia: Institute of Social Sciences.

Roter, Z. 1986. *Religiousness and Irreligiousness in Slovenia.* Nis, Yugoslavia. Gradina, 1-2.

Rubinstein, S. L. 1957. *Being and Consciousness* (in Russian). Moscow.

Salom De B., Columbia. 1984. "Expectativas de exito y fracaso en Venezuela." Paper presented at the Fourth Venezuelan Conference on Social Psychology, Caracas.

Sanford, N. 1973. "Authoritarian Personality in Contemporary Perspective." In J. Knutson, ed., *Handbook of Political Psychology*. San Francisco: Jossey-Bass.

Sapir, E. 1924. "Culture, Genuine and Spurious." *The American Journal of Sociology* 29(4): 401-429.

Scheibe, W. 1970. *Beliefs and Values*. New York: Holt, Rinehart and Winston.

Schein, E. H. 1985. *Organizational Culture and Leadership*. San Francisco: Jossey-Bass.

Schermerhorn, J. R., Jr., Hunt, J. G., and Osborn, R. N. 1988. *Managing Organizational Behavior*. New York: John Wiley and Sons.

Sheppard, H. L., and Herrick, N. Q. 1972. *Where Have All the Robots Gone?* New York: Free Press.

Šiber, I. 1974. *Social Structure and Political Attitudes* (in Serbo-Croatian). Zagreb, Yugoslavia: Narodno sveučilište.

Siehl, C., and Martin, J. 1984. "The Role of Symbolic Management: How Can Managers Effectively Transmit Organizational Culture?" In J. G. Hunt, ed., *Leaders and Managers: International Perspectives on Managerial Behavior and Leadership* (pp. 227-239). New York: Pergamon Press.

Simmet, H. 1990. *Neue Informations-und Kommunikationstechnologien im Marketing des Lebensmitteleinzelhandels*. Stuttgart.

Skinner, B. 1971. *Beyond Freedom and Dignity*. New York: Knopf.

Smirnov, V. Y. 1929. *The Psychology of Youth and Age* (in Russian). Moscow-Leningrad.

Smith, M. B. 1969. *Social Psychology and Human Values*. Chicago: Aldine.

Smolić-Krković, N. 1970. "On the Measuring of Interests" (in Serbo-Croatian). *Pedagoški rad*. 1-2: 37-46.

Sokolov, V. M. 1986. *Sociology of Moral Development of the Individual* (in Russian). Moscow.

Soriano, Graciela. 1988. *Venezuela 1810-1830: Aspectos desatendidos de dos decadas*. Caracas: Cuadernos Lagoven, Serie Cuatro Republicas.

Staehle, W. H. 1987. *Management*. 3d ed., München.

Stankov, L. 1977. "Some Experiences with the F-Scale in Yugoslavia" *British Journal of Social and Clinical Psychology*. 16 (2).

Steege, G. 1986. *Gesellschaftliche Werte und Ziele*. Frankfurt am Main.

Supek, R. 1963. *The Psycho-Sociology of Youth Voluntary Work Drives* (in Serbo-Croatian). Belgrade, Yugoslavia: Mladost.

Szalai, A., and Andrews, F. eds. 1989. *The Quality of Life*. London: Sage.

Tajfel, H. 1981. *Human Groups and Social Categories*. Cambridge: Cambridge University Press.

Tietz, B. 1982. "Die Wertedynamik der Konsumenten und Unternehmer in ihren Konsequenzen auf das Marketing," in *Marketing (ZFP)*. 4(2): 91-102.

_____. 1990. *Euro-Marketing-Unternehmensstrategien für den Binnenmarkt*, 2d ed., Landsberg.

Toffler, A. 1970. *Future Shock*. New York: Bantam Books.

Tomanović, V. 1971. *The Young Workers and Students* (in Serbo-Croatian). Belgrade, Yugoslavia: Institute of Social Sciences.

_____. 1977. *Youth and Socialism* (in Serbo-Croatian). Belgrade, Yugoslavia: Mladost.

Töpfer, A. 1989. "Euro-Management, Erfolgsvoraussetzungen für die neunziger Jahre." In *EG-Magazin*. (10): 12-18.

Toš, N., Roter, Z., et al. 1987. *Public Opinion in Slovenia* (in Slovenian). Ljubljana, Yugoslavia: Delavska enotnost.

Trommsdorff, V. 1989. *Konsumentenverhalten*. Stuttgart.

Ungeheuer, Frederick. 1991. "Can France Compete?" *Time International* (Special issue: "The New France"). July 15: 36-42.

Urbaneja, Diego Bautista. 1988. *La Idea Politica de Venezuela 1830-1870*. Caracas: Cuadernos Lagoven, Serie Cuatro Republicas.

Uslar Pietri, Arturo. 1991. "Venezuela esta en un momento muy dificil de su historia." *El Nacional*. November 11, D-4.

Uznadze, D.N. 1961. *The Basic Thesis of the Attitude Theory*. Tbilisi, Georgia.

_____. 1969. *The Psychological Problems of the Motivation of the Individual Behavior* (in Russian). Moscow.

Vasović, M. 1988. "Values of the Members of Informal Groups in Youth." In S. Joksimović, et al., *Youth and Informal Groups* (pp. 174-216). Belgrade, Yugoslavia: IIC SSOS.

_____. 1991. "Value Priorities of the Yugoslav Public" (in Serbo-

Croatian, summary in English). In Lj. Baćević, ed., *Yugoslavia at a Turning Point in Crisis* (pp. 197-233). Belgrade, Yugoslavia: Institute of Social Sciences.

Viana, Mikel. 1990. "Ethos y valores en el proceso historico-politico de Venezuela." Paper presented at the Third Venezuelan Congress of Sociology, Porlamar.

Vinokurova, S. P. 1988. *The Individual in the the System of Moral Relations* (in Russian). Minsk, 1988.

Vrcan, S., et al. 1986. *Social Position, Consciousness and Political Behavior of Youth* (in Serbo-Croatian). Zagreb, Yugoslavia: CIDID SSOJ and IDIS.

Vušković, B., et al. 1987. *Some Characteristics of the Political Profile of Youth*. Split, Yugoslavia: Pogledi.

Walsh, James. 1991. *Time International* (Special issue: "The New France"). July 15: 8-11.

Webber, R. A. 1969. "Convergence or Divergence." *Columbia Journal of World Business*. 4(3): 75-83.

Weber, M. 1956. *Wirtschaft und Gesellschaft*. 2 vol., Tübingen.

Williams, R., Jr. 1968. "Values." In E. Sills, ed., *International Encyclopedia of Sciences*. New York: MacMillan.

_____. 1969. "Generic American Values." In V. Rogers, ed., *A Sourcebook for Social Sciences*. London: Macmillian.

_____. 1979. Changes and Stability in Values and Value Systems: A Sociological Perspective." In M. Rokeach, M., eds., *Understanding Human Values* (pp. 15-46). New York: Free Press.

Windhorst, K. P. 1985. *Wertewandel und Konsumentenverhalten*. Münster.

Yadov, V. A. 1983. *Attitude to Work: Conceptual Model and Real Tendencies* (in Russian). Sociological Researches, no. 3.

Yakobson, P. M. 1969. *Psychological Problems of the Motivation of Human Behavior*. Moscow.

Yankelovich, D. 1981. *New Rules! Searching for Self-fulfillment in a World Turned Upside Down*. New York: Random House.

Yaroshevsky, M. S. 1966. *The History of Psychology* (in Russian). Moscow.

Yaroshevsky, T. M. 1973. *Individual and Society* (in Russian). Moscow.

Zaninovich, G. 1970. "Party and Non-Party Attitudes on Societal Change." In B. Farrell, B., ed., *Political Leadership in Eastern*

Europe and the Soviet Union. Chicago (pp. 294-334).

_____. 1971. "The Case of Yugoslavia: Delineating Political Culture in a Multi-Ethnic Society." *Studies in Comparative Communism* 4(2): 58-70.

_____. 1973. "Elites and Citizenry in Yugoslav Society: A Study of Value Differentiation." In C. Beck, et al., *Comparative Communist Political Leadership* (pp. 226-297).

Zdravomyslov, A. S. 1986. *Needs, interests, values* (in Russian). Moscow.

Županov, J. 1970. "Egalitariansim and Industrialism" (in Serbo-Croatian). *Sociologija.* 1: 5-45.

Županov, J., and Tadić, N. 1969. "Economic Aspirations and Social Norm of Egalitarianism" (in Serbo-Croatian). *Sociologija.* 2: 279-304.

Index

About the Authors and Contributors

NINA ANDREENKOVA (1945) received her Ph.D. in Sociology from the Institute for Sociological Research (ISR) in the USSR Academy of Social Sciences in 1971. She currently is the President of the Institute for Comparative Social Research of the Russian Academy of Sciences, head of the Department of Sociology of Work in the Institute for Social and Political Research of the Russian Academy of Sciences, the Director of the Center for Sociological Training, and a member of the Soviet Sociological Association. Her major areas of research focus on social problems of work and labor collectives, problems of management and marketing, and the training of sociologists and managers on sociology and social problems. She has been a member of the Fund for the Assistance in Social and Work Research (member of the Board); Sociological Association "Sodruzhestvo" (President, 1992); Society of Sociologists and Demographics of Russia (member of Presidium, 1989-92); Committee of Work SSA (Chairman, 1990); Soviet Sociological Association (member of the Board and Vice-Chairman of Moscow Division, 1972-1987); and Russian Fund for Development of Social Sciences (Vice President, 1989-91). She has published numerous books, monographs, and articles dealing with Russian and Soviet sociological, social, and political issues and topics. Moreover, she has served as the principal investigator on numerous research projects dealing with these broad topical areas.

LJILJANA J. BAČEVIĆ received her B.A. in Psychology from the University of Belgrade, her M.A. in Communication from the University of Ljubljana, and her Ph.D. in Political Science from the University of

Belgrade. She was a visiting scholar to The Bureau for Applied Social Research, Columbia University, New York, and to the University of Amsterdam. She is a senior research associate, and since 1989, Director of the Center for Political Studies and Public Opinion Research, Institute of Social Sciences, University of Belgrade. She is involved in professional research of international, intercultural and political communication, media audience and effects, and political attitudes. She has published a number of books and articles in the fields of communication and public opinion. She was a double winner (1977 and 1985) of the national Radio-TV Net Annual prize for the best mass communication study.

PETER J. BALOGH is completing his Ph.D. in business at the University of Wisconsin-Madison and holds an MBA from the same university. He also studied business, economics, and languages at Ludwig-Maximilians Universitaet, Munich, Germany and the University of Minnesota-Minneapolis. Presently, he is an Assistant Professor of International Business and Marketing at Florida State University. His research focuses on the governance of international technology transfers, the relationship between cultural values and marketing management issues, and the assessment of market potential. Moreover, he serves on the Board of Directors of Spectrum Research, Inc., a Minnesota based firm that conducts business in the areas of research contracting, data management, and software and systems development. He was the chief financial officer and a vice president in this company between 1986 and 1990.

FREDERIC BRUNNEL has been a Lecturer in business at the Ecole the Superieure de Sciences Comerciales d'Angers (ESSCA) in Anger, France. He is currently completing his doctoral degree in the United States.

MIJAT DAMJANOVIĆ received his Master of Arts in Law and his Ph.D. in Political Sciences from the University of Belgrade. He is currently a faculty member in the Department of Organization and Management, Faculty of Political Sciences, University of Belgrade. Moreover, he has been a member of the Institute of Social Sciences in Belgrade for a number of years. His special fields of interests include: theory of organization, management science, public administration, and political sociology. His publications include articles in *Gledista*

(Belgrade), *Politicka Maso* (Zagreb), and *Revija za Socioligiju* (Zagreb). Also, he has published a book, *Organizacija i Upravljane* and is a co-editor and contributor in a book of essays: *The Impact of Culture-Based Value Systems on Management Policies and Practices*, New York: Praeger.

ALEKSANDAR FIRA received his B.A. and Ph.D. in Law, University of Belgrade, Yugoslavia. He has served as professor of Constitutional Law and Comparative Political Systems at the University of Novi Sad. Currently, he is a professor of Constitutional Law, University of Belgrade. He was a member of The Federal Government of the Socialist Federal Republic of Yugoslavia (SFRY), president of the Federal Committee for Legislative Affairs, president of the Constitutional Court of Vojvodina, judge of the Constitutional Court of Yugoslavia, and twice the president of the Constitutional Court of Yugoslavia. He has been a member of the Academy of Science and Arts of Vojvodina since 1979, and from 1987-1989 its president and the president of the Council of Academies of Science and Arts of Yugoslavia. He is a member of the Academy of Science and Arts of Serbia. He has published more than 400 papers and articles and eight books in the fields of law and political science. For his scientific contributions to the theory of constitutional law he received the highest prize of Vojvodina 1988. He took part in numerous international scientific meetings and congresses and was a visiting professor at universities in Europe, Asia, Africa, and America. At the 13th World Congress of Jurists, he was elected for vice-president of the World Association of Judges.

VLADIMIR GOATI received his B.A. and M.A. in Law, and his Ph.D. in Political Science from the University of Belgrade, Yugoslavia. He is a senior research fellow in the Institute of Social Sciences, University of Belgrade, and was the Director of the Center for Political Studies and Public Opinion Research from 1977-1983, and thereafter, chairman of the Managing Board and Director of the Institute of Social Sciences until 1988. He was a professor of political sociology, University of Nis 1974-1975, and a visiting professor at the University of Ljubljana and at the University of Zagreb (1982, 1983, and 1989). He was elected professor at the University of Ljubljana 1991. He was editor-in-chief of the journal "Gledista" 1971-1973, member of editorial board of the journal "Sociologija" 1982-1984. Currently, he is the head of the project "Emerging of Parliamentarism in Central and Eastern Europe and

Yugoslavia". He has published a large number of articles, took part at numerous international scientific conferences, and is the author of twelve books. His current interests are the problems of consolidation of democratic order in post-communist countries. He received NIN Award 1984 for the book "Modern Political Parties" and "Vjesnik" Award 1989 for the book "Political Anatomy of Yugoslav Society".

ROSALIND GREAVES DE PULIDO is a sociologist (1964) from the Universidad Catolica Andres Bello, Caracas, Venezuela. She is a professor in the School of Social Sciences of the same university. Her experience includes two years postgraduate courses (1964-66) in Social Psychology in the Ecole Practique D'Hautes Etudes in the University of Paris, France. She has held directive positions in Venezuelan Public and Private Institutions which include: Director of Social Welfare in the Ministry of Health and Social Assistance; member of the Board of Directors of the National Child Institute; Secretary of Education of the International Institute for Advanced Studies; General Secretary of the Social Solidarity Fund Foundation; and the Neumann Foundation. She has carried out research and studies mainly in the field of Social Planning and Programme Evaluation. Presently, she is Director of Continuous Education Programmes in the Universidad Metropolitana Caracas.

HANS GÜNTHER MEISSNER received his Ph.D. and habilitation in business administration from the University of Cologne. He is the former director of the institute for foreign trade and served as president of the European International Business Association in 1978 and 1988 and as president of the "Deutsche Werbewissenschaftliche Gesellschaft" from 1981-1984. He is the holder of the chair of marketing of the University of Dortmund since 1973 and professor titulaire at the L'Ecole Superieur de Commerce et d'Administration des Enterprises (ESCAE) in Amiens, France since 1990. He has written and edited numerous books and articles on international and European marketing, in particular.

JOEL D. NICHOLSON graduated from the Florida State University with a Ph.D. in Business Administration. He is currently the Director of International Business Programs at Illinois State University, where he also teaches seminars in International Management. Previously, he served as the Director of International Programs at Gonzaga University. He has taught at Washington State University, Florida State University, and Gonzaga University. His research focus is on cross-cultural management with a geographical focus on Latin America, specifically including Mexico, Venezuela, and Chile.

DRAGOMIR J. PANTIĆ has been a senior research fellow at the Institute of Social Sciences of the University of Belgrade, Yugoslavia, and its director since 1989. He received his B.A. in Psychology from the Department of Psychology, Faculty of Philosophy, University of Belgrade, where he also won a Ph.D. in Social Psychology with the dissertation: "Value Orientations, Personality Traits, and Class Structure". He was a visiting scholar at the BASR, Columbia University, New York (1969) and in Canada (1974-1975). He has taken part in several international projects concerning problems of national commitments, public opinion, political culture, and values. He was elected a full member of the International Association for Applied Psychology in 1974. For his contribution in the field of psychology - works on the nature of interests and values - he received the annual award of the Psychological Association of Serbia in 1982. Since 1992, he has been a member of the Scientific Council of the Republic of Serbia.

YOLETTE RAMIREZ received a Master in Business Administration (1991) and a Sociology degree in 1978 from the Universidad Catolica Andres Bello, Caracas, Venezuela. She has been Coordinator of the specialty of Sociology in the School of Social Sciences in the same University and is currently teaching there in the areas of Social Theory and Research Methodology. She has been General Coordinator of Pre-school Centers in the Child Foundation and Senior Consultant for the relation with the multilateral financing institutions in the National Planning Office (Cordiplan).

ALFONSO RODRIGUEZ-COSS is a professor of ITESM, Queretaro, Mexico.

HEIKE SIMMET received her Ph.D. in business administration from the University of Dortmund. She is assistant professor at the chair of marketing at the University of Dortmund and teaches at the L'Ecole Superieur de Commerce et d'Administration des Enterprises (ESCAE) in Amiens, France. Her research interests focus on European market research and international retail strategies. She has written and edited various articles related to these fields of research.

E. RAY SOLOMON received a Bachelors Degree in Business (1951) and a Master of Science (1958) from Florida State University and a Ph.D. in Business (1962) from the University of Wisconsin. He served as Dean of the College of Business at Florida State University from 1974-1991. He is currently the Payne H. Midyette, Sr. and Charlotte Hodges Midyette Eminent Scholar Professor of Insurance at Florida State University. Dr. Solomon's special areas of interest include: risk management, employee benefits plans, life and health insurance, economics of insurance, business ethics and business education accreditation. His publications include articles in the *Journal of Insurance*, the *C.P.C.U. Annals*, the *Life Association News*, the *Life Underwriters* News and in various professional journals, and has authored two books, *Industrial Fire Insurance*, University of Florida (1986), and *Motor Vehicle Physical Damage Insurance*, University of Florida (1986). He has served on the Board of Directors of numerous business and non-profit organizations. Dr. Solomon has also participated in several programs, conferences and research activities of the Cooperative Center for Yugoslav-American Studies, Research and Exchanges involving Florida State University, the University of Belgrade and the University of Zagreb.

LEE P. STEPINA received his B.S. Degree in Psychology, M.A. in Labor and Industrial Relations, and Ph.D. in Labor and Industrial Relations from the University of Illinois. His major areas of interest include human resource management, labor relations, culture and management, and compensation. He is currently a faculty member of the Management Department and the Director of the Center for Human Resource Management at Florida State University. He has published numerous articles in various journals such as the *Academy of Management Journal*, *Journal of Personality and Social Behavior*, *Industrial Relations Journal of Organizational Behavior*, *Journal of International Psychology*, and others. He has been the principal investigator and research associate on a number of grants dealing with compensation and human resources related to information technology. Also, he has served as a consultant for a variety of business and non-profit organizations.

MIRJANA VASOVIĆ graduated from the Faculty of Philosophy, University of Belgrade, with a Ph.D. in social psychology. She has been senior researcher in the Institute of Social Sciences, University of Belgrade. Presently, she occupies post of the Assistant Minister in the

Federal Ministry of Education and Culture of the Federal Republic of Yugoslavia. She has been publishing widely on the political socialization, on social values and behavior, and on public opinion. She is also an author of numerous articles and several books.

DAN VOICH, JR., received a Bachelors Degree in Business (1961) and a MBA degree (1962) from Florida State University, and a Ph.D. in Business (1965) from the University of Illinois. He is currently a Professor of Management in the College of Business at Florida State University. He has served as the Associate Dean, College of Business at Florida State University from 1979-1991. His special areas of interest include: systems theory and analysis, organization and management theory, comparative systems, and policy formulation and decision making. He has co-authored the following books: *Principles of Management: Resources and Systems*, 1st Ed., Ronald Press (1968); *Organization and Management: Basic Systems Concepts*, Richard D. Irwin (1974); *Information Systems for Operations and Management*, South-western (1975); *Principles of Management: Process, Structure and Behavior*, 2nd Ed., Ronald Press (1976); *Management: Process, Structure and Behavior*, 3rd ed., John Wiley & Sons (1984); *The Impact of Culture Based Value Systems on Management Policies and Practices: Yugoslav and United States Issues and Viewpoints* (Co-editor and contributor), Praeger (1985). Dr. Voich has been an active participant in various programs, conferences, and research activities of the Cooperative Center for Yugoslav-American Studies, Research and Exchanges involving Florida State University, the University of Belgrade, and the University of Zagreb.